KANGAROOS
AND CHAOS

JULIA BROOKE

Kangaroos and Chaos

Copyright © 2013 by Julia Brooke.

All rights reserved.

Cover art and formatting by damonza.com

KANGAROOS AND CHAOS

Kangaroos and Chaos is the tell-all, true story of the year I spent backpacking around Australia. It's a very honest and personal account of my travels with all the debauchery left in (I'm still coming to terms with the fact that my grandmother has read every detail). I hope it will inspire budding backpackers, take ex-travellers on a trip down memory lane and entertain anyone who enjoys a giggle and a gasp as they read.

Should you wish to see any photos from the trip, please hunt down *Kangaroos and Chaos* online. I'm prepared to reveal shots from any part of the journey, with the exception of my naked mountain moment! Equally, should you require some dubious words of advice for your own Aussie adventure, I'm more than happy to assist. And of course, feel free to get in touch at any point during your read to share thoughts or stories of your own. I absolutely love receiving messages from readers—bonus points for sending me pictures of you and your book/device in random/picturesque locations.

AUTHORS NOTE

To protect their privacy and in some instances their dignity, I have changed the names of the people who feature and also those of the farms. However, the Australian place names remain the same and are out there waiting to be explored.

To Dad, Hollie, Faye and Erin.

*Thank you for always being there, no
matter which country I'm in.*

Chapter 1

Cows Gone Wild

THE FOUR-WHEEL DRIVE disappeared into the distance. I was now alone and panicked. Soon I would be the only human for hundreds of kilometres. Although I hadn't technically been abandoned, I had been left to run an Australian cattle station. I had no experience and no idea how I was going to cope.

I had only arrived on the property 24 hours earlier. The owners, Sarah and Shaun, had foolishly believed that after a quick tour I would be capable of caring for their 2,000 beef cattle, six dogs and two horses. Before they departed I had tried to communicate my concerns. I had never owned a dog or dealt with a horse and I didn't even eat beef, let alone know how to look after the live version. For a moment Sarah looked apprehensive, but Shaun patted her on the shoulder and casually announced, 'She'll be right!'

I highly doubted it.

I was just a backpacker looking for some work in-between

exploring the country. Although I wanted people to see past my highlighted hair and girly ways, this was a little too far in the opposite direction. However, like it or not, the station was now my responsibility for the next week. I had no choice but to get on with things.

My first job—on a list that included, rugging horses, checking reservoir pumps and baking bread—was to move a herd of cattle. Shaun had given me a demonstration the previous day and admittedly he'd made it look easy. With the farm map in hand I headed to the shed and jumped on the quad bike. At least they hadn't expected me to ride a horse.

I managed to start the thing first time and even felt a flash of adrenaline as I headed down the track. It wasn't every day a girl from a built-up suburb of Kent got to drive such an unusual mode of transport. Nervously I bumped and weaved along the muddy trail while somehow keeping control of the bike. Having survived the first kilometre my anxiety began to dissolve and I started to enjoy the ride. The air had a pureness about it and I inhaled deeply. Duck's Meadow wasn't your usual dirt and dust station. I was surrounded by lush, green fields and hilly picturesque views that could have rivalled the Yorkshire Dales. Except the Dales don't have clouds of exotic coloured birds or kookaburras making laugh-like calls from up in the trees.

Suddenly my mind was jerked back to the task at hand as a kangaroo shot out from the bush. For a few magical seconds it bounded alongside me before turning into the shrubbery. I couldn't believe my luck. What an incredible encounter and how very, very Aussie. Cattle stations, kookaburras, parrots and roos—this was fast turning into a Walt Disney film.

And then I saw them. The colour didn't so much as drain from my face, rather it dropped straight to my feet, as pure terror ebbed through me. Across the paddock were hundreds upon hundreds of cattle, all pounding, galloping, thumping and thundering towards me. Oh. Fuck!

Thankfully between the mob and my current location stood an electric fence, which I seriously hoped would stop them. It did. And so, at a much slower pace and with a lot more caution, I continued on. Shaun had informed me that this herd consisted of two-year-old stock, the cattle equivalent of teenagers. It seemed they had the attitude to match. They stood en masse—varying from black, brown or white to a muddle of all three—huffing, puffing and snorting loudly. There were a mix of males and females. The evil looking, pointy horns made it easy to distinguish between the two. I had been told the herd would be excited to see me. They were moved on a regular basis and had learnt that the sound of the bike meant a fresh field of food. However, the cows which Shaun and I had mustered the previous day had been older females, and a little more tranquil to say the least. They certainly hadn't greeted us with this much vigour.

I had been instructed to park the quad a good distance from the gate in case it made the animals too nervous to come through. Nervous?! These things were practically baying for blood. Moos, moans, cries and what can only be described as screams, erupted from the crowd as they stamped their feet in frustration. I ducked under a fence and stood in a triangle of space, which was surrounded by three electrified gates. The first field held the new grazing ground, the second led off across the station, while the third held the cows. The electric gates were a thin strip of tape, which looked like those used to cordon off crime scenes. Thankfully the farm version had a rubber handle and a hook on each end which would allow me to disconnect it from the supply without being electrocuted. I would then pull the tape back across to the opposite fence post. First I would open the gate which led through to the new field and then do the same for the one with the cattle behind it. The creatures would apparently wander through into their new pastures enthused by the prospect of tasty grassland. The problem was that this lot didn't look like they were in the mood for wandering. They looked as if they were ready to stampede.

My main concern was that as soon as I unhooked the tape the herd would trample me before I had chance to reach the adjacent post. The noise and aggression was increasing by the second. I approached the gate on foot as 500 pairs of eyes watched my every move. The deadly horns upon the fiery males looked even more terrifying up close. As if sensing my fear the bull closest to me let out an almighty shriek. The pressure was on and I was too scared to keep them waiting any longer, yet too scared to move.

In the end I had no choice. Grabbing the rubber handle, I fumbled, before finally disconnecting the tape and hurrying across. My heart pounded in my chest, surely any second now I would be crushed. But somehow I managed to complete the crossing alive. Relieved, I leaned on the post trying to catch my breath. For a split second I really thought everything was going to be alright. Then, to my horror the cattle heaved forward, ignored the open field of grass and broke straight through the third fence. NO! NO! NO! Powerless to stop them, I looked on as the entire herd poured through the forbidden gate and vanished over the horizon.

10 Months Earlier...

I looked around the aircraft and noticed several other backpackers. Well I couldn't be sure, but the khaki trousers, slouched positions and t-shirts with Thai beer logos certainly gave that impression. For all of us, the thrill of adventure had been dulled and then stamped on by hours of planes and airport lounges. We sat like battery farm hens, caged by an inch of personal space, preparing for another twelve hours of cramping.

Thankfully, it was the last leg of my journey. Soon I would be arriving in Sydney to begin my one year trip around Australia. As the flight bounced off the runway I tried to rest, but my mind had other plans. I was en route to start an unpredictable adventure, in a foreign land, normally half a world away. I had read the guidebook and listened time and time again to advice given by friends, family and random strangers.

It seemed that everyone had an Australian pearl of wisdom to share. I gave up telling people about my trip for fear of hearing, 'Oh you must speak to my great aunt's second cousin…' one more time. I wanted to discover the country in my own way and doubted that good old Dorothy would be able to recommend the best hostel, cheapest pub or where to meet other backpackers keen on some debauchery.

I had notes, books and maps, but in Australia I planned to let go of the girl who was usually organised, thorough and occasionally a little anally retentive. It was time to discover the real me. Under the practicalities I could be a wild child and had a feeling that my recklessness was about to be released in full force.

Sleep eluded me, but after seemingly endless hours of contorted shifting, tense muscles and with the onset of insanity, the plane finally began to drop down into Sydney. The air below was clear blue and out of the window I had an aerial view of the city. Straining my eyes and stretching my neck, I peered at the deep blue water and tall metallic buildings. Then, to my surprise, picture-perfect and lit up by glorious sunshine, the infamous Opera House and Sydney Harbour Bridge came into sight. Somehow it didn't feel real and just for a second my emotions overwhelmed me. I couldn't believe it. I was really here, on the other side of the world, all by myself. I was in Australia.

*

I flashed a weary smile at the customs officer who looked equally tired and dutifully stamped my passport. I had a one year working holiday visa, but there was no need to check my papers, everything was electronic. Admiring the fresh ink on the page, I looked at the date quizzically. I had left the UK on Thursday the 12th November. The mark gracing my passport read Saturday 14th. This had to be a good sign. By the magic of time travel or some confusing science, I had now lost an entire day. More importantly, I had completely skipped Friday the 13th and any bad luck that may have come with it.

Breaking free into the arrivals hall I was greeted by a sea of faces. All of them instantly looked up and directly at me, wide-eyed and hopeful. Some of the awaiting crowd bounced little signs up and down, others turned their gaze away disappointedly. Rather startled by all the attention, I almost wanted to do a little dance so as not to let them down. The walkway out of the sliding doors was sectioned off and the barriers gave it somewhat of a red carpet feel. But instead of being fresh and glamorous, my face was as crumpled as my clothes and my hair looked as if I had spent the flight with my head stuck out of the window. Any remnants of make-up that had been applied over 24 hours ago, were now sitting in oil like pools under my eyes. I put my head down and scuttled off to find the transfer desk.

A pre-booked bus was to take me to my hostel. These were the only things that I had prearranged for my trip. For the rest, I had the freedom and flexibility to take it as it came. Following the receptionist's directions I joined the queue of fellow tourists. The bus arrived and we all piled on. The other travellers stayed silent, so I spent the drive talking to the bus driver, who had no idea where my hostel was. We eventually found it and I unloaded my luggage outside the backpackers accommodation in Sydney's Kings Cross district.

After a few formalities at the reception, I checked in and heaved my bags up the stairs. Reaching the top I held my breath and opened the door. A huge sigh exhaled as I took in the neat and clean six bed dormitory. Three bunk beds were pushed up against the walls, a large fridge sat in one corner and a door led through to an en-suite bathroom. Piles of clothes and photos taped to the wall told me that the other beds were already occupied, but the room was currently empty. It was early morning in Australia and I still hadn't been to sleep, but with a new city and indeed a country waiting to be explored who would want to lie in bed.

*

I removed the British pounds, euros and other now useless currencies from my wallet. Travel certainly wasn't a new pastime for me. I had grown up in England but had spent years living on various Spanish islands and occasionally ventured off on backpacking trips. Now, at the age of 27 and after a year of saving, I had finally made it to the land down under. Ahead of me were twelve months of touring and sightseeing, with the possibility of working along the way. I would start with a few weeks in Sydney to explore the city and recover from the jetlag, before heading off into the unknown.

Having packed my small rucksack with water, a guidebook and camera, I stopped to pick up a map from reception and set off in search of the Opera House. My first impression was that Sydney appeared to be just like any other city apart from it was bathed in glorious sunshine. Huge towering buildings were set against the skyline and the streets were heaving with traffic. After patiently waiting to cross at a million sets of traffic lights down

William Street, I finally came upon some greenery. The grass in the Botanical Gardens was luminous in colour and I quickened my pace excitedly. A slightly worse for wear tramp muttered something as I passed by. I wandered on contemplating what he had said when abruptly I stopped dead in my tracks.

Crossing the path was a large white bird with a ridiculous, curved beak as long as my forearm. It strutted like a stalk on its skinny, dark legs. From its plump body stretched a long, slim neck, upon which sat a tiny black head. Suddenly it hit me. Sydney wasn't just another city, this was Australia, land of the outback, adventure, Steve Irwin and Skippy the bush kangaroo—and I was free to explore it all.

The wildlife continued to fascinate me. Cockatoos squawked noisily as they flew overhead and brightly coloured parrots flitted about between the shrubberies. Under a crowd of trees I heard some high-pitched squeaking and presuming it to be a flock of birds turned my eyes upwards. What I actually saw came as somewhat of a shock. Bats. Hundreds of them and nothing like the tiny little things back in the UK. These were huge. Big ginger bodies with thick fur flew from tree to tree powered by a wingspan easily over a metre long. Transfixed, I watched them circle in the air before making impressive landings, wrapping their claws around branches and hanging upside down. A sign explained that they were in fact flying foxes and considered a pest to the local environment. All this within my first few hours in the country and there was plenty more to come.

Following the path I meandered through the park, taking in the tropical plants dramatically set against a backdrop of skyscrapers. Eventually the grass gave way to a walkway and beyond that the famous Sydney harbour. The water shimmered a deep sapphire blue and waves made a gentle rippling sound as small boats flew past. I couldn't help but smile to myself. I felt totally alive.

I stopped at a pond and was once more surprised as I noticed large eels in the shallows. A sign informed me that the eels ate the baby ducklings and were not considered a pleasant feature. Occasionally the pond was drained and park staff returned them to the harbour. However, within weeks the eels always came back, having overcome the large stone wall and dry pathway. They had even been seen slivering across the grass at night.

Following the water's edge, I was enjoying the fresh breeze soothing my jet lag when the Sydney Opera House came into view. Exactly as I had imagined, it gleamed in the sun, the shiny white armadillo shape crisp against the blue sky. Behind it loomed the enormous Harbour Bridge like a protective older sibling. The two landmarks made a striking scene. It was a strange sensation to be standing in front of icons that although I had never seen in reality, triggered a feeling of familiarity within me and I stood transfixed for some time.

In photographs the Opera House appears to be one solid unit, but I was taken aback to find that it consisted of several buildings. I rounded them before coming to a railing where I could take in the bridge by itself. I wanted to continue, but by now I had covered quite a distance and the jet lag was kicking in with force. It was only early morning in Australia but the sun was getting hotter and hotter. This was day one of many. I had plenty of time to explore and so headed back for some rest.

*

After many hours of much needed sleep, I awoke to find that one of my roommates had returned. I politely introduced myself to Chad, a young guy from Turkey. He was also new to the city and here to study and catch up with friends. My sleep had left me refreshed and revitalized. I asked Chad if he would join me and see what an evening on Kings Cross had to offer. He already had plans but invited me to come along. I opened my luggage, recovered my make-up and attempted to make myself look fresh and attractive, choosing a dress from my creased wardrobe.

Kings Cross was a colourful place to say the least. Prostitution was legal and Darlinghurst Road upon which my hostel was sat was famous for sex, nightclubs and criminals. In the years gone by, organised crime and police corruption, mixed with addicts and sex workers, formed a dangerous territory. Now the streets were far cleaner and the dealers and brawls had been curbed, at least to the public eye.

Neon lights advertised places with names like Porkies and Dreamgirls; burly bouncers stood arms folded at the entrance of nightclubs and bars. Touts or even the prostitutes themselves called out to potential clients as they passed by. A line of Harley-style motor bikes were watched over by their long haired, tattooed riders. The atmosphere was electric and I felt a buzz run through me.

We met Chad's friends and queued to enter a bar. I laughed as a doorman asked me for ID. I certainly wished that I still had the youthful looks of an 18-year-old, but my giggling soon stopped as the bouncer enquired how many drinks the boys had consumed. This seemed a little intense for entry to a fairly average looking bar. Thankfully security seemed happy with their answer, and we were allowed through. The lads explained that this rigid screening was common practice in Sydney, and if door staff had a reason to suspect drunkenness, you could be asked to go and sober up or be straight out rejected.

The four of us walked through and I paused to take in my surroundings. It was a fair sized bar with a small dance floor, and a popular hangout for backpackers. The décor was bright and modern but didn't have anything special to offer. As we queued for drinks I tried to loosen up but the jet lag still nagged away. The music certainly didn't help. The DJ's idea of mixing was simply to play two tracks at once. I'm an avid lover of almost any genre of music, but my ears cringed as one terrible mix after another belted out of a dodgy sound system. For the sake of the lads I tried to have fun. Even attempting to dance to the musical atrocity. Chad grabbed my hand and spun me around wildly, but as a remix of The Fresh Prince of Bel-Air blasted, I knew I had to get out.

To one side of me was a young American, and we had been casually chatting. He shared my disappointment, but told me there was a great club down the road which he could take me to. Relieved to have an escape plan I invited Chad to come along. He declined and told me that he didn't like my new friend. I was a little bemused and asked him why. 'Because he is talking to you,' came the reply.

Hmmm, this didn't seem good.

Having freed ourselves from Chad and the tacky club, the American and I passed through another lot of security and stepped into a lift which took us to the penthouse bar. As we entered the atmosphere hit me instantly. The vibe was young and trendy and groups of people chatted away in softly lit lounges. From the balcony was an incredible view of the street, illuminated by the famous Coca-Cola sign which took up a good part of the skyscraper opposite. We ordered beers and soaked up the house tunes that drifted through the crowd.

It was certainly a much better location, but before long my eyes were drooping once more. An hour later, I mentioned that it was time for me to leave and the American took that as his cue to shove his tongue down my throat. Thankfully he only managed to sneak in a few seconds before I got my wits together and pulled away. It was day one and I had already scored my first kiss. Hopefully any future mouth on mouth action would be more pleasurable. I made my excuses and wearily said good-night, before returning to my dormitory for some much needed shut-eye.

*

Over the next few days I spent my time walking around the city. In fact I walked so much that my feet became so sore I could hardly stand. I visited the Aquarium, rode an elevator up a huge tower overlooking the city and wandered around the modern but beautiful St Mary's Cathedral. In among the skyscrapers, parks and wharfs, were shops to die for. Yes, my name is Julia and I am a shopaholic. Not usually too much of a problem as I'm more Primark than Prada, so I could normally afford to treat myself. However, in the land down under money was not the only issue. I was now a backpacker and my bag could only take so much. Sydney must have cottoned on to this and I could almost hear the clothes taunting me as I passed by. These were no ordinary fashions. It was as if someone had gotten into my head, taken everything I loved and turned them into garments.

The people of Sydney were a melting pot of cultures and life-styles. Tourists, suited city workers and travellers came together in a jumble of bodies on George Street shopping strip. Fitness was clearly a big trend and along the harbour side women, who made Lycra look sexy, bounded past, and almost every man I came upon was built to perfection. Inspired, I attempted a few early morning runs but after ten minutes I felt as if I needed an ambulance. It was blisteringly hot, my legs hurt like hell and I looked ridiculous with my face puffing and panting like a steam train as I half jogged, half limped around the Botanical Gardens. From then on I saved my energy for sightseeing and toning my biceps as I lifted beers to my lips.

*

I had been in the hostel a few days and Chad was my only friend. He was nice enough and although we had established that we were just good friends and nothing more, he was becoming a little clingy. I broached the subject of trying to meet new people and he agreed we should be more social. As Chad pointed out, the common room wasn't the best place in which to socialise. A large TV sat on the wall and everyone seemed permanently glued to it making polite conversation hard. Luckily a Canadian girl was organising a hostel night out. She was a little loud, very funny and seemed like my kind of person. Chad complained that she talked too much. It seemed there was no pleasing him.

I got ready for my night out and a large group of us were led across the street to a bar. I spent the evening chatting and circulating among the crowd. Chad followed me around like a sheep, crossing his arms moodily and glaring at everyone I introduced him to. I would be sure to do some serious distancing over the next few days.

He was in Sydney to learn English and I always made the effort to slow mine down or help him translate words. I think he had mistaken my friendly guidance for full-time tutoring. Where he came from, life had been a little different. His eyes widened as we walked past posters advertising Miss Bikini competitions and strip shows. I love to shock and this opportunity to corrupt an innocent man was too good to miss. I dragged Chad into a pub and volunteered him to be a water boy for the wet t-shirt contest. I don't think his life will ever be the same again.

Shortly after, the hostel became overbooked and he decided to move in with his friends. I was happy to no longer be his personal translator and relieved to finally hold a conversation without his thinly haired head popping up over my shoulder.

*

Free from Chad's presence, I found myself surrounded by new

friends. Many of the travellers staying at the hostel were working. Most of them had been there for at least a few months. My favourites were a group from Ireland. I would rise early and head off for a walk. They would still be up drinking.

'How's the sightseeing going?' they would ask.

'Not bad. How's the drinking?' came my reply.

The drink of choice among backpackers was cheap boxed wine affectionately known as goon. Every morning the hostel common room would be littered with empty goon boxes with a frustrated cleaner clearing them away. Holding the wine inside the box was a sliver foil bag. Many times I came down from my room to find passed out partiers, sleeping peacefully, using their air inflated goon bag as a pillow.

I began to look forward to my early morning trip down the stairs. There was always something different to see. One day I came across a man with a sofa on top of him. Yes, seriously. He seemed totally unaware of the armchair pinning him down. Some kind person had even thought to write 'TWAT' on his forehead in permanent marker.

The side effects of drinking were just the start of early mornings in The Cross. As I exited onto Darlinghurst Road things became even stranger. Badly dressed transvestites would wobble past in their stilettos, make-up smeared around like drunken clowns. Prostitutes high from the night before, tottered about, eyes wide and glazed.

One morning, I came across a man who must have been in his sixties. He seemed to have taken a little too much. It was 7 a.m. and the sun was shining brightly in the sky. The pensioner in question was in a shop doorway, wearing Ray Ban style sunglasses, a bright pink headband and appeared to be dancing to some imaginary music while bouncing literally off the walls.

However, I never felt threatened in The Cross, merely intrigued and amused.

For years the murders, drug abuse and corruption had become so commonplace that a royal commission was sent in to clean the system and area up. Now there were security cameras and police on every corner, but the place still had an air of randomness about it, especially on a Sunday morning. If it's free entertainment you're after I highly recommend it.

ICONIC EXPERIENCES

Not a city girl by nature, I was now feeling the urge for some means of escape. The wonderful thing about Sydney is that not only is it a happening, vibrant city but a touch of paradise and freedom is never far away. The Blue Mountains are a perfect example. Only a couple of hours from the central business district, the mountains stretch as far as the eye can see. I had arranged to visit them on a bus tour and it began with a stop to see one of Australia's well-known icons.

After a couple of hours on the road we traipsed off the mini bus and I ran my eyes over the field ahead. About a hundred metres in front of us were a mob of kangaroos chewing peacefully on the grass. Mothers with babies were bent forward with their heads down, continuously munching away as we inched closer. They were a couple of metres tall, beige grey and very furry. I watched them move forward to fresh food, using only their tail and hind legs, not even stopping to lift their mouths from the ground. They were the first kangaroos I had ever seen, and we spent a good twenty minutes being captivated by their presence.

Back on the bus we headed to a waterfall which ran through the mountains. Disembarking at a viewpoint, I strolled over to the rail where an outlook of green lush forest was framed by a perfect blue sky. It was more valley than mountains but on the horizon were several ridges. Directly below me was a dizzying drop and looking over the edge made me feel ill. It was certainly breathtaking imagery and I hadn't even seen the water yet.

We began a steep descent down a rocky cliff side which followed a creek as it cascaded and tumbled over rocks and fallen trees. The stream was crystal clear and I longed to cool off in it. Down and down we went, but as our guide constantly reminded us, there was no time for a rest. We crossed the water many times, walking over it and even under it, as it poured across a ledge above our heads. All the while spectacular views across the gorge could be seen from gaps between the trees. The other people on the tour seemed quiet, reserved and a tad dull. I chatted with the guide but learned very little about the area.

Before long we headed back up via a steep path paved by a seemingly endless set of stairs. Huffing and puffing we began the climb, every now and then I would pull out my camera and turn towards the scenery, any excuse for a rest. Eventually we made it to the top and with the waterfall finally conquered I collapsed back onto the bus.

Pulling up at another lookout (Aussie for viewpoint) I paused to read a plaque. It declared that the falls were named after a man called Govett, as he had, and I quote, 'first come upon the spot'. I found this hysterical and stood there giggling away with the class of a naughty schoolgirl. No one else found it even the slightest bit funny so I straightened up and carried on.

Next up were the Three Sisters, three huge, orange tinted chucks of rock that stood towering over the forest below. Crowds of tourists hovered about admiring the landscape and snapping up pictures. I meandered among the families, backpackers and Asian tour groups trying to find a gap along the railing, but before long we were being herded back onto the mini bus.

The need for speed was justified as our guide happily announced that we would have time to stop at a bottle shop. Bottle shops are the only places in Australia, other than licensed bars and restaurants, where the public can purchase alcohol. I would personally have preferred refreshment via a waterfall swim, but it seemed we had no choice. Not one to turn down a beer, I grabbed a couple of bottles and savoured their cool crisp taste as we sat on a rock face, taking in the vast mountains stretching out infinitely below. The day had been picture-perfect and I was certainly glad to have gotten some country air into my lungs, but all too soon we were returning to Sydney and the hustle and bustle of The Cross.

*

Many of the backpackers staying in the hostel were looking for employment. Quite a few had previously worked on farms and were now looking for something with a higher earning potential in the city. Apparently it was possible to gain an extra years working holiday visa after the completion of three months farm work. It sounded interesting, but I was warned of long hours, hard labour and lots of snakes and spiders. Anyhow, surely a year to see the country was more than enough?

In the common room a noticeboard advertised cars, camper vans and station wagons for sale. Many backpackers bought them to travel the country and most came equipped with camping gear. I couldn't help but read that board most days, wishing I had a travel companion to accompany me on such a journey.

Australia was so vast that even with a partner, I wasn't sure I would cope with driving such long distances.

I was sharing my room with two very sweet German girls who were nearly fluent in English and a French guy who didn't speak any. As none of us knew any French our contact with Francois was limited. Chad's bed had been filled by another German. A very tall, extremely camp, apparently straight guy called Christof. We hit it off instantly, both of us a little crazy, bonding through our shared passion for partying. We hit the clubs, went for long walks, sunbathed in the park and the friendship quickly turned to romance.

The hostel dorm was decorated with our posters and photos. The German girls who were working in the city had photos of their boyfriends, back in Germany, proudly displayed. I had a picture of my father sticky taped to the wall, while Christof had porno posters. He was working in a sex shop. A perk of the job was an unlimited supply of posters, advertising DVDs of various tacky and sometimes scary natures. On the door to our room was a sign declaring that the bus stop had temporarily been moved. It had been stolen by Christof during one of our drunken nights out.

*

Having been captivated by kangaroos, it was time for me to witness another of Australia's natural icons, the beaches of Sydney and in particular the infamous Bondi Beach. Christof had to work so I headed out alone. I had been prewarned that the beach was overhyped and overpopulated. Wanting to see the place for myself, I boarded a train from Kings Cross station. The train ride was short, but at Bondi Junction I had to find the connecting bus which would take me to the ocean front.

The bus was packed, as surf boards, tourists and backpacks fought for any remaining inch of space. I distracted myself from the claustrophobia by staring out of the window until it was time to break into the fresh air of the Australian coast.

Bondi was a large arch of creamy yellow sand with a cobalt blue ocean breaking upon its shore. As predicted it was jam packed with people, but I was happy to breathe in the smell of ocean spray and feel the sand between my toes. I was due to meet some backpackers from the hostel who were waiting for me on the promenade. We all piled down onto the soft sand, laid out our towels and I relished the warm sun and refreshing breeze as it rushed over my body.

Out in the waves were hordes of surfers and I was eager to see the typically Australian pastime in action. They made the jump to standing on the board seem effortless and a horde of wetsuit clad figures rode the waves, cutting in and out of the surf before tumbling into the foam. Life guards used a megaphone to call to people swimming in dangerous areas and the sound echoed across the wind. Backpackers sat in groups, families built castles in the sand and sweaty muscular bodies pounded up and down as locals set about their fitness routines. It may have been busy and crowded but there was a definite, vibrant buzz that floated about on the shore. I had only been in Sydney for a short time and I had already come to love the hostel and its inhabitants. Every night there was a group outing to a different bar. Great music, dance floors and girls wearing dresses to die for, came together, to complete a fantastic night in The Cross. During the day I would chat while I cooked in the shared kitchen and eventually it took me half an hour just to get down the stairs. There were always people I recognised who wanted to swap stories or say hello.

I continued my wanderings around the city, exploring the glamorous Darling Harbour and frantic Paddy's Markets. The wildlife continued to astound me and one day a large, scary looking lizard caught my attention. A big white flap hung under its huge jaw, black stripes lined its back and the belly was coloured brick orange. From a distance I took photos, when all of a sudden another one, equal in size, jumped out of a bush and the two began to fight. They were easily each a metre long.

Together Christof and I visited Coogee Beach which was still beautiful but a lot quieter than Bondi and we watched a plane draw pictures in the sky. We also spent a day in Manly which I loved as much for the journey as for the beach itself. Instead of the trains and buses that we caught to Bondi, Manly was accessed by a ferry leaving from Circular Quay. As the vessel pulled away all on board were treated to a spectacular view of the Opera house and Harbour Bridge. The beach itself was unlike those in the east. Instead of a small bay, Manly's sand was long, stretching and stunningly beautiful.

*

It was my last few days in Sydney and by now I'd had enough time to acclimatise. It was time to move on. I had been invited to stay with a very good friend in Adelaide for Christmas but as always the Yuletide had snuck up far too quickly. Long gone were my childhood habits of excitedly counting down the days, but this year at least things would be a little different.

Before my flight I had a few days left to fill with adventures and sightseeing, so Christof and I made the long walk to and across the Harbour Bridge. It had been on my to-do list since arriving, so I was full of energy and excitement as we set off. My enthusiasm didn't last long. Although the view of the bridge was not far from The Cross, the stairs up to the structure certainly were. The sun was pounding down and the air thick with heat. We lightened the atmosphere by purchasing some matching reindeer horns and having our photos taken in front of anything

Christmassy. In fact we hardly took them off for the remainder of my time in the city.

The view from the bridge was worth the trek, and we stood looking down onto the harbour and Opera House before battling the ferocious wind, that had appeared from nowhere. We fought against it, straining as it pushed my body back in the opposite direction. This was far from the romantic walk I had imagined. Next to us a stream of traffic honked and screeched and petrol fumes fogged the air managing to survive the wind better than we were.

Finally with the bridge conquered and crossed, I insisted we treated ourselves to lunch. After, I casually suggested that we should catch the train home. Christof shot me down in a second; it seemed my aching feet would have to retrace their steps. At least the wind would be behind us this time. Once again I heaved my sore body up the steps and braced myself to feel the now helpful gale against my back, but the air was still and nature, clearly against me.

*

It was now my last night in the city and I was not the only one. Phil from New Zealand was also leaving and had decided to hold a hostel Christmas party. Christof and I were delighted that our reindeer horns would finally get an official wearing. Our hostel kitchen was usually a chaotic, messy nightmare. If you could find a saucepan with a handle, it was best to hold on to it for life or risk never seeing it again. In fact things had become so bad that I had bought my own cup which I kept hidden under my bed.

On the night of the party you could hardly recognise the place. A large leg of ham sat at the head of a long buffet, no less than ten different types of cheese graced a platter and a bread basket hosted a selection of rolls. The surrounding horde of back-packers, who had been surviving on a diet of pasta and goon, crowded the table with hungry eyes and rumbling stomachs. A few made a grab for the food but were stopped by Phil's helpers.

I had already eaten more than my share. Christof had been helping to prepare the buffet while I swanned around the kitchen filming on my video camera and stealing blocks of cheese. With the preparations complete, Phil gave a speech thanking everyone for their company, drunkenness (whilst winking at the Irish) and good times. A cheer went up and at least fifty greedy hands dived at the table. It was possibly the best meal ever eaten in a hostel, certainly in Kings Cross.

I went up to bed early as the airport shuttle bus was due to collect me at 4 a.m. A few hours later, I begrudgingly got up to the sound of my alarm. I tried not to wake the rest of the room; we had already said our goodbyes. Christof was working in the sex shop so I crossed the road to see him. Amongst the dildos, anal beads and crotchless panties we embraced. Christof assured me he would be waiting for me when I returned in a couple of months. By this point I had planned some of my travels. I don't know who cried more, but I do know that I was the only one able to hold back until I had left the shop.

It had only been a few short weeks. We were both from different worlds and we both knew the relationship had no future, but it didn't stop us caring deeply for one another and I will always hold a place for Christof's friendship deep in my heart.

CHAPTER 2

A VERY WARM CHRISTMAS AND A SWELTERING NEW YEAR

A SCREAM ROSE UP as the two girls embraced. Emma and I were finally reunited. We had first met four years earlier when she arrived in Tenerife, one of the Canary Islands. I had employed her in the bar I managed and we bonded quickly, causing chaos and laughter wherever we went.

Just as, if not more outrageous than myself, Emma was a free spirit. In fact she was the reason that I had come to Australia in the first place. I had previously ignored the land down under. It was so common for Brits to travel the country, and with the same language and a similar culture I didn't see what I would learn from the place. I was more than happy to be proved very, very wrong.

Since our first meeting, Emma had flown to Europe on several occasions and together we had terrorised Italy, Ireland and the inhabitants of Amsterdam. Now at last I was going to see where this blonde ball of energy originated from.

Who would have thought that the quiet and upmarket suburb of Athelstone, Adelaide would be home to such a reckless but loveable girl. She collected me in her gorgeous blue convertible and I gasped as I saw the family home. Emma was currently living with her parents, having just returned from studying in France. The place was beautiful and could have come straight from the pages of a magazine. The two storied house was decked out with exquisite artefacts and paintings which had been collected by Emma's parents as they travelled the world. The garden was equally as stunning and backed on to a wildlife park. I was thrilled to hear that they often had koalas and kangaroos visit the yard.

Finally free from the hostel dorm, I was to have my own air-conditioned room with a double bed. Oh the luxury. Emma's parents were warm and welcoming. I had met them during a visit they had made to Sydney shortly after my arrival in Australia. Bill, Emma's father had been there on business and had wanted to meet the girl their daughter talked of so often. That day I had been nervous as hell. I felt as though I was meeting my in-laws for the first time. Thankfully there had been no awkward moments, although Sharon, Emma's mother had told me:

'I can see why you and Emma get on so well. You don't stop talking either.'

I'd been so nervous that I hadn't shut up throughout the whole lunch. This time around big hugs were exchanged as they welcomed me and warned me to expect a busy day this Christmas. Twenty-five of us would be having dinner, three houses would be visited, with a trip to church squeezed into the middle.

We spent that afternoon at Emma's friend's house and I swear it was like a home from the set of Neighbours. A one storey, wooden panelled house, complete with a pool and a couple of teenagers playing with a beach ball. It was just the day I needed and gave me a chance for some rest before Christmas was upon us.

*

I wasn't expecting much from Christmas Day; it wasn't my family after all. So imagine my surprise when I came down the stairs to find a stocking with my name on it next to Emma's. Father Christmas hadn't visited my house for years; Emma must have bought out the inner child in me. Not only had Sharon, I mean Santa, brought me gifts but had gone one step further and been thoughtful enough to buy me things I could actually use. Useless presents are frustrating at the best of times, so imagine having to lug them around a mammoth of a country to boot. Thoughtful Santa had provided me with shampoo, conditioner, mozzie repellent, a silk sleeping bag liner and a posh bottle of Champagne. Coming from a small family and normally spending Christmas abroad, this kindness meant an awful lot to me. Emma gave me a slip of paper promising to pay for one of our days out, and I handed over a goody bag full of things for the festival we would be going to. Everything from party poppers to New Year's hats and glow sticks, it was an entire bag of tack and she loved it.

Australia itself had sent me a gift in the form of a very cute koala sitting in a tree in the backyard. Grey and furry with little white tufts on its ear, the darling thing was gorgeous, but not particularly entertaining. It seemed they spent most of their time sleeping, saving all the moving around for when the gaping audience were sound asleep themselves.

I was most impressed to see Sharon cooking a big hunk of meat on the BBQ. It may not have been throwing a shrimp on the barbie but it was Australian enough for me to whip out my camera. The whirlwind continued as we headed off to church to keep Granddad happy. Emma and I sniggered like children as the lady behind me sang very loudly and somewhat out of tune. She was later introduced to me as one of the relatives. The day flew past and we returned to Emma's house for a huge lunch, so huge in fact, I had to lie down for an hour after eating. They say family keeps the magic of Christmas alive and I must say that year it really did.

*

It was now time to hit the road for our New Year's celebrations. For this epic journey we were going to borrow Emma's father's silver Volvo and it was overflowing with food, drink, camping gear and clothes. There would be four of us setting off at the unreasonable hour of 5 a.m. Emma and I were to be joined by her boyfriend Bruce, who was flying in from Sydney and her friend Jenny. I hadn't met either of them before, but it didn't matter in the slightest as any friend of Emma's had to be up for a good time.

Jenny was in her early twenties, classic and classy with beautiful porcelain skin and long dark hair. Her elegant manner matched her look, but she still seemed more than happy to camp in a field with riffraff like myself. Bruce had met Emma in France. He was in his early thirties, lean and muscular with a passion for the outdoors, surviving on a strict vegan diet. I was intrigued by his dietary choice as I had been a vegetarian for years, but didn't have enough willpower to make the leap to veganism. Emma was blonde with the personality the size of an atomic bomb and the devastating good looks to match. Between the four of us there was certainly some diversity.

The festival was held approximately 1,000 kms away on the outskirts of Melbourne. We set off, but as the car turned out of the street we noticed a cloud of smoke and then to our horror, flames engulfing hills behind the house. This was my first encounter with a wild bush fire, and I seriously hoped it would be my only one. Jenny and Emma called their families who promised to make sure the authorities would be alerted.

With home for many Australians surrounded by wild bushland, one spark or dropped cigarette had the potential to leave whole towns homeless, and the same can be said for the local wildlife. Most Australians were aware of the dangers, and the whole country was covered with signs which predicted the daily fire risk. The scale started with green for a very low—moderate risk, leading up to high, very high, severe, extreme and finally a bright red section with the word catastrophic across it in bold letters—which probably meant the sign was on fire while you were reading it. The government advised that if you lived in a fire risk area you should have a fire evacuation plan. Most bush fires could be controlled and were often accidental but occasionally, despite all efforts from home owners and the fire service, the flames took over with horrendous consequences.

In 2009, a vicious bush fire led to a terrifying ordeal that became known as Black Saturday. On February 7th, approximately 400 fires took hold in Victoria destroying over 2,000 homes, damaging many more and shockingly, killing 173 people and injuring over 400. I was very aware of how dangerous those angry flames on the hill could be. Fortunately, we later heard that the helicopters managed to contain the blaze using water bombs. I was disturbed to hear it had been started by arsonists, a fairly common occurrence. What kind of sick person would do something so dangerous?

With the drama behind us we relaxed into the drive; between us and the festival stood a ten hour journey. Emma took the wheel only stopping for a lunch break and to see the Giant Koala. No, not a real life fluffy kola but a big tacky plastic replica. The Big Things around Australia started with the Big Banana at Coffs harbour and from there on spread like the plague. Australia was home to the Big Prawn, the Big Guitar, the Big Milkshake, a whole variety of Big Fruit and even a Big Bull. The landmarks served no other purpose than to attract tourists and fill the tills with cash. Sadly for the proprietors we skipped the gift shop laden with postcards and ironic mini statues of the Big Koala. Preferring to take our pictures, go to the loo and save our cash for something more substantial, such as alcohol or party hats.

The night before the festival we were staying at a house in Wonthaggi. It was owned by a friend of Jenny's family who were currently away on holiday. We were sharing with the house-sitter, a very friendly lady in her fifties. She had blue shining eyes, a welcoming smile and informed us that she was a Jehovah's Witness.

Meanwhile as she explored the back garden and tried out the trampoline, Emma was bitten by a bull ant. Even the ants were different in Australia ranging from yellow and green to hard black armoured. They varied in size from the tiny but vicious, to evil looking ones the size of a matchstick. Apparently they also gave a nasty bite. On the bottom of Emma's foot was an angry red welt which continued to sting for the next few hours.

*

Wonthaggi didn't have much nightlife to offer, but after a day in the confines of the car we were desperate to stretch our legs. The local RSL club seemed our only option. RSL stood for Returned and Services League, and it reminded me of working men's clubs back in the UK. On entry we filled in a visitors form, and I cringed at the school canteen style restaurant and room full of arcade machines. After grabbing a well-earned glass of wine, Emma headed for the flashing lights of the fruit machines. Pokies, as they were known in Australia, were a national obsession. According to a BBC program, Australians spent more on gambling than on alcohol and petrol. Quite a statement for a nation with a huge country to drive around and a passion for beer. Government sponsored signs warned that eventually the machine would always win. This didn't seem to bother the current patrons, and several retirement age women, sat transfixed in front of the blinking lights, repetitively pumping machines with coins. I had no idea how to operate the things, let alone win, but the others took seats, so I tried my luck. One by one I slotted in five dollar coins. Wheels spun, lights flashed and chirpy noises led me to believe I was in with a chance. A few minutes later, the previously excited contraption called out an abrupt *uh err! Dooooooooooollp!* Before falling silent.

In the meantime Bruce, Emma and Jenny had all come away with various amounts of winnings. Emma, ever the professional gambler (you should see the girl in a casino), had won the highest prize, four times what she had put in. Everyone had stuck to $5 bets, but $20 was certainly enough for a few glasses of wine.

Then it was off to join the grey haired masses in the canteen room for a drink or ten. A crackly microphone announced a raffle with the opportunity to win a large tray of meat. Bruce and I shuddered at the thought, but perked up at the next prize.

'Win your weight in beer,' came a shaky voice, echoing through the ancient speakers. Sadly we were too late to take part, but a rather large lady did well out of her winning ticket. A few hours later, slightly worse for wear, we wandered back to find the house-sitter still wide awake. We three girls crashed into bed, while Bruce sat up learning about Jehovah.

*

I awoke with excited butterflies in my stomach; we were off to my first ever camping festival. This time Bruce took the wheel as the house-sitter waved us off. She had been very helpful, mentioning a derelict housing estate where we could camp for free if we needed to. Apparently sometimes her group went there to witness. I have no idea what that would involve, but some things are better left a mystery.

All four of us were looking forward to the festival, but couldn't relax completely as we still had to get our secret stash into the grounds. We had concealed a highly valuable, possibly dangerous and definitely banned cargo. Hidden among pillows and camping chairs was a copious amount of alcohol. The event banned party-goers from bringing their own booze, but after spending a fortune on tickets we had been forced to take our own.

To avoid confiscation we, and by we I mean Emma, had come up with some cunning ideas. The first had been to siphon out the sugary juice from a screw top jar of preserved peaches. The liquid was replaced by a potent mix of white rum, vodka and gin. A large box of bagged water had been careful opened only to be resealed with a sack of goon sitting in its place. A bottle of vodka had been stuffed in with Emma's luggage and Bruce had a bottle of Jägermeister gaffer tapped to his leg. We were fully loaded.

As the silver Volvo turned into the ground, men in florescent jackets indicated for us to join one of four long queues. The sun was shining, the sky was clear and we couldn't wait to start the party. We climbed out of the car to stretch our legs and Bruce headed to the front of the line to find what was causing the delay. He returned with bad news, searchers were going through every vehicle, bag and boot hunting for forbidden booze. Girls had to empty their toiletry bags, spare wheels were being pulled out and festival goers were driving through the gate devastated at having their stash confiscated.

The queue crawled forward, our suspense and anxiousness building as it went. As we reached the front a tired looking worker approached our car to check our tickets and ID. As one of the last cars, we were hoping he would have lost enthusiasm for a full search. Either way we had a plan worked out. Our biggest concern was Emma's bottle of vodka, it wouldn't be difficult to find. We opened our bags, but as the inspector headed towards her luggage I pulled out my underwear and loudly asked if I really had to empty my dirty knickers out for inspection. The distraction worked and soon enough we were sailing on through to freedom.

Arriving at our designated camping spot we set up our tents. I had borrowed mine from Emma's parents. Rather than the normal sausage shaped pack, it came in a circular flat bag. This was no ordinary tent; this was a pop-up tent. Possibly the best invention I have ever come across. I simply released it from the confines of the bag and hey presto, within seconds the tent popped itself up. All I had to do was peg it down and unzip the fly screened air vents, saving valuable minutes of party time. Bruce poured us an unusual cocktail of vodka, goon and cream soda which tasted just as bad as it sounds. Emma and I filtered it into our children's batman flasks which we clipped around our waists, before heading to the main stage. The heat beat down, the pure blue sky making a picture-perfect day.

The stage was set against a backdrop of green hills, soaring cliffs and deep blue ocean. A subtle electric buzz ebbed through the crowd who were milling around, taking in the sights and sounds. A spray of water cooled festival goers as they walked through a mist tent, and water stations were dotted around to refill empty bottles. A scattering of clothing, jewellery and food stalls formed a shopping area, and a first aid stand stood waiting for anyone overcome by heat, drink or drugs. Stretching as far back as I could see, a variety of flags fluttered in the breeze. Rising up from tents and vans they would help the owners locate their beds among the jungle of tents. We watched a few bands, most of whom I had never heard of. The Australians had a vast amount of musical talent, but sadly much of it never reached Europe. I was in for a tuneful education.

Several hours later we returned to base to fill up the flasks, paint pictures on each other with zinc (a coloured sunscreen stick) and play with our bubble blowers. The place was awash with randomness. Someone had set up a children's paddling pool by the arena entrance, a blow-up doll bounced around in the crowd and Emma set off on a spree of chaos. Upon seeing a game of giant ten pin bowling she became a human ball, interrupting the participant's turn and just missing out on a strike. Emma and Bruce then cartwheeled off to the tents and danced on the roof of her dad's Volvo.

*

That night we partied hard, possibly too hard, judging by how I felt when I awoke on New Year's Eve. It was far too early and far too hot. Sadly the pop-up in all its wonder didn't come with an air conditioning unit. I wanted to curl up and go back to sleep, but the tent was rapidly turning into a sauna and my head a pounding ball of pain. There would be no more rest for the wicked. I grabbed my batman flask which I had managed to fill with water the night before. I took a big gulp, waited for refreshment to hit, but instead retched in disgust as water with a hint Jägermeister hit my taste buds. Unfortunately the 'Julia must not drink Jäger' rule had not been enforced. My alcohol tolerance was simply too low and shots always ensured a vile hangover. I was later informed that when offered the potent liquor I declared:

'Jägerbombs!!! Awesome!!! Fill me up. Wooooooooooo!' without a moment's hesitation. I couldn't even palm off the blame. The odour never left that flask, and subsequently the flavour of it haunted me for the rest of the festival.

The previous evening was a blur, but I remembered jumping around like crazy to bands I had never heard of. Gazing in awe, mesmerised by the brightly coloured lights as they whirled around the DJ tent and making a variety of weird and wonderful friends. One in particular stood out. A very hot, buff, nineteen-year-old called Doug, whom we renamed 'Doug the disappointer' for reasons I am not prepared to reveal.

Faced with being cooked alive inside my polyester home, I begrudgingly opened the tent flap and screwed up my eyes in agony as the sunshine hit. Staggering around like a plane crash survivor, I attempted to make it across the field to the toilets. I only narrowly missed Doug's pool of vomit that he had inconsiderately planted between my tent and the Volvo. On my return from the very fragrant portaloo, Bruce and Emma also emerged. The looks on their faces told me everything I needed to know, no cartwheels today. But not everyone had overindulged in festival madness and Jenny waltzed up to the camp as fresh as a daisy, making us feel even sicker.

We did all share one common need, the luxury of a shower. As with most festivals, the toilet situation was a disgusting mess of trailers and portaloos. Revellers had to queue for a lifetime in order to wade through urine, vomit and worse before balancing themselves precariously over the bowl. The showers were also in one of those trailers. Rumour had it that there was only one shower block for the entire festival. I approached it, but the queue itself was enough to stop me, let alone the thought of the grimy floors that were no doubt already clogged with hair and dirt.

Armed with shower gel, toothbrushes and plastic tubs, Emma, Jenny and I headed for the nearest water tap. We refreshed ourselves under its stream, washing each other down with the tubs much like a mother with a child in a baby bath. We drew some curious stares but we were clean (ish), cool and ready for our next hit of New Year's fever.

The sun blazed and I swear I could hear the grass crackle in the heat. The four of us sat under a sunshade eating breakfast, as we enjoyed wafts of music drifting from the stage and took in views of the deep blue ocean beyond. My hangover began to slowly ebb away or maybe it was just masked by a fresh intake of alcohol.

After breakfast we headed down to explore the art tent. A selection of paint and brushes were available to put our own personal mark on a poster wall. Emma found it much more entertaining to paint Bruce. He ran away, but was chased by the mad brush-wielding South Australian. The art tent volunteers looked on in dismay as Emma disappeared into the crowd, leaving a trail of decorated bodies and ruined clothes in her wake. The sun continued to pound down, and I continuously made attempts to cool off, but any moisture from the mist tent or hoses evaporated in seconds.

On one of her adventures, Emma fell down the toilet truck stairs. Nursing her injury she made friends with the attendant, as the kind lady offered her a plaster. We were all taken to meet the thoughtful woman, who spent her day sitting under the stinking truck and clearing up various disgusting disasters. Emma was very proud of her new friend who let her pretend to drive 'the poo truck' while we took photos and attempted to look pleased for her. Emma was much like a child who would innocently bring home a used condom as a treasure for her parents. She was easily pleased by the most random and occasionally disgusting things. Sadly that wasn't the end of her dirty antics. From having someone's half eaten watermelon on her head, to running around wearing an odd work glove while waving a manky, chewed, corn cob. We were certainly never short of entertainment.

At one point we returned back to camp for a break, but feeling restless I started a solo silent iPod party in one of the walkways. In my head I could hear the tunes pumping away; to the rest of the crowd I must have looked deranged. However, a few people joined in with the dancing, trusting me to set the pace to the otherwise unheard sound. One fellow dancer caught my attention. He was wearing a t-shirt with a to-do list on it. The list was all festival related and he informed me that there was still one task to be completed. They had yet to build a human pyramid.

I turned off the iPod and set out as project manager for the dangerous construction. I began by recruiting as many strong looking men as I could. Quite a pleasurable task I must say. Five guys, including Bruce formed the base, lined up on their hands and knees. Four more followed suit on top, then three, then two. But just as I instructed a slim girl to climb to the top, the whole thing literally fell to pieces in a jumble of hot sweaty bodies. It was a devastating moment and only later did Bruce confess to being the cause. Trust it to be one of my own letting the team down.

*

Emma's mother had texted us with a storm warning, but we all prayed she was wrong. It seemed so implausible with the sky a solid block of perfect blue, but as the afternoon progressed a breeze picked up. Although we welcomed its fresh relief, I knew it was a signal of what was to come. We tried not to let it ruin the mood and back at the main stage I fell in love with a group whose music still takes me back to that moment. I couldn't wipe the smile of my face, we were all so ridiculously happy. Then everything changed very quickly.

The clouds didn't exactly sneak up, more rushed across, thick, black and angry, coating the sky. Having been prewarned we headed for the shelter of a giant sunshade before the masses joined us. The refreshing breeze picked up to a furious wind, before finally becoming a howling gale. Partygoers began running around manically, desperate for shelter. The heavens opened and the clouds spat out a vicious torrent of water, while forked lightening violently punctured the gloom.

From our increasingly cramped shelter we could see the lighting rig on the main stage swinging around precariously, the performers had been called off. The area under the 'sun' shade was ram packed, but various revellers made a break out into the storm to save their tents as the gale battered on. Others danced around, half or in some cases fully naked, in front of the empty stage, ignoring the loud speaker warning them to move away. It was now 10 p.m. and New Year's wasn't looking promising. After an hour of enduring English lads belting out tuneless songs and starting doomed Mexican waves, the rain began to slow.

It was now or never, we would run to check on our camp. It was a long way back to the tents and I shivered as we ran. My face stung as the wind battered sharp rain against it. All around flattened tents lay like corpses and wreckage blew across the field. I was dreading what we would find at our camp. Jenny and I jumped straight into our tents. I breathed a sigh of relief as I found only a small pool of water in my tent. Bruce and Emma had a larger problem on their hands. The waterproof top sheet had blown off their tent, leaving only the flimsy mosquito net. Fortunately the tarpaulin was plastered against a nearby car, but I felt for them as Bruce faced the blustering winds and pounding rain to fix up their battered shelter. From the warmth and safety of my sleeping bag I called to see if he needed assistance and was more than happy to hear him decline.

Snuggled up and finally getting some warmth into my body, my excitement and adrenaline started up once more. Storm or not, this was New Year's Eve at a huge festival and it was now 11 p.m. I cranked up my music and waited for the others to regroup so we could make our next move. At last the rain slowed and then finally stopped. Thousands of people all breathed a collective sigh of relief, and those of us who still had tents, emerged back into the open. Luckily for Bruce and Emma the top sheet must have torn free just before we made it to our tents. Their bags and bedding were only slightly damp. Jenny had managed to escape without a drip of water inside hers and within minutes we were heading back up towards the main arena.

Hordes of others had also congregated. We had missed out on a few acts, but the stage was being cleaned and the microphones tested, so we were sure the headliners would be walking on at any moment. The minutes ticked by. Nothing happened. 11.40 p.m., 11.50 p.m., they must be coming on at 12 a.m. for the count-down we all decided. 11.57, 11.58, 11.59, nothing. Eventually at about 12.03 a.m. someone in the crowd boldly started a half-hearted countdown and we all cried, 'Happy New Year,' with as much enthusiasm as a class chanting their times tables.

We had been let down, badly. It wasn't the lack of entertain-ment that annoyed everyone, so much as the organisers leaving us all standing hopeful. They tested working microphones which could have announced the lack of performance or even simply given us an official countdown. They did however play Prince's famous song with the line, 'gonna party like its 1999'. If the lyr-ics rang true he must have endured a pretty shit party that year. Some people waved sparklers, we all hugged and some even attempted to dance, but our spirits were almost as damp as our tents.

In an attempt to make up for the disappointing New Years, Bruce, Emma, Jenny and I headed over to the DJ tent to dance it out. My mood was lifted by a New Year's kiss. After pressing myself against a washboard stomach and being held in muscular arms, I felt much better.

Later that night I walked around the camp site making friends and trying to help the washed out homeless, many of whom had taken to sleeping in uncomfortable cars. In my boozy haze I kindly invited anyone and everyone who needed somewhere to sleep, a place in my tiny, two man tent.

'The tent down by the big white van,' I cried. 'It's dry and cosy. I just want to help.'

The soggy campers looked on in dismay, probably swearing to avoid the tent at all costs, as the drunken English girl staggered past.

I did get one taker, in the form of an 18-year-old big mistake who was very attractive and enthusiastic. I probably should have taken a little more time to get to know him, but in my alcohol ridden state logic had abandoned me. It was New Year, I was single, I might as well have a good time. If only I had known what I was letting myself in for as we made our way to 'mine'.

The lad had clearly been studying a copy of the Karma Sutra, probably giggling over it with his teenage mates. As a result he left me feeling dizzy, dazed, disoriented and disappointed as he flipped me from position to position for a maximum of thirty seconds in each one. After several demands of, 'Have you come yet?!'

I tried to look convincing as I replied that I had. Hopefully, having 'satisfied' me he would now stop. Within seconds he made a grunting sound, finished and in an instant the blonde haired bombshell was gone. I felt as if a tornado had just ripped its way through my body. Surely this wasn't how sex at a festival was supposed to be. Unconsciousness couldn't come fast enough, and I fell in to a deep, dark sleep—away from storms, teenagers and drunken haziness.

*

The next morning I awoke with a bit of a shock. I was not alone and it wasn't the returning teenager. Next to me lay a rather sweaty, ginger haired man. Thankfully he was fairly skinny which enabled us to have an inch of space between our bodies in the humid cocoon. The man himself didn't concern me. I knew who he was, or more importantly that he wasn't some crazy rapist. What I found more worrying was that he had managed to clamber into my tent undetected, at some point during the night. Note to self—be sure to find a locking system for tent if planning to fall into a drunken coma.

My new bed mate was Ryan, one of the many homeless who I had generously offered a place to crash. His tent had been washed out, and I'd discovered him and his friends searching through the mud looking for their car keys. The car, now their only form of shelter, had sat smugly in the boggy grass tormenting them with its potential warmth, cosiness and dry surfaces upon which to sleep. Who knows where the other two boys had gone, but Ryan had clearly decided to take up my offer of a bed for the night.

I lay still for as long as I could, not sure of the correct morning greeting for the current situation. 'Sleep well?', 'How do you like your eggs?', or a gentle neck nuzzle, were all firmly out of the question. I just prayed he wasn't one for a case of morning glory. While my mind pondered, my bladder nagged me to get up. Fortunately my dilemma was answered as Emma's voice roused Ryan from his beauty sleep. Loud and clear her South Australian accent bounced around the muggy confines, 'Hey, Julia! There's a used condom out the front of your tent!'

Ryan's eyes pinged open and stared directly into mine.

'Errrr, well it's nothing to do with me,' I called back unconvincingly. Two men in one night was a little much to explain during already questionable circumstances. My teenage tornado had obviously left me a memento, what a little charmer.

Sweaty ginger man and sweaty backpacker, plus even sweatier tent, equals get me out of here now! My full bladder was now being backed by a strong desire to vomit. Unplastering the foam camping mat from my moist back, I crawled out towards the zipper, taking care not to come into contact with Ryan's half naked, pimpled body. Finally reaching freedom, the breeze hit me like a shot of morphine. The nausea left, my body relaxed and I breathed in the wonderful freshness.

The cool day wrapped itself around me and I finally felt ready to lift my head and take a look around. Out of the thousands of festival goers it seemed we were the last to leave. Closer inspection showed that from the endless sea of cars surrounding us the night before, we were one of only three remaining. The entire neighbourhood had upped and left while we were sleeping. Wow, that really was a deep, deep sleep. In place of the cars and vans was an ocean of debris. Soggy tents, broken camp chairs, mattresses and scattered randomness littered the site. Bruce and Emma were in their element playing camp site cricket, which involved Bruce launching anything he could find in Emma's direction as she attempted to hit it with a tent pole.

My hangover washed away with excitement as I ran around searching for treasures. I have always loved other people's junk. As a child I remember staring from the car window dying to explore the ripped sofas and broken wardrobes piled up at the dump. I saved my pocket money to spend at boot sales. Then as an adult I explored charity shops (Op shops as they are known in Australia), hoping to find a valuable vintage jacket but coming home with a load of useless tat. So to me this vast stretch of chaos was actually a field of gold.

Ryan had surfaced and we strolled towards the toilet block praying it would still be open. He confided that he could do with an extra camp chair, and once our bladders had been emptied I was off on a mission. I returned to the Volvo with two chairs in perfect condition for Ryan and a table for us. By this time Emma had moved on from cricket and was now spray painting 'POO!' onto a giant piece of plywood. Who actually brings that kind of stuff to a festival? A car bumped past and Ryan and his mates waved from the window. The recommended departure time had been 10 a.m., it was now 1 p.m., but what was the hurry? I was glad to have been lying in my tent instead of sitting in a queue of traffic which surely would have formed as everyone departed at once. Eventually packed up and ready to go we gave Emma a few extra minutes to run and bellyflop herself onto an abandoned tent, before we set off back to the real world.

*

As it turned out normal existence actually felt like heaven after our few days surviving in alcoholic tramp-style conditions. Jenny, who was currently my heroine, had booked us a motel room for the night. At the time we had all objected, saying that we would find a campground, but as I stepped into the piping hot shower I was happy to be wrong. The water washed away all traces of teenage boys, sweaty dancing and alcoholic fumes. When I got out all that remained was a happy glow, memories to last a lifetime and some dirt under my toe nails that didn't move for weeks.

Back in the room we stretched out on our beds lolling around in comfort. Bruce and Emma ran out onto the grass to play Frisbee while I remained true to my British roots and made everyone tea. Once we had cleaned up, feeling human once more, we took a stroll down to the beach and enjoyed a late lunch. Happy and full we headed back to spend the evening lying in bed watching films.

I turned on the television and paused, it was the news. Footage of the previous night played as Trafalgar Square erupted with cheering and hugs when the clock turned twelve. Moscow danced as crazy Russians tried to keep upright on the icy streets while sipping vodka from hip flasks. The Eiffel Tower lit up, as a blaze of fireworks illuminated Paris. And then in dramatic contrast, the camera cut to a field of brown trampled grass and abandoned rubbish. It was a very familiar scene.

A female news reporter stood among the wreckage, speaking gravely into a large black microphone '... but it wasn't all fun and festivities. Last night this area behind me was hit by a vicious storm washing out and cancelling performances at the famous New Year's festival ...'

While the rest of the world had been partying we had sat crouched ironically under a giant sunshade. Oh well, at least our shelter had stayed firmly on the ground. Apparently one of the others had blown over, in the 100 kilometre per hour (kph) wind, almost crushing the people who had been taking refuge under it. Glad that the cold and wet was behind us we munched on chocolate as a romcom played on the TV and one by one we fell into a well-earned sleep.

THE GREAT OCEAN ADVENTURE

From here on four would become three, as we dropped Jenny off at Melbourne airport. She had to return to work while the rest of us would continue the trip back to Adelaide the long way round. Between Melbourne and the Festival State (South Australia) stood one of the country's most popular and striking features. The Great Ocean Road was a 263 km drive edged by stunning beaches, dramatic rock formations and hopefully clear skies. Starting just outside of Geelong, an hour from Melbourne, it would provide a wonderful backdrop to our long drive.

The first place of interest was a small town named Torquay.

Much like its namesake back in the UK, Torquay down under was very popular with surfers and day trippers due to its beaches. However, it wasn't the prospect of sunbathing and a swim that had caught my attention. The place was filled with discounted surf wear shops. Emma and I excitedly bounced from Rip Curl to Billabong, gathering around brightly coloured purses and cute summer dresses while Bruce poured over racks of wetsuits and board wax.

Then it was off to the Surf Museum. Small, but interesting, the history of surf was portrayed via photos, video and boards. Impressive pictures of huge waves which dwarfed the surfers, lined the walls, pushing home the power of the ocean. To Bruce these were images of heaven, to me the thought of playing mercy to a huge volume of water, supported by a slice of fibreglass coated foam, brought on visions of total and utter pounding fear. Further on we came to a surf board balanced on springs where we could pretend to ride a wave. Photos taken, Emma and I headed for the gift shop while Bruce lagged behind gazing at black and white pictures of surfers past.

*

Finding a camp site that night proved to be harder than expected as most places were full. A site in Torquay's centre informed us that they might have a spot behind the pub, but due to some bikers who were embarking on a loud drinking session, it might not have allowed for much sleep. We decided to continue cruising along the coastline and beaches, dotted with postcard perfect towns. Finally in the small village of Jan Juc, we found our own slice of harmony in a wooded camping ground only a few minutes' drive from the legendary Bells Beach.

Bells was one of Australia's most notorious surfing beaches, with the waves being ridden by locals and tourists alike. The beach rose to fame with the surfing competitions which had been held there every year since 1962. With a few hours of daylight left, Bruce hit the waves while Emma and I headed to the supermarket to organise a veggie BBQ.

Shopping completed, we collected our brave surfer who must have peed repeatedly in his wetsuit just to keep some warmth in his limbs. The sun may have been shining but the breeze had an icy chill. The Southern Ocean was well known for its cool temperatures, not surprising considering the next mass it hit after Aussie waters was the ice of the Antarctic. The three of us enjoyed a tranquil BBQ with kookaburra birds laughing at us from the trees. They really did sound like they were laughing or perhaps imitating a monkey. One of the girls I met later in my trip had been fooled into believing that there were wild monkeys living in the Australian bush. Finally we fell asleep surrounded by nature, peacefully far away from drunken biker brawls.

*

The Great Ocean Road wound on and on past the stunning but busy towns of Lorne and Apollo Bay. We made a few stops for supplies and cafe breaks. As far as camping was concerned we agreed to avoid the masses and their sweet but screaming children. However, there was one tourist attraction that we could not miss, the lighthouse at Aireys Inlet. Never heard of it? I'm not surprised, most Australians haven't either, but to me it was very much a part of my childhood.

The lighthouse itself was white with a red top like most others along the way, but Aireys Inlet had something special. It was used for the filming of the children's TV show *Round the Twist*. Never heard of that either? Never mind, but some of you who grew up watching kids TV in the 1990's may remember it and the catchy theme tune, which I sang for the rest of the day, much to the annoyance of Emma and Bruce. Even without the show, the view overlooking such beautiful but rugged coastline was worth stopping for. Sadly the same can't be said for the $120 parking fine that we incurred there.

*

We spent a few days in the Cape Otway National Park, a huge stretch of forestry and wild bush edged by a vicious coastline and beaches littered with shipwrecks. We stayed at a gorgeous campground that was to become my favourite. With a field of horses next to our tents, kookaburras that swooped down to catch a snack and an ocean view just a few minutes' walk away, the place was perfect. Koalas sleepily chewed on leaves above our heads and possums played chase with each other around the grounds. There was also an open air cinema which even sold popcorn and the reception offered a variety of cheap walking tours.

The next day I booked a shipwreck tour, leaving Emma and Bruce for some time as a couple. The tour was led by a stocky local called Mark. Mark had the most Australian accent I have ever heard. It didn't resemble the sound of the other locals and I wondered if he had turned it up a notch or ten for the tourists. As his moustache bristled in the breeze, Mark taught us how to find bush tucker. I sampled a variety of grasses and berries trying my best to make pleasant faces while lying through my teeth as Mark enquired if I loved the strong lemony flavours. More like two day old fox pee with sand I thought, but I smiled and made *mmmmm* noises to please.

I was delighted to see kangaroo tracks on the beach but disappointed that there were none hanging out on the shore. I heard of the tragic ends met by ships in the Bass Straight, the mass of water between the mainland and Tasmania. Many of the boats having already travelled across the globe sank with their destined land in sight.

I'm not sure how embellished Mark's tales were, but either

way I found them enthralling. Apparently most of the wreckage scattered up the beach came from boats trying to hurry through the Straight, in the hope of beating the masses to the gold rush which drew a variety of nationalities to Australia. I had my photo taken by a large rusty anchor and watched in wonder at the power and ferociousness of the ocean as it crashed and sprayed against the rocks. The day was now overcast, as if the weather had changed to fit the tales. As the sky darkened I looked for the blinking eye of Cape Otway lighthouse which stood proudly on the headland a short distance up the coast. Piles of seaweed lay in thick rubbery mounds like grotesque sea creatures crawling from the foaming waters. Mark picked one slimy looking plant up from its sandy bed and showed us the piece of rock clamped to its root. The weed's grip on the ocean boulder was so strong that the rock had broken against the pull of the water long before the plant did. Nature really is an amazing force. Clambering over barnacled rock pools, we saw small squares where fossils had been cut from the stone. It seemed the Great Ocean Road had been a prime spot for dinosaurs long before us tourists made an appearance.

*

I enjoyed Mark's tour so much that I insisted that Bruce and Emma join me for his evening glow-worm walk. For dinner we grilled corn cobs on the BBQ, washed down with a few vodkas. I had been sober for at least a couple of days now, so it was time to get back on it. Several drinks later I realised that this may not have been the best idea. I had been fully aware that we would need to follow Mark by car up to the forest. I was also banking on the fact that there would be some unsuspecting holidaymakers with enough room in their vehicle to drive us.

We filled our Batman flasks to the brim with more alcohol and headed up to the meeting point. On greeting Mark I treated him like an old friend, hoping our morning bonding session would excuse the slur in my speech. Apparently not. Mark was not impressed as I informed him that we didn't realise (*ah hmm!*) that we would be required to drive and had enjoyed a couple of beers over dinner. I knew he had a whole car to himself, but instead of offering a ride he briskly shrugged us off. Thankfully a kind man stepped up, and we crammed into his four-wheel drive, trying to act sober in front of his twelve-year-old son. Oops!

On the way into the forest, Mother Nature put on an impromptu show for the tourists as a koala crossed the road up ahead. I had never seen one on the ground before. It moved along with no regard for the waiting queue of traffic, keeping a slow pace with its bum up in the air comically swaying from side to side.

Once in the blackened forest, everything seemed very dark and scary. We were armed with small torches which were constantly being turned on and off so that we didn't scare the glow-worms. Emma, Bruce and I tried to avoid falling over trees, families, each other or down the steep bank on each side as we stumbled through the night. Mark's talk seemed fairly dull, probably due to my drunken inability to pay attention, but the glow-worms were amazing if not slightly blurred through my enhanced vision. After a couple of minutes of Mark droning on, a voice from the dark, easily recognisable as Emma's, piped up, 'How many are there in that bush?'

In front of us was a mass of glowing dots. Bruce and I giggled, along with the twelve-year-old who was happy to be joined by someone on his level.

An angry Mark sarcastically replied, '150 to be exact,' before carrying on with his monologue for another five minutes. The terrible three tried to stay upright and the young boy seemed half asleep, when another interruption came through the night. '148, 149, 150 …. Wow you were right!' cried Emma. The crowd laughed while Mark growled, not happy with his authority being undermined.

*

On our return to the campground we found another surprise. Waiting for us, a koala sat at shoulder level in the fork of a tree and seemed more than happy to sit around whilst we *ooohed* and *awwwed* over him/her. Before bed, Bruce and Emma slouched around a fire as I chased possums around the park, vodka in hand. It certainly beat drinking in the pubs and clubs back home.

Once ensconced in my tent I discovered that although koalas are cute little critters in person, they actually make some very grotesque noises. During the night I could hear the male mating call which resembled a pig grunting, although much, much louder. The females let out a high-pitched scream which according to Mark, was because a male was mating against her will. So our cute, cuddly friend in the tree could actually have been an evil rapist.

*

The next day, the three hungover amigos begrudgingly packed up and headed on to the Cape Otway Fly Treetop Walk. It wasn't the best activity, considering our pounding heads, but it had to be done. This man-made tower of metal had been constructed so all could feel at one with nature while wondering through the forest at tree height. The forest was captivating, but being 30 metres in the air, held up only by a few bars of steel, combined with a bottle of vodka less than twelve hours before, made it all seem a bit painful. The sun pelted down humidifying the surroundings, and I think we were all glad to be back on solid ground and heading once again towards the ocean.

*

The next stop was one for the photo album, albeit online these days. The Twelve Apostles were one of the country's most famous tourist spots. Like another of Australia's defining landmarks, The Apostles were rock formations, but these were far from the desert. In fact they stood in the glory of the Southern Ocean. I had seen the postcards and read the guidebook but nothing prepared me for the beauty of these natural giants as they stood towering above the waves. The wind whipped my hair and I could taste the salty spray floating on the air. The sun shone down, perfectly illuminating the spectacular scenery. The limestone stacks stood haggard and eroded in the choppy ocean, yet they were stunningly beautiful.

Not all twelve remained, the last to fall victim to the seas was in 2009, leaving only seven now standing. Originally called The Sow Piglets, the stacks were renamed in 1950, apparently Apostles attract more tourists than pigs. Even back then there were only nine intact. Hordes of bus trip crowds filled the viewing platform, but it didn't take away from the soaring glory. Returning to the car I felt refreshed, revived and alive. Something about the place had invigorated me.

Further along the coast we stopped at Joanna Beach, a yellow strip of sand sheltered by looming cliffs. Well, it would have been sheltered had the wind not been tearing, very annoyingly, across the ocean towards us. I shivered and hugged my cardigan as Bruce and Emma dove into the chilly waters. Coastal Australian's couldn't seem to resist the call of the ocean.

*

The next eventful evening was spent at Port Fairy which was 'only' 600 kms from Adelaide, our destination. Sadly the Great Ocean Road was now behind us, but the adventure was far from over. Once again we succumbed to alcohol, making the crucial mistake of choosing a dodgy bottle of fizzy wine as the beverage of choice. The drink was extremely cheap, filled with an amazingly fake fruity flavour and probably loved by teenagers. If it was being given away in a raffle they would refer to it as Chateau Del Shite. It was possibly on the same level as goon, except tasted much better, and the hangover it gave me was twenty times worse. As an innocent backpacker I had no knowledge of these facts. Emma and Bruce should have known better. The night was a blur, we were in a pub, and then the fateful bottle shop run was completed. We returned to camp where I made friends and smoked weed with a country boy called Grant while Emma randomly decided to jog around the campground.

*

The next morning I woke up in a Turkish Haman, formally known as the pop-up tent. Gasping for air I ripped the zipper open and temporarily blinded myself in the blazing sunshine. My head pounded and pumped in objection. The world before me began to spin. Would I ever learn? Emma however was having a miracle moment. Having extracted herself from the tent opposite she turned around and came face to face with her dream scenario. Right in front of her, shining like the gates of heaven was her hangover cure and all-time favourite food. A pie van had pulled up and was sat waiting, metres from their bed. Two minutes later the van was gone, leaving Emma happily holding a pie, a doughnut and wearing a big smile. Unfortunately my condition was not so easily cured. After a trip to the beach and vomiting behind the Volvo, I fell asleep in the back of the car for the next few hours.

Groggy from my snooze I woke up to find Emma and Bruce debating where to stop next. At the last minute, at literally the last minute—the high speed turn was somewhat terrifying—we pulled into Tower Hill. It was supposedly a green wooded area, very scenic and beautiful, however it looked pretty dull from the car. We decided to take a stroll anyway and I'm so thankful we did.

As we began a steep climb up to the viewpoint Emma cried out, pointing wildly. Crossing the road behind us were some very scary looking emus. Skinny legs led up to oval shaped feathery bodies, from which long necks protruded, topped by tiny heads with evil eyes. Emus have wings, but as the birds are five foot tall and 150 kgs, the chances of their 6 inch appendages lifting them is as likely as, heard of pigs joining them in the sky. However, they can run at a speed of almost 60 kilometres an hour and have extremely mean looking beaks and claws. I was glad we were at a safe distance.

Emus feature on the Australian coat of arms along with a kangaroo. I had been told that the creatures were picked because they are the only Australian animals that can't move backwards. A strange way to choose the creature that will represent your country. Although someone later explained that, like the nation, they are always moving forward which made more sense.

Emus quickly forgotten, the three of us froze in surprise as a family of kangaroos bounded across the path a few metres above. Reaching the peak of the hill our animal spotting continued as I noticed wallabies hopping among the trees. Australia was giving me a tour of its native wildlife all within a few minutes. 'All we need now is an echidna,' Bruce joked.

These spiny creatures resemble the English hedgehog but with long pointy snouts. Rather bizarrely their rear feet are on backwards. When threatened, echidnas dig holes and bur- row into them leaving only their spines available for predators. Unlike hedgehogs they cannot roll into balls. I had never seen one and as they are extremely shy, our chances of spotting one in the wild were slim. However, by some miracle, as we started the descent back to the car, lo and behold there was one of the crea- tures crossing our path. What a wonderful place and all of this within half an hour.

Back down in the picnic area we stopped for a toilet break. I had a moment of panic as two emus came over to investigate me while I was distracted by a koala. The chubby ball of fluff was running away from some tourists and up the nearest tree. Fortunately both the koala and I escaped unharmed. Then, more than satisfied with our impromptu stop we set back onto the main highway where I dozed off the rest of my hangover.

*

When I awoke, Bruce and Emma were in deep discussion trying to decipher a map, as Emma simultaneously tried to keep the Volvo on the tarmac. Seeing my raised head they informed me that I had missed seeing my first wild wombat, albeit dead and stiff, by the side of the road and oh, also, that we were lost. I wished that I had woken earlier to see the wombat, and also that I could sleep until we arrived at our planned campground, but the road was now too bumpy for any more rest. Getting lost often rewards travellers with a treat. Ours came in the form of a tiny but stunning beach. We had a swim, and Emma collected shells which she later used to make bracelets for each of us.

*

Once back on the road I took a glimpse of the map. We were trying to find our first national park campground. Emma had told me about these places, where in payment for your stay the driver is required to fill out a form and pop five bucks into a box. Emma commented that it had been a few years since her childhood camping trips and that maybe they had updated the system. They hadn't and after returning back past the dead wombat, a flattened brown snake and a live tiger snake, we found Old Man's Lake camp site. We tucked our cash into the envelope provided and being honest people, slid it into the collection box. I did note a sign that warned of $200 fees if the car was found unregistered. According to the notice, park rangers did come round and check, but we never saw one.

Old Man's Lake was promptly renamed Old Man's Balls due to the pungent cheesy odour it emitted, but smells aside, the place was beautiful. The tents were pitched with extra caution due to the sighting of two deadly snakes on the way in. We tucked into a meal of salad wraps, entertained ourselves making animal hand shadows on the tent and enjoyed the unspoilt view of stars above. It was our last night on the road, in the morning we would undertake the final stretch, arriving in Adelaide by evening.

Unable to avoid it any longer I hesitantly retired to my tent, Bruce and Emma were off to bed and I didn't fancy sitting in the darkness by myself. I had never felt uncomfortable sleeping alone, but in the middle of the woods in the middle of nowhere, I felt unsafe. Visions of rapists and axe wielding murderers fluttered before my closed eyes. Before I could even think about sleep, I had to drag my tent door to door with Bruce and Emma's while loosely tying my zippers together so they couldn't be opened from the outside. I woke up alive and alone but with some interesting sounds joining the morning chorus. Putting my tent against the happy couple's hadn't been the best idea.

It may have been the last day of our trip but we still had time for a few stops. In Robe we played in the ocean with a ball that bounced on the water, a present from Emma's parents. Then it was on to the Giant Lobster for some photos, before pulling up at a pelican breeding ground. There wasn't a pelican in sight, but in their place were at least three billion flies. A huge fish head sat on a post which was amazing for several reasons. Firstly, it was being completely ignored by the flies. The fact that we were surrounded by an army of buzzing insects preferring us to a dead fish, said something about our now severely poor personal hygiene. The other unusual thing about a giant decapitated fish head was that the lake was a dry empty crater. So unless the entire thing had evaporated that morning, how anyone had caught a fish here we had no idea. However, it made for great photos as I forced Bruce to kiss it before he and Emma pretended to be walking on the moon inside the cracked bowl of the lake bed.

We piled in the car for one last ride, and as we pulled away, Emma, who was at the wheel, pointed excitedly to the sky. In response, I pointed anxiously to the road. Once I was sure that the Volvo wasn't going to veer off into a ditch, I leaned out of my window to see a flock of pelicans flying along directly above us. I sat back in my seat, watching the sun glazed, bright skied world go by, sad that our trip was coming to an end. However, this blow was considerately softened by the thought of a comfortable bed without axe men lurking nearby, air-conditioned rooms and home cooked food. I can safely say that the shower I took when we collapsed back into the family home was the best I've ever had.

*

A few days later at the end of a very drunk fancy dress party, a Moulin Rouge dancer and Pocahontas said goodbye to their Indian Chief, as Bruce left for the airport praying he was sober enough to get through security. He had to return to work back in Sydney. Much to my excitement, Emma was planning to follow him there and live in the city. I was also planning to return to Sydney at some point during my trip, so our paths would cross again. I had no doubt that there would be many more exploits to come.

Island of Attraction

Just off the South Australian coast was Kangaroo Island, named after a unique breed of kangaroos which inhabited it. To give Emma's family a break from my constant chatter I had booked a two day trip there. I waited in the dark at an ungodly hour of the morning, praying I had the right time and place. There was no sign of the bus. I tried to relax. Then I panicked. Then I called the tour company, who for some reason actually staffed the office before the sun rose. The bus was running late.

When it finally arrived I was pleased to meet our guide, the rather gorgeous Marko. He had exotic dark looks, beautiful long brown hair and a very strong Aussie accent. Also on board the bus were two English girls who mostly ignored me. I guess they didn't come to Australia to meet more English people. Two Korean girls who ignored everyone due to their lack of English. And a delightful Irish family: a mother and father with their rosy cheeked boys aged ten and twelve. I thought I must have been the last pick up, but thankfully I was wrong. Just around the corner we stopped outside a flash looking hostel and a fit man in his fifties climbed in. He was followed by a tall, broad and extremely hot guy who hopefully was around my age. The tour guide had just been outdone and I was enjoying the scenery already.

We set off on the two hour drive to the ferry port. Most of the group fell asleep, but I became a little distracted. My gaze constantly flickered between the window, my book and the sexy man. Fields, book, man, fields, book, man. Until we pulled up for a toilet and coffee break. I, 'coincidently' ended up next to the hottie and 'by chance' we began chatting. His name was Martin, he was from Holland and the older man was his father. Martin had been travelling Australia for some time and his father had come over to visit my future husband/his son. Martin was 24 years old and I was in lust. This was going to be even more exciting than I had hoped.

Back on board the bus we chatted in hushed whispers so as not to disturb our fellow travellers but before long, arrived at the ferry terminal. By the time the two of us were on deck, with the breeze blowing in our hair, the conversation had moved from the normal meet and greet to full on flirting. Just as Kangaroo Island came into sight I had asked him to kiss me. The ferry crossing was only 45 minutes long, I had worked fast. I had to. We only had two days and then Martin would be flying to Melbourne. It was certainly the first time I had ever managed to pull a guy before ten o'clock in the morning. Martin declined the kiss, but not for the sake of rejection. He wanted to make things interesting. I would get my kiss at some point during the day. I wouldn't know when, but it would be worth waiting for. My heart leapt once more, this guy was gold.

The day passed quickly. We stopped at a viewpoint where I took in the scenery which was tall, dark and handsome. Photos were taken while Marko made some entertaining comments and managed to sound as if he hadn't repeated them a million times before. Next was a lunch stop and we all chipped in, helping with setting up and clearing away. The Irish kids were very mature for their age and so fast thinking. They were able to come up with on the spot jokes and quips that had the whole group in stitches. Their parents were amazing too, so friendly and fun, you've got to love the Irish.

Another highlight was stopping to see the seals. We sat on the beach only metres from them and watched as mothers and babies gallivanted up and down the sand. These were the cute cartoon creatures with little snub noses and wide pleading eyes. From shades of brown, white and grey, they were everywhere, and babies yelped loudly as they waited for mothers to return and give them a feed. It was so captivating to watch that I may have forgotten about Martin's kiss for at least twenty minutes.

Sandboarding was next on the agenda. I wasn't looking forward to it. It seemed a fun idea, but the prospect of plummeting down a dune on a thin piece of wood with no brakes made me a little anxious. After an exhausting hike up the tallest sand dune, Marko showed us how it was done. With a few metres run-up he threw his body into the air, clutching the board to his chest, before angling downward, hitting the sand and hurtling into the desert stretched out below. Well maybe desert is a slight exaggeration but there was at least three hundred metres of stopping distance between us and the car park. Marko made it look easy. Easy, but nevertheless still terrifying. The worst aspect had to be the return journey. After what I anticipated as ten seconds of pure fear, we would have to reclimb the dune which nearly killed me the first time and pass the board onto the next rider. If only I could go last.

The Irish children were waxing up the boards excitedly, and Martin was trying a small slope behind me, STANDING UP! The Koreans tried to take photos on cameras which were currently protected by clear sandwich bags to keep them away from any nasty grains of sand. My camera was battered but girly and would not be faffed with. I firmly told Marko that this pink toughie had been coming to the beach with me all summer in Europe, it would survive, and I certainly wouldn't need a plastic bag.

The kids flew down the hill and then ran back up at almost the same speed. Their Dad whizzed off, followed by Martin. I stood with the Irish mother, both of us hoping that no one would offer us a turn. The Korean's even yelled out with glee, whether it was due to the rush of flying down the slope or the excitement of another photo opportunity who knew. The English girls took a turn, no doubt having been practicing on a sledge back in the UK. Then it was my go. Don't get me wrong I didn't want to miss out; I just didn't want a face full of sand, followed by some serious grazes.

'Remember,' Marko told me, 'don't put your fingers around the edges of the board. You could cut them off and you need them for the rest of the tour and life in general.' Sound words, good advice and now one more thing to worry about. Excellent.

With the Irish mother clutching my camera to capture the moment, I cautiously lay on top of the board and jerked my body forward, hoping to tip over the edge as slowly as possible. Down I went. It wasn't exactly terrifying, but I did spend the entire time concentrating on staying on the board and not losing my fingers. I certainly didn't feel fun fuelled adrenaline which the others seemed to enjoy so much. I finally slowed to an uneventful stop, climbed to my feet, held a big thumbs up for everyone to see, before beginning the hike up while every grain of sand underfoot was determined to slide me down. With eleven people watching and waiting for my ascent, I tried and failed to make it quick and seem effortless. Eventually making it, I handed over the board so the kids and Martin could take a few more turns.

By this time we had been joined by a rival tour group. Marko knew the guide, and they were about to continue a competition to see who could get the furthest before stopping. Apparently this was a regular event, and the other guide was currently champion. Much to our pleasure Marko won, before both guides looked on in bitter surprise as Martin flew past the pair of them. After everyone had exhausted themselves and the Irish mother had been pushed over the edge, both literally and metaphorically, we set off back to the bus.

I was casually strolling along when Martin grabbed my hand, 'I can't wait,' he whispered, 'I need that kiss.'

It must have been the way I handled the board. We hung back until our group had disappeared behind the trees, for some reason we had both silently agreed to keep this our secret. I guess we didn't want his father or any of the others to know that we were hooking up with a relative stranger within half a day of meeting them. Families and fathers don't always understand the travelling way, where life moves at a fast pace. In the back-packing world good friends are made in an hour, a relationship is formed in a week and every second counts towards memories that last a lifetime. Finally he kissed me and as he did so I melted as the anticipation ebbed out of me. I suppose I could go on to describe the look as we caught each other's eyes, the way his tongue explored every detail of my mouth, etc., etc., but that would be sickening. I felt like a naughty schoolgirl as we rushed to catch up with the group, both of us blushing with pleasure.

*

The last stop of the day was a dip at the beach. The water was freezing but I went in anyway hoping for some more lip locking action. Unfortunately, Martin and I were also joined by the Irish children keen to play with someone other than their parents. The ocean current was strong and a rip pulled us quickly down the beach in only waist deep water, so my eyes stayed firmly on our young companions. Any thoughts of kissing had to be put on hold.

The final destination for day one was our sleeping quarters, a quaint cottage in a field surrounded by woods and kangaroos.

There were bunks and plenty of sleeping room inside, but the bedding arrangement causing excitement was a circle of swags being set up outside the house. The swags were essentially a VIP sleeping bag. They rolled out onto the ground and were made out of thick tent canvas, reminding me of my Girl Guide days. The inside was lined with a thin mattress and some form of blanket. As with a sleeping bag the idea was to crawl in via a hole in the top. They were designed for outdoor use. So if you awoke to find the view of the stars had been replaced by thunder clouds, a large flap would keep off the water without suffocating the inhabitant. Marko assured me that he had slept out in a storm the previous week and stayed dry as a bone. I listened patiently to his story while inwardly deciding that if a million creepy crawlies dancing on my face hadn't already done the job, then I was sure to dash inside before the second drop of rain had time to hit.

Martin was currently hunting for fire wood so I went over to join him. The two Irish boys were helping fill a wheelbarrow with branches, in-between deciphering a scheme to walk their mother onto a crawling mass of termites. Thousands of the insects were running around in a frenzy because the lads had thrown a rock at their nest. My Dutch hunk was a star with the children, showing them what kind of logs and sticks to collect and how to build a fire. I looked on dreamily thinking what a great father he would make.

The Irish mother and I hit the booze, and before long we were all gathered around the fire toasting marshmallows on sticks. Possums ran around in the dark, and Marko told us about one who used to grab sausages off the BBQ and then dart through a hole in the roof. However, the fast food affected the creature's health and one day it darted towards the hole to find it had become too fat to fit through. It slipped, fell onto the hot grill below and learnt a lesson on greed while coating the remaining meat in fur.

One cheeky possum clearly hadn't heard this tale or maybe it was the very same animal. Seeing the Irish child wave his toasted marshmallow in pride, the quick furry ball darted across and gobbled the melted mallow from the end of its stick. Not content with that, the possum then ensued in a tug of war with the boy, trying to pull the twig away and lick off the remaining sticky sweet goo. Possum verses ten-year-old didn't seem a fair fight, but the animal was clearly experienced and for a moment it looked as if he might win. After an unsure moment, the Irish child recovered from his shock, snatched the stick away and the hungry creature shot off into the dark.

*

Night may have fallen but the day's adventures were far from over as we piled on the bus for a kangaroo hunt. They weren't hard to find, in fact the field was full of them. Babies, mothers and huge males hopped around among an array of wallabies. The difference between wallabies and kangaroos was easy to spot when they were metres apart but harder to put into words. As far as I could tell wallabies were smaller, a slightly different colour and had a much cuter hop. I'm sure if you can be bothered to look it up online there would be a far more intellectual answer, but I'm quite content with mine.

Everyone took photos but without a flash to protect the creature's eyes. As the Koreans snapped away, my camera simply made a bleeping noise and shut itself off. Again I tried. *Beep errrr!* The lens seemed unable to extend. *Beep, errrr! Beep, errrr!* Oh bollocks, damn bloody camera.

Seeing my frustration the Koreans looked over. Waving their plastic bags from sandboarding they solemnly declared, 'Sand veey bad fo camra, must use bag.'

No shit! Having decided it was nicer to view wildlife without a lens in front of my face, I enjoyed the rest of our adventure before crawling into my swag. Marko was right, it was warm and comfy, so warm that I had to ask Martin to return to his own bed halfway through the night.

*

The next morning we all rose at 6 a.m. and after a cup of what was essentially Aussie hot chocolate and in my mind by no means suitable for breakfast, we headed off for our next stop. The unimaginatively named Remarkable Rocks were indeed that. Sitting on a high cliff top, the rocks were a natural playground. Martin, the children and I crawled into a cave, before entertaining ourselves around the other chunks of stone which formed different and unusual shapes. There was even one which we could slide into. Once inside, we found various holes and stuck our arms and legs through them, giving the impression that we had been squashed under the giant stone. I asked one of the Irish kids to pretend to lift the rock as if he were saving me from its weight. Fortunately, my camera may have perished but my video camera was capable of taking grainy stills so I was able to capture our antics.

Signs warned us to stay away from the cliff edge after several dangerous accidents had occurred at the spot. Sadly the most recent had resulted in a tragic loss of life. A tourist had ended up in the huge swell below. The strong currents and ferocious waves soon overpowered him, and had two brave men not jumped in to save him, he surely would have died. The tourist survived, sadly his rescuers did not. A powerful reminder of the oceans strength and a lesson to all.

I heard many other similar stories during my time down under. A man in his twenties lost to the water on the Gold Coast. A husband drowned as he tried and failed to save his wife as their three children watched from the beach. Then most recently, an American backpacker who lost his life while moonlight swimming off Fraser Island. I do not mean to sombre the mood but it certainly pays to respect the ocean, especially one full of gripping currents, sharks, jellyfish and crocodiles. Australia has 26,000 kms of coastline and included in this are hundreds of patrolled beaches where you can enjoy a relaxing swim or play in the waves. As for the rest, I highly advise you stick to hanging out on the sand and taking in the scenery.

Fortunately, the only drama we encountered was as Marko climbed to the top of the highest rock and then struggled to find a way down. 'Don't worry,' the oldest Irish boy cried out, as Marko crossed a small ledge. 'We have a towel down here to stem the blood flow when you fall.' Where did they get this stuff from? We all laughed as Marko gave him a sarcastic smile before hopping across with the ease of a mountain goat.

The rocks conquered, Marko led us on a magnificent walk through beautiful hillsides and along a creek. The stream bubbled and flowed over smooth, black, shiny rocks all the way to the ocean. Just before it hit the sand we clambered up to a cave overlooking the beach. A tiny hole apparently led to an even better view. Wonderful, we agreed, if only we were small enough to fit through it. Then much to our amazement Marko turned his back to the gap, lifted his right leg in, followed by his left arm and slipped through. One by one we did the same, and as promised the scenery was even more spectacular. I chased the children down to the beach and although the day was overcast we enjoyed the sea air while exploring rock pools and sandy inlets.

Lunch was followed by a trip to see some koalas. Having seen so many already I concentrated on spending some final moments with Martin. Our time together was nearly over. Eventually we had to reboard the ferry and the crossing flew by as we all exchanged email addresses. During the return bus trip to Adelaide I fell asleep on the Dutchman's shoulder and awoke groggy and exhausted to find it was time to say goodbye. Martin and I shared a kiss agreeing to stay in touch, but the chances of either of us moving halfway across the world for a 48 hour relationship were slim to say the least. Oh well, there was always Facebook. Then one more kiss, a shy wave to his father and I was whisked off in Emma's Saab. I had been away less than two days, but it felt like weeks.

Aussie, Aussie, Aussie*

The return to Adelaide was short-lived, but as always Emma kept it fun packed. We visited the Big Rocking Horse and stopped by an animal park. I held a koala and yes, they really are as fluffy as they look. They also stink of eucalyptus and have big evil claws that made a slicing, scratch mark across my left shoulder. On our way out of the enclosure we were encouraged to pat a baby koala which was learning how to deal with human attention. Hopefully it wouldn't inherit the death lock, blood drawing grip its mother had displayed.

In the next paddock we fed kangaroos. Albino white ones with red eyes hopped among both grey and red specimens. They were adorable, taking peanuts from our hands as joeys shyly crawled into pouches. All very serene. Among this haven of God's creatures, Emma noticed some unrest. A small grey kangaroo, whose head was no higher than my waist, had become agitated and seemed a little anxious. In gesture of peace I held out a peanut at arm's length. It seemed that in kangaroo culture this was a sign of aggression, or maybe it was sick of being force-fed by tourists for years on end. Anyhow, it moved in for the kill. Using its puny little arms it began to box me. Shock took over. How are you supposed react when being attacked by a teenage marsupial? It was far too small and fluffy to fight back against, but its claws were razor sharp and it sliced my arms. Fortunately being the hardened Australian, Emma took charge dragging me away before we ran out of the enclosure.

The rest of the day passed more peacefully and I was treated to my first Golden Gay Time ice cream. The happy named snack came with the slogan, 'You can't have a gay time by yourself'. Feel free to snigger as much as I did. Battered and bruised I had certainly gotten a feel for the Australian wildlife and decided that from this point on I would admire it from afar.

It was the 26th January, also known as Australia day, and Emma had promised to give me a local experience. Aussies tradition-ally celebrate by drinking slabs of tinnies, throwing some snags on the barbie and dancing around in their thongs (beer, sausages and flip-flops in case you were wondering). Groups of mates would hang out at the beach, the backyard or pool while Triple J's hottest one hundred played on radios all over the country. Triple J was a hugely popular station that broadcasted and supported Australian bands and artists. They were responsible for helping many local groups rise to fame and tour throughout Australia. Europe and America are closely linked in their popular music, but the land of Aus had a sound of its own. Rock and electro pop dominated the airwaves as home-grown bands with names like, The Hungry Kids of Hungary, blasted their latest tracks to the masses. Emma told me that each Australia day Triple J count up listener's votes and broadcast the hottest one hundred tunes from the previous year.

We ended up at five different parties that day, all of them a drunken blur, but I clearly remember two things. Firstly, at one stage and for no apparent reason boys began playing with chainsaws. Secondly, that Mumford and Sons peaked the top one hundred list with their song 'Little Lion Man'. That day was to be one of my last with Emma. Our time together had been unforgettable, and I was so sad to leave both her and the comfort of a clean shower and my own room. Once again I would be heading off alone, released into the wilds of the Aussie backpacker circuit. Emma and I would catch up in Sydney but as travel waits for no girl, soon enough I found myself on a plane to Brisbane.

CHAPTER 3

MUSHROOMS AND MAYHEM

ARRIVING IN BRISSY, as the locals call it, I made my way to the hostel. I had been told that there was a nightclub, swimming pool and a hot tub; the elite of backpacker accommodation. As it turned out my room was clean but cramped with eight beds and a small en-suite bathroom. Next to my bunk I discovered a wall light and my very own plug socket. Such luxuries are highly valued when sharing a room with seven other people, all with irregular sleeping patterns and a phone, computer and camera needing to be charged.

The following day I woke early and set off to explore the city. Brisbane didn't have Sydney's defining landmarks, but I passed the time wandering around the shops and walking along the river. As with many cities in Australia there were botanical gardens, and although there wasn't a beach, a lagoon had been built.

A spare tyre had appeared around my waist following a

month of constant eating with Emma. I decided that from now on I would make an effort to shift it. Emma had a super fast metabolism, allowing her to consume the everlasting packets of chips and lollies (crisps and sweets) without an inch of fat appearing on her. My body seemed to enjoy junk food so much, it clung to it with no plans on letting go. In an attempt to get fit, I walked for hours and purchased a child's skipping rope. With the iPod on full blast I attempted to jump off my fat intake while the heavens opened and rain poured down from above. It was quite invigorating.

I spent a couple more days in the city wandering about and eating nothing but apples and salad, still desperate to shift some weight. On one of my walks I met a group of young Brazilian boys. We spent the afternoon hanging out in the hostel hot tub, but I hesitantly turned down their offer of a fivesome sex session. If my last 18-year-old at the festival was anything to go by, then one was more than enough. There were certainly plenty of sexual opportunities in the backpacker world.

*

Then finally I was leaving the inner city life once more and climbing on board one of the legendary Greyhound buses, heading south to Byron Bay. Byron was well-known among backpackers and locals alike. Renowned for its beaches, hippy-like atmosphere and pubs with tables made for dancing on, I couldn't wait to see it for myself.

Once again I had picked a modern and slightly nicer hostel. These places were known as flashpackers. The bright, air-conditioned reception had its own internet cafe and tour office. When I checked in, the girl handed me a pass that opened my room and activated the lift. It was certainly very, very flash. Unfortunately I had been put in a twelve bed dorm. I preferred to stick with six–eight beds cutting down the chance of ending up near a chronic snorer, but they had all been fully booked.

The dorm seemed reasonable but the inhabitants were rather surprised to see me. As I enquired which bed was mine, I began to understand the issue. My bed was still covered in the previous occupant's belongings. Apparently the guy had checked in the morning before and had gone to the beach. He hadn't been seen since. His unopened backpack and mobile phone sat on the bunk. Rather than take the advice of my roommates and chuck his stuff on the floor, I decided to report the missing lad to reception. The girl on the desk thanked me and agreed that it would be best for me to take another room. I would be getting a free upgrade to a 4 bed dorm. Perfect.

I don't know what happened to the missing boy, but if it had been something terrible then I'm sure I would have heard about it. Out of the four beds, only two were taken. One, by myself and the other by a cheerful Scottish guy, John. I told him my upgrade story and the Scot joked, 'Maybe he went to Nimbin.' Nimbin was famous for having people openly sell marijuana on its streets. 'He probably got too fucked and didn't make it back,' John suggested.

Little did I know the very same thing would happen to me the following day.

Excited to be staying within walking distance of the beach for the first time since my arrival, I headed down to take a look. The sky clouded over, but I sat for an hour or so watching the surfers. The beach was stunning. I couldn't wait to see it in the sunshine, but for now an early night was due. I would have to be up at 8 a.m. to catch a day trip that I had booked to Nimbin.

*

As the tour bus arrived I quickly realised that the guide, let's call him Joe (I'm not writing this to promote tour companies, nor to get the good man in trouble for some of his dubious advice that day), was absolutely off his rocker. I made a few friends on the bus and we chatted as Joe peppered the journey with funny stories and a funky 70's soundtrack. After an hour of negotiating country roads we arrived and Joe educated us on where to buy drugs while reminding us that they were illegal.

The small village consisted of one street lined with cafes and hippy-style shops. Posters of Bob Marley were on sale alongside bongs and pipes. The place was covered in the Rastafarian colours of red, green and yellow which adorned shop signs as well as beanies, t-shirts and belts. Some of the bus meandered around tie-dyed laden rails and jewellery stalls, while the majority set on a mission to buy pot. I didn't entirely understand the logic behind the towns 'legal' system, but somehow, someway, it had become acceptable to sell marijuana on the streets of Nimbin. Joe explained that although it wasn't technically legal, the police seemingly overlooked the selling of weed. Sure enough a scruffy local talked to a couple of Swedish tourists, offering his wares undeterred by the police strolling along the other side of the street.

The town even had a festival, Mardi Grass, where an enormous papier mâché spliff was carried up the street in a parade. Joe had warned us about younger lads who would try to sell us small amounts at extortionate prices. Instead he advised, we were to find the oldest, most decrepit, drugged up hippies around, in fact people who probably came on a tour 20 years ago, got stoned and never left. I had expected to be harassed constantly as we walked along in the sun, but by the time we reached the end of street, no one had approached us. It seemed that an endless train of tour buses had made sales so easy that dealers waited for the trade to come to them.

Taking heed of Joe's warning I wandered over to a ruggedly

aging man, taking along Bryan, a loud Canadian boy who wished to share whatever we could buy. My potential dealer was the epiphany of hippy. Long dreadlocks hung from his bony head, his mouth was a dark hole of gaps left by missing teeth and he wore fisherman's pants. Breaking ourselves in gently we handed over $20. The old man reached into a string pull bag and produced three hash cookies. His hands were long and spindly, with yellow nails to match his three remaining teeth. He reminded me of a wizard, a real life Gandalf from the sixties.

I'm quite certain that most of the backpackers on the trip had smoked pot/weed/skunk or whatever you wish to call it, before, but for some reason buying it in Nimbin took the transaction to a new level of excitement. Bryan devoured his first cookie before I had put my purse away, and determined not to be left behind I followed suit. Somehow we strayed into a side alley, where, as predicted younger guys hovered around. They made us offers of weed for a minimum of $200 a bag, much more than we were willing to spend. Having asked around, we gave up on buying marijuana, pleasing ourselves by finishing the cookies and hunting for something a little different.

Magic mushrooms, Joe had informed us, were also easily obtainable. A long bearded man, who was more biker than reefer, took us around the back of a pub. From his ancient car he produced a brown paper bag. Three or four mushrooms, he assured, would be enough to get us going. Another $50 spent and we had a total of ten brown, slimy looking mushrooms hidden in my handbag. Our new friend had generously chucked in a couple of small extra ones for free.

Meeting by the bus we all exchanged stories and a joint was being passed around already. Bryan was starting to look a little wasted. I was slightly disappointed with my cookies as I felt completely normal. Twenty minutes later Joe arrived at the bus.

We were already two tourists down. The drama was unrelated to drugs, one of the Swedes had eaten in a café and set off his nut allergy. Who knows what Joe had done with them, but they were nowhere to be seen and we were setting off without them.

We drove on and Joe changed the soundtrack to match the scenery. Wafts of pan pipes filled the bus as we passed through rainforest, before pulling up at a viewpoint overlooking a waterfall. Meanwhile Bryan was acting stranger and stranger. I had become a little light-headed after our smoke but nothing more. Bryan however had totally lost it. He walked off and sat on a bench. He was alone, other than a couple of roosters whom he appeared to be talking to. Then as we stopped to pick up some munchies, he appeared with arms full of jumbo packets of crisps, Pringles and an assortment of chocolate bars. I secretly wondered if he was enjoying the attention or more worryingly, if my tolerance to drugs had become too high. I had spent the usual teenage years smoking pot down the local park, but those days were now far behind me. Drugs were certainly not a part of my normal routine. I didn't see how his state could be so extreme compared to my own. Sober or not, I didn't worry too much. There was plenty more fun to come as I still had the mushrooms sitting in my bag.

The bus rolled on. Joe announced that the ride was about to begin as the vehicle lurched down a steep slope before rushing over a hill, rollercoaster fashion. Stopping on the brow of the next peak, he told us that we would set off at the start of a Pink Floyd song and hit the T-junction precisely as the last beat finished. The bus rocketed up and down hills as we screamed in an intense mix of excitement and fear. After ten minutes of thrills, the bus ground to a halt as predicted in time to the final note.

The last stop of the day was enough to drive even those sober among us crazy. We had been warned that the place was a little unusual, but nothing prepared me for what was to come. Strange sculptures lined the driveway, built from everything from micro-waves and bath tubs to decapitated Barbie dolls. Forest sur-rounded us as we meandered past old wheels, bicycles and tall exotic trees. We finally came upon a small structure by the side of a lake. It was very quaint with a blue and green roof but no solid walls. This strange and curious place was home to an even stranger man. Having lived in the forest alone for an undeter-mined number of years, Bob was an interesting character. No taller than my chest, he was small and toned with long scrag-gly hair, a grey beard and John Lennon style glasses. He wore nothing but a pair of fisherman's pants and spoke with a strong American accent. I had no idea what the purpose of this trip was, but I had a feeling that Joe enjoyed freaking us out. Bob was from a very wealthy area of New York but had decided to give up the shallow life and move to a place of inner peace.

Although bizarre, the place was certainly beautiful. Lily pads coated the lake and a turtle swum among them. We sat on the deck of the house, although everyone declined the kind offer of a swim in the murky water. I felt like Alice in Wonderland. No doubt the exact effect Joe had hoped for. Just before we reboarded the bus, Bob gave us a five minute talk on protons and neutrons and the way the universe flows, until we were so confused that our heads spun. These two were definitely having a laugh at us, but we loved it.

As we neared Byron Bay, I had to make a decision. Returning to the flashpacker hostel seemed an inappropriate end to the day. Most of the others, including Bryan were staying at a well-known campground and hippy-style hostel just outside of town. I decided that I should see the place for myself.

*

Bryan and some other bus trippers walked into the bar where we were supposed to have dinner. Somehow after a few beers I forgot about food and set about making friends. Bryan had pretty much disowned me. As far as I could tell, he was now roaming about annoying the shit out of everyone. The time came for the mushrooms to be taken. Well, I had to eat something. I located Bryan and shared them between us. Sitting at a table of strangers who now felt like close friends, I chewed on my first piece of disgusting brown mush. A kind American took the time to video my face. The words 'dog chewing a bee' came to mind when I later reviewed the footage. A mix of slime and gritty dirt, I swallowed the vegetable as quickly as I could.

Time passed, nothing happened. An hour later I ate another. Nothing happened. Bryan flew up to the table in a ball of energy. I enquired how his mushrooms were, only to find him high as a kite having consumed all five. Oh well, down the hatch my last three went.

I'm not sure how long it took, but one moment I was playing cards with a group of travellers, the next I had cards in my hand, a table full of strangers staring at me and no idea of what was going on. To me this was the funniest thing to ever occur, and I could not stop laughing. No really, I could not stop. The rest of the table looked on, half amused, half horrified. A kind Norwegian picked up my video camera to record some more.

It was at this point that I made a close bond with Patrick the American and Sean from Ireland. They were both a little crazy, but fun and sported matching sunburn. At first I thought their intention was to freak me out. I was wary of being used as entertainment as Patrick suggested we explored the camp site. The hostel had many different sleeping options, from dorms and camping, to teepees. I had no choice but to trust the boys. I was in no condition to speak to anyone else. Thankfully they only had good intentions. Things moved from explorations, to trying out various uses for an empty goon bag. For example, as a hairdryer, floatation/life saving device and of course a pillow. Then it was outside for some drinking games. Irritatingly Bryan, who was still hanging about, managed to confuse and obstruct the game at every possible moment.

As more time passed my head became fuzzy and the world felt extremely floaty. Then I began to notice the jellyfish stings up my arm. Yes, that's right jellyfish stings. Long tentacle trails going up my forearm. Of course everyone else thought I was mad. My arms were fine. Rather than freaking me out, this latest development excited me further. The whole time I was very aware that my visions were a long way from reality. This knowledge seemed to allow me to stay in control, although I am in no way suggesting that you should ever take drugs. They are of course dangerous and highly unpredictable, plus I'm happy to take the risks on your behalf so just sit back and enjoy the show. I had met a guy with jellyfish stings in Brisbane a few days previously. I realised this was most likely my minds inspiration for the illusions, probably sparked by the stinging mosquito bite on my finger.

Having come to terms with my 'injuries' the boys and I continued our mission of stupidity. Traditionally when drinking goon the bearer must hold up the bag and slap it before pouring their drink. This is known as 'slap the goon'. For our version we decided to reverse it and slap people with the goon. Unsurprisingly the only participant we could find was Sean. He made receiving his slap very dramatic introducing his own sound effects and falling to the ground in slow motion as if in a gunshot scene. I loved his attitude.

We sat around the edge of the lake before putting Sean to the test once more. Patrick and I spun him around and around in a swinging chair hoping that when he attempted to stand up, he might stagger towards the water. Unfortunately the experiment backfired as Sean walked in a perfectly straight line, while our arms ached for hours from all the pushing. It was now around 4 a.m. and there was no chance of me being able to find my way home. I found an empty bed in the dorm shared by Patrick, Bryan and Sean and hopped in. Within minutes I fell sound asleep as my head fluttered away with the fairies.

*

The following morning, I awoke to see Sean and Patrick snoring away. Bryan had half his body precariously hanging off the edge of a top bunk. I crept out and made the short but uncomfortable walk through the sunshine, back to flashpacker heaven and air conditioning. The heat and hangover were a bad combination.

My roommate, Scottish John, was still in bed. I decided that sleep looked amazing and tried to fall back into it. But even in a clean bed and cool room I couldn't seem to drop off, and soon enough John began to wake. I gave up on the napping and invited him to join me on a walk to Byron's lighthouse. I knew the track followed a coastal path and thought that the fresh air and sea breeze would do me the world of good.

I was wrong. The sun pounded down and the path wound up exhausting hills and unforgiving steps. The sea breeze was nowhere to be seen. I hadn't managed to get any breakfast and my hangover was getting worse by the minute. Fortunately, my jellyfish stings had disappeared along with the other effects of the mushrooms. The headache I blamed entirely on the goon, something I normally avoided like the plague. Then again the mushrooms had let me drop my guard and drink the goon … *hmmmm.*

Anyhow, the walk was painful but wonderfully worthwhile. Beautiful beaches formed in small curved coves. Waves broke far from shore, forming numerous lines of white froth that smoothly rolled towards the sand. It was paradise. We stood at a viewpoint and I let the imagery soothe my pains away. The path continued on, running up and down past houses, beaches and forestry.

I stopped as we came upon a huge goanna. The lizard was well over a metre long and was thrashing its dark scaly body about in the bush. Nervously trying to get a better look, we saw his jaws jammed open, a clump of feathers stuck between them. It seemed the goanna had swallowed a bird but was unable to fit the fantail down his gullet. To no avail, it bashed the feathers against a tree in an attempt to snap them off. I concluded that the only solution was to vomit it up and start again with some serious chewing. However, I didn't feel my advice would be appreciated or understood, so we headed on.

Much moaning, groaning and sweating later we finally arrived at my goal. Not the lighthouse itself but at a sign that I had seen in Christof's photos, months before. I stood behind it proudly smiling for the camera. We had reached the most easterly point in Australia. After our photo session, hungry and tired we set off to the lighthouse hoping to find some ice cream. Nothing. Someone was missing out on a serious business opportunity. Desperate for food we began our descent back to town, this time taking the inland path. Even downhill it was a long way, but once again we were treated to spectacular views.

Finally back in the town centre I set about finding breakfast or what by now would be lunch. Byron was a haven for vegetarians, the small vegan, organic and veggie cafes making it almost too difficult to choose. John returned to the hostel, and having eaten at last, I found myself revived enough for a shopping trip. I knew I needed to keep my luggage as light as possible but the shops were irresistible and I wanted to equip myself for my next tour. Anyhow, I needed that bikini and thongs and cap and … well, let's stop there and just say I was well prepared.

*

Back at the hostel I bumped into a Canadian guy, Ches, whom I had met in Brisbane. With millions of backpackers taking the same route up and down the east coast, the chances of running into someone familiar were always pretty high. Ches and his crew were making a TV show about backpacking. They were financed by tour operators and hostels in return for advertising. The team were getting free trips, rooms and camper van hire wherever they went. I was sure the show would only ever be aired in hostels and tour agencies, but the boys were confident they were going international.

My hangover was quickly forgotten as we started our recording session in the hostel common area. Then led by the TV crew, everyone was rounded up and taken to a local bar. Much dancing, drinking and talking ensued before Ches and another couple invited me to join them on a walk. The four of us trouped down to the beach, and then moved on to the compulsory skinny-dip. Even through the alcohol, I was acutely aware that this could turn into a dangerous situation. We agreed to keep in shallow water safely away from rips. We sat in the knee-deep ocean laughing as the waves splashed over us and chatted away.

Eventually we decided to move on but upon exiting the water couldn't find our thongs, and in the end we gave up on the search. Luckily our clothes were closer to the water's edge. We had also picked up some towels on the way down. By now Ches and I were so drunk that getting dressed was too much effort; the towels would be enough to keep us warm. The other couple returned to their accommodation, and I headed to mine with the Canadian in tow. Drunk and giggly we dropped our towels just before reaching reception and made the walk to the dorm completely starkers. The receptionist didn't even flinch, she must have been used to such behaviour, but others in the corridors laughed and blushed. Ches and I thought we were hilarious. We said goodnight at my door and I never heard of him nor the TV show again.

*

My last day in Byron was spent binging on the healthy, tasty food, revisiting the shops and meandering the beaches. By a miracle I found our lost thongs on a rock. Whether we had left them there or someone had put them on it, I had no idea. I couldn't remember that part of the evening too clearly, but I honourably delivered the footwear of the others to their hostels. My final night in Byron Bay was an early one. My body could not handle any more alcohol, plus I had to rise at 7 a.m. My next adventure was about to begin.

LEARNING FROM THE LOCALS

The five day surf camp promised that I would learn to ride a wave, meet new people and judging by the pictures, get smashed every night. I had no expectations as my ability to learn any physical activity was practically non-existent. I stood waiting for the bus at the unearthly hour of 8 a.m. The time passed, 8.15, 8.30, still nothing. Fortunately, there were others also waiting, otherwise I would have probably panicked that I had the wrong dates or missed my pickup. Finally concern moved to annoyance and then the large coach with the company's logo plastered along the side, pulled up. It was 8.45 a.m., but the delay was about to be explained and instantly forgiven.

I met two of the instructors, Eco and Duster. Their looks matched their alternative names. Someone had broken into the bus overnight. For some reason the boys had left their bags on board and had lost money, passports and some other irreplaceable personal items. They were angry and frustrated, commenting about fucked up druggies and plotting their revenge. One of the girls waiting with us enquired if any surf boards had been taken. In shock, the boys hadn't even thought to check the rear of the bus. As we loaded on, Eco returned down the aisle just about holding off tears that were brimming around his eyes. Their beloved personal boards were gone. More swearing ensued, along with apologies to us for the wait and atmosphere. I felt for them having to deal with their loss while trying to play happy tour guides to the backpackers.

The trip was to take us from Byron to Sydney with overnight stops at various places. Settling onto the bus we headed south, and before long most of us were asleep. Thankfully there were only five in our group so we all had room to stretch out. Just before I began to doze I inwardly groaned as the grey clouds opened and it began to rain.

All too soon we were awoken and arriving at our surf beach for the day. Piling off the bus we waited in the drizzle to be allocated a soggy wetsuit. Mine was cold, damp, unflattering and undid any attempt at sexiness that my brand new bikini was hopefully portraying. The rain continued as we were each handed a large blue surf board. They were nothing like the sleek looking ones often seen being carried by hot, buff men. These boards were far taller than me, too wide to fit under my arm and made of horrible scratchy foam. They even had masking tape wrapped around the top to minimise damage caused by previous riders.

I trudged down to the sand as my arm threatened to fall off with the strain. Plonking the boards down on the beach we sat in a circle while Eco explained the basics of catching a wave.

We were not to attempt to stand up at first. We would wait in the white wash, the area just after where the wave had broken, until we saw a wave of foam heading towards us. We then had to lie on the board and as the froth hit our toes paddle three times and ride the wave to shore. Eco also warned that the conditions were unusually rough, due to the tail end of a cyclone lashing the shores. Things were not looking good. But somehow even with genetic laws and the weather against me, I managed to complete the task with amazing ease.

With big grins on our faces the five of us were regrouped for another meeting on the beach. Alongside me were two French guys and two German girls. Both couples were speaking their native tongue but sadly my language skills were limited to,

'Wo ist die orgie?'— Where is the orgy? and

'Je suis une cochonne.' — I am a dirty pig/slut.

The story behind these phrases is another travel tale in itself. Anyhow, not feeling that these sentences were appropriate, I stuck to talking with the instructors.

Our next challenge was to push ourselves up and stand. Battling the incoming waves, I headed out into the foamy waters. Ironically I almost fell off with shock, when upon catching the wave, I stood up and rode the whale of a board to shore. I ran straight back in for another go. Several trips later my body ached and heaved. Continually forcing myself and the board against the pushing water was leaving me exhausted. Duster told me to take a break, but I was determined to do well and continued for as long as I could. Soon we were learning how to turn the boards in the surf, and then it was time for a well-earned lunch. Sandwiches were gobbled greedily filling our hungry stomachs before we launched ourselves in for one more lashing from the ocean.

An hour or so later we were drained and fell into our seats on board the warm coach, happy to be out of the torrential drizzle. We drifted off once more before seeking some R&R in a nearby pub. The beer soothed my soul and went down a little too well. Before long Eco, Duster and I were buying a crate to take away.

That night we stayed at a lodge. After dinner both instructors and backpackers crashed out in the cinema room to watch surf movies. Too many beers combined with the exhaustion of the day meant that the movie faded into dreams. The next thing I knew was that the sun was rising, and I had spent the night on the couch.

*

On the way to our second beach we stocked up on beer and Savlon. My hands, feet and knees were scabbed from my determined efforts to ride the abrasive board. That afternoon was spent declaring war on the ocean and continuing to pursue my dream of becoming a relaxed and effortless surfer. I had a long way to go.

By evening we arrived at camp base, a beautiful wooded location not far from the beaches. A swimming pool sat in the middle of a courtyard, surrounded by a bar and shower block. Across from a paddock filled with horses and wild kangaroos were dorm rooms. I started to interact with my group using beer in an attempt to befriend the French boys and loosen up the German girls. After trying to stop the friendly horses coming into our room, we joined Eco for a beer at the edge of the river.

Then it was up to the bar area for dinner. The staff or 'helpers' were backpacker volunteers providing labour in return for food, accommodation and the chance to surf. They informed us that up to eighty guests would stay at the camp. For that night they only had us five, so it would be a quiet evening. But then again, I never have been one to do things quietly.

One of the helpers, Nik from Germany, came over to sit with

us. I suggested we played cards, and so we all grabbed beers and sat around a table. Nik and I chatted and laughed as he bought jugs of sangria and kept us all topped up. At only 21 he was young and fresh faced, short but toned, with a crop of light brown hair. I don't know if it was the sangria or those hazel eyes that kept drawing me in, but once again I was well and truly in lust. I have no idea who won the card games, but I do remember that I didn't care. Cards were the last thing on my mind and I didn't return to the dorm until the following morning, having spent a very enjoyable night in Nik's tent.

*

After breakfast it was off to the beach, this time with unbroken blue skies and sunshine that matched my mood. We had a new instructor Mick, who taught us about the dangers of rips and how at times they could be helpful when surfing. Nik came along and we spent the day talking and gazing into each other's eyes. We even took the Jeep out for a romantic drive up and down the beach, returning with sand stuck in some rather intimate places.

The golden grainy shore stretched ahead for miles and miles and our group were the only humans around. Pods of dolphins swam by and everything seemed perfect. Everything except my surfing that is. I can't entirely blame Nik's distractions for my lack of enthusiasm. My hands, knees, feet and arms were covered in more cuts, bleeding wounds and scabs. Fighting to get a huge foam board out against the pounding waters, only to get washed up on the sand, was proving a painful experience.

Back at the dorm we fought to keep the horses out once more while a large goanna attempted to break in through the window. Other surf groups had arrived, and the atmosphere was building. Later there was music and drinking games. I have always loved games but sometimes forget that I can't handle much drink. Two glasses and I'm pretty much gone, a cheap lightweight, but pure entertainment. Nik had to work, so I sat with my group watching the activities.

I decided that for once I would keep quiet and let the others take part in the action. I volunteered Lauren, the French boy to represent our team. Eco grabbed the microphone and explained the rules. Unfortunately, Lauren needed help translating the Aussie accented instructions. I had to assist him and you guessed it, before you could say 'sangria' I was up playing too. Having already swapped clothes and generally run around like idiots, we were instructed to grab a wetsuit and both get into it. Eco had been expecting us to each insert one of our arms and one of our legs into the normal holes. However, in Julia's drunken world and Lauren not understanding anything at all, the resulting tangle even surprised the seasoned instructors. We hopped back to the stage both of us completely inside the suit. The rubber stretched and pulled against our skin as we wriggled along with two arms and two legs in each space, grinding up against each other in an unintentionally provocative manner. Eco nearly fell over laughing, and much cheering and drinking ensued as we won a non-existent prize. The drink was free-flowing for the entire night each of us having prepaid twenty bucks.

Nik finished work, and we danced together among the crowd. The instructors had reputations as womanizers. I'd heard that they often picked up girls only to return to the party an hour or so later for another. Nik seemed different, although he was honest about having received a few tips from instructor Mick, and I was about to enjoy the benefits. As we slipped away from the party and climbed into the Jeep, a thrill of excitement ran through me, I had no idea where we were heading. Finally the car stopped in a paddock where Nik produced a blanket and climbed onto the roof. We lay on top of the car staring at the stars, talking about our lives and travels before finally succumbing to our desires. Eventually we returned to Nik's tent on the edge of the forest and fell asleep in each other's arms.

*

The last day of surfing was by far the most eventful. I made a few more attempts to conquer the ocean, practicing riding the board in the white wash, before resting at the water's edge. A pod of dolphins appeared around a group of surfers out behind the wave break. I had never managed to get past the waves, the huge tumble of foam always pushing the giant board, swiftly back towards the sand. Duster caught me gazing and as if reading my mind, inquired if I wanted to go out there. He didn't need to ask twice and within seconds his strong arms were pushing me through the water, over and under the waves. He Eskimo rolled the board to avoid being washed backwards, my adrenaline pumped as I closed my eyes and tried not to inhale the mass of ocean forcing itself against me.

Finally reaching the calm water, I gained enough breath to sit up my board just in time to see the dolphins swim past me and off up the coast. I can't even describe the feeling. It was totally intoxicating. For that split second, it was just me and nature out there in the ocean and I couldn't thank Duster enough for his help. We sat out in the stillness talking for a while and relishing the moment before he mentioned the inevitable. I had to get back to shore.

Between me and the serenity of the sand was the huge thunderous wave break. Apparently I was going to surf back. 'Hahaha! Very funny!' Dusters face was stern. He was serious. 'Oh shit!'

I argued that he could take the board and I could swim, but apparently this was not an optional activity. Duster was going to push me off and all I had to do was stand up on his command. Simple eh? I braced myself, praying for a miracle.

Duster pushed and yelled at me to get up. Unfortunately I was taken by surprise and having expected to paddle three times first, I basically fucked it up. The whole world went upside down and inside out. Water went up my nose, in my mouth and possibly a couple of other orifices. I waited for air and finally surfaced in a sea of foam. I tried to grab the board attached by the leash to my ankle but heard Duster yelling. I was to forget the board until it was shallow enough to stand. Finally gripping the chunky foam board, I sulked up the sand like a drowned rat, as Nik chirpily informed me that I had just performed an impressive nosedive over the edge of the wave. My career as a surfer was over before it had even started.

*

As the saying goes, all good things must come to an end and too soon our group were collecting our luggage and preparing to set off for Sydney. Moving on had become normal, but this time I wasn't just saying goodbye to a place and an amazing experience. This time there was Nik.

I had been preparing for the inevitable goodbye, but for once it wasn't to be. He had arranged to join us on the four hour journey, having promised Mick he would take the wheel for the drive back. Not only that but Nik was quitting surf camp the following week and was coming to Sydney. The sad goodbye turned out to be an optimistic see you later. We certainly made the most of our last few hours in the back of the mini bus while the others tried to ignore our heavy breathing and Mick turned up the radio. We got a few strange looks from passing cars along the freeway. Even bus journeys were full of thrills down under.

Chapter 4

Chance or Cheek?

ONCE AGAIN I was in Sydney. You may find it a questionable move. I had done my fair share of sightseeing around the city but there was one more thing to see. I had returned for the famous Mardi Gras. The yearly event saw thousands of people flock together to parade, petition and celebrate gay and lesbian rights. Based around Oxford Street which is well known for its gay clubs, the festival lasts for over two weeks and is a blur of parties, tight t-shirts, high-heels and glitter. On parade day, huge crowds of people come to watch floats, dancers and campaigners march, skip and even hula-hoop down the street. I was immensely excited and had even purchased a pink wig, fairy wings and ten tons of glitter for the occasion. Just to top things off, Emma, who had now moved to Sydney was coming to meet me after the parade so we could hit the pubs.

I was staying in the same Sydney hostel as before and had even secured a place in my old room. I knew that Christof was still there and upon my arrival he came down to greet me. Although, a little saddened to realise that I had found myself a new German man, he took the news well and enthused about all the parties and general drunkenness I had missed during my two month absence.

*

On parade day I awoke full of butterflies. Christof was at work, and my other roommates had risen early and left. I would be meeting them at another hostel for a pre-parade party. A welcome new addition to the room was a surround sound system which belonged to an English couple, who had moved from a shared house. I plugged my iPod in and began applying my overly bright make-up in between strutting my stuff and singing into my stubby (Aussie for a bottle of beer).

Three beers later I was off to the party brandishing a bottle of wine. Everyone was dressed in drag, sequins or both, and most were well and truly blotto. An hour later, the music finished up and everyone headed towards the parade route. As we walked, I polished off the wine and purchased a pack of Smirnoff Black, the alcopop version of extra strong beer. In hindsight I realise that due to my severe lack of alcohol tolerance, the three beers were enough to get me sufficiently pissed and the wine would have pretty much topped me off. Buying the extra strength Smirnoff was practically social suicide.

My lovely roommates had been waiting at the roadside barriers for the last four hours. Wanting a good spot they had arrived early, even bringing some crates for us to stand/sit on. The parade started and I jumped onto my crate delightedly blowing the plastic whistle someone had given me. I was having a fantastic time in my increasingly hazy, sparkly world. Although I was later informed that I was the only one enjoying the constant sound of my whistle blasting.

From this point on things became a bit blurry. I remember falling off my crate at least three times. I also remember that the crowd only caught me once. I remember peeing in the street and not caring who saw and then that some lovely guy, who I had met a few hours earlier, had to half walk, half carry me home. Upon meeting me the poor bloke had probably thought, given the amount of alcohol I was carrying, his luck might be in. I'm pretty sure a few hours later, as he literally dropped me into my room, he was most relieved to hear me slur, 'Wellz Ims not ficking fucking you ... I'm too pizzzzed.' Before I passed out, pink wig still upon my head. I never saw him again, although to be honest I couldn't remember what he looked like anyway.

*

The next morning I woke up with a very sore head and eleven missed calls from Emma. Apparently I was the only one not woken by the constant, irritating old school Nokia ring tone during the night. My wings were gone. During the parade I had taken them off as they were constantly knocking and blocking the people behind. I had apparently stowed them in an empty carrier bag. I had a vague recollection of throwing the bag in the vague direction of a bin, wondering why I was still holding it when all my booze had gone. My roommates also informed me that I had shared out my Smirnoff cans and then minutes later panicked wondering where they had gone. The increasingly concerned travellers had reluctantly handed them all back to me. Oh the shame.

I had been taken home before the parade had even finished, stood up my friend and annoyed the crap out of all my roommates. I was twenty seven years old and making mistakes I should have learnt from when I was fourteen. This time was definitely going to be the last ...

*

A few nights later, I was out with the hostel gang. Still recovering from Mardi Gras, I was sober but taking pleasure surveying the parade of drunks fall over, trip up or in one case get dropped. I stood on the balcony, staring down at the throng of dancers, cringing as one worse for wear young guy, jumped off the stage and into the masses in an attempt to crowd surf. He went up with a big cheer only to hit the ground seconds later as the crowd dumped him on the floor.

Tired, I wandered over to the sofas and sat down. I scanned my surroundings. It seemed that the backpackers were on a mission of self-destruction—bottles smashed, beers spilled. I helped a glass collector pick up some credit cards, which must have been dropped as their owner haphazardly tried to pay for a drink.

Abruptly, a very drunk girl entwined with an even more intoxicated guy, stumbled over, before collapsing onto the seat next to mine. For some time they continued with their ever growing throws of passion. It was a fairly common occurrence in a world where most drinkers were backpackers and most backpackers stayed in shared hostel rooms. Sexual encounters quite often had to be taken on the spot as there was neither a 'your place' nor 'mine'. Then a man with a Mohawk hairstyle came onto the scene and put himself between me and the couple, as someone, who I presumed to be his mate, took photos on a giant camera. They were clearly amused by this increasing display of public affection. I asked if he knew the lovers, who now had their hands thrusting wildly inside each other's clothing.

'It's my sister,' the mohicaned man replied, before disappearing into the crowd. Not believing him but not really caring either, I continued to people watch, debating if it was time to call it a night and head home.

Within seconds, another drunken girl fell into the chair on my other side. It was definitely time to go. But before I could stand up, the girl introduced herself as Melissa. I knew that name, I asked her to check her handbag and sure enough she was missing her credit cards. I headed off to find the glass collector before Melissa embraced me gratefully as we returned her lost cards and ID. Good deed done for the day, I was really ready to leave, but once again I was intercepted. The glass collector grabbed my arm.

'That was really nice of you to help that girl get her cards back,' he said.

'No problem, hopefully someone would do the same for me,' I replied, wondering where this was going. I wanted to get to bed.

'Seeing as you're a nice person, I've got a little tip for you,' he told me mysteriously.

'Oh?' This sounded interesting.

'See that man over by the bar with the Mohican, that's Trey Cool, the drummer from Green Day.'

I couldn't believe it, the guy who had been sitting next to me less than half an hour before, was the drummer of an international hit band. World famous. Wow. I paused to thank my new best friend, before watching Trey for a minute or two and hatching a plan.

Convinced I needed to say hello, I wondered over to the bar 'accidentally' ending up next to Trey. I turned my head, faking surprise as I caught his eye. 'Oh, you're the man from earlier. I think your sister left with that guy.'

'It's not really my sister,' came the reply. No surprise there.

'Oh.' I tried to look disinterested and called the barman over, before casually asking if Trey wanted a drink. He declined, telling me that he had to leave as a mini bus was on its way to pick him up. He disappeared outside, but I was determined not to let this one go.

Nabbing who I now realised was a professional photographer, I innocently batted my eye lids. 'Do you have to leave too?'

'Yeah, we're on the Green Day tour, gotta get back to the hotel.'

Again I faked surprise. 'Oh wow, that's awesome. When's the gig?'

'Tomorrow's the last one, it's gonna go off. Wanna come?'

I thought he'd never ask. Taking my number he promised to text me, before following Trey to their bus. Now that's what I call an interesting night.

The next day, I was on one of my stints wandering Sydney, trying not to buy any clothes, when my phone beeped. With bated breath I hunted around in my bag before pulling out my dodgy Nokia. It was from Greg the photographer, he wanted me to text him the full names of the people coming to the concert so he could get us VIP tickets and passes. I thought I was going to explode. This meant I was allowed to bring friends, it just kept getting better.

I knew exactly who I wanted to join me. When I returned to the hostel the night before, one of the Irish girls had gone crazy. She couldn't believe I had met a member of Green Day, she loved them. So Keely would be coming for sure. The other would be her partner in all alcohol related crimes, a sweet girl from Denmark, Karmil.

I rushed back to the hostel, taking Sydney's underground, metro train system. The novelty of walking had worn off with the appearance of each new blister. The girls screamed like crazy when I told them. The concert was that night. In fact, we were going to be late. After enquiring at reception, I discovered the stadium was an hour and a half away, and we would have to take three trains to get there. I guess Greg had taken it for granted that we had a car. The three for us pounded down the steps at Kings

Cross station and fidgeted constantly throughout the painfully slow train ride. We wouldn't be missing Green Day but we were too late to watch their support act, Jet.

I queued at the VIP desk for our tickets, but they had nothing under my name. My heart stopped for a second before my brain kicked into gear. I had put Karmil's name first, and thankfully our tickets were there under her name. The white envelope also contained three VIP passes for the after party. Excitement bubbled as we went through security and finally found our seats. We were very close to the stage on a raised platform which gave us a perfect view. Jet had finished and Green Day were due on at any moment. Admittedly I wasn't a dedicated fan, but I loved their music and had a few of their albums.

Suddenly the lights flared up, fireworks exploded and the band ran onto the stage. They started playing and I instantly recognised one of their biggest hits. The crowd in the standing zone below went wild, jumping around, screaming along to the lyrics and climbing over each other to get a look at their idols. Green Day were electric on stage. Several times they pulled fans up out of the crowd to sing with them. Then Billy Joe, the lead singer, fired t-shirts up into the balcony areas using a gigantic air gun.

*

As I looked around the stadium I was thankful for our seats, people at the top were so far from the stage that they were using binoculars! The three of us jumped around like crazy, while all the other VIPs stayed firmly glued to their seats like stone statues. The night wound up with Billy Joe singing solo, accompanied by only his acoustic guitar. I sang along, as my voice joined thousands of others echoing around the stadium accompanied by the glow of swaying lighters.

During all this time I hadn't heard anything from the photographer. I had texted him to say thank you for the tickets but hadn't received any reply. I didn't think too much of it as he was currently working but presumed we would be meeting later for a drink so I could thank him in person. After the show we walked around the stadium to find the bar indicated on our passes. I imagined it packed with the band and crew, plus all the other VIP ticket holders. The reality was somewhat different. A doorman waved us through into an empty glass fronted restaurant. Only one other table was occupied. My heart sank but we decided it was too early and that everyone must still be backstage. Grabbing some beers we waited and waited. No one appeared.

Eventually Trey walked in but he simply spoke quickly to the people at the other table and then abruptly left. I called Greg but his phone was off. Not only were we in an empty and now closing bar but we were also stranded miles from the city, as the trains had stopped running.

Frustrated, I herded the girls towards the taxi rank. They were grateful for the evening but this wasn't how I'd envisaged it ending and things were about to get worse. The taxi queue was at least twenty people long and after standing in the cold for ten minutes, we hadn't made any progress. No cars came and no one moved. I overheard someone at the front say they had been waiting over an hour.

This was not happening, I could not wait here, with no taxis in sight, getting colder by the minute. From the corner of my eye I noticed a white mini bus leaving from behind the stadium. It was very much like the one that I had seen Trey get into the night before.

'Stay there,' I told the girls, as I dashed up the road. I was too late to catch the van but it had given me an idea. Around the back of the stadium I found a group of roadies loading up. 'Excuse me,' I enquired 'I'm looking for Greg the photographer ...'

'Sorry everyone's gone,' said a gruff looking bearded man, cutting me off mid-sentence.

'But please I just need to get back to Sydney, my friends and I ....'

'Everyone is gone, the band has left. Go home.' He clearly thought I was a desperate groupie trying her luck. Desperate maybe but all I wanted was a lift.

'Thanks anyway,' I called over my shoulder, as I stalked back up to where the girls waited. The taxi queue hadn't moved.

Another ten minutes passed. One cab approached but swiftly drove past without stopping. What the hell was going on? Then the people ahead of us turned round and told us that the front of the line had been waiting an hour and a half. That was all I needed to hear. I walked off around the stadium once more. The roadie saw me coming.

'I told you the band has left!'

'Please,' I asked with pleading eyes. 'Just listen for one minute.' I told him the story, making sure he knew how big bad Greg had left the poor little backpackers waiting alone in the dark. Five minutes later the three of us were backstage being told to help ourselves to cold beers.

'Make sure you take a few for the ride,' called my bearded friend, just before we piled onto the bus.

The two girls couldn't believe our luck or should I say my cheek. Well, I'm a big believer in the saying, 'If you don't ask you don't get', and I had been driven by the two things I hate most, being cold and being bored. The taxi queue already a distant memory, we headed off towards the city. The original plan had been to drop us off in Kings Cross. Then I heard the words 'Sheridan Hotel' and 'Nightclub after-party.' It wasn't long before I casually mentioned that I wasn't really tired and actually quite fancied a drink.

The next thing we knew we were walking into a mirrored lift and heading up to a suite in the Sheridan to finish the rest of our now pre-party drinks. The other two girls were *oooing* and *awwing* at the beauty of the place, but I kept quiet. If you lead someone to believe they have extensively impressed, then they can lose the will to try so hard. I was hoping that we were still far from the evening's highlight, the after-party. Maybe our new friend could help get us in. Although I must admit beer does taste a lot better when drunk from a balcony overlooking the city.

We had a fabulous time and I couldn't wait to hit the clubs. The other two girls weren't as enthusiastic and were actually ready for bed, well I guess it was nearly 2 a.m. Never one to leave my friends I insisted that myself and a roadie took them back to Kings Cross before continuing our night. In this case my loyalty may have been my downfall, and by the time we reached the nightclub they were on lock out.

Lock out was a Sydney rule used to keep late night drunks out of the clubs, if you're not in by 2 a.m. you're not getting in. I encouraged the roadie to push the subject some more, but the doorman said there was nothing he could do and the bar was closing at 3 a.m. anyhow.

Disappointed but not discouraged we went to another club, and band or no band, we partied the night away. Greg texted me to say that he was sorry, but his phone had run out of battery and he couldn't come out as he had to photograph Billy Joe surfing on Manly Beach at 6 a.m. I guess I could have gone to watch, but I wasn't in any state to walk by, then let alone catch a ferry to Manly. The whole 48 hours had been incredible and I still break into a massive grin every time I hear a Green Day song.

A Journey Mapped By the Heart

A week later I was reunited with Nik. He was going to spend some time with me before looking for work outside of the cities. Nik was a farm boy at heart, and when he wasn't driving the surf camp buses, he preferred to be at the wheel of a giant harvester or some form of tractor. I wanted to find somewhere more romantic than The Cross for us to enjoy together and my guidebook recommended a small place named Jervis Bay. Located a couple of hours south from Sydney, it was described as a naturally beautiful and peaceful area with pristine beaches. To get us there I hired a car but insisted that Nik drove. I had spent most of my adult life on the Spanish islands and had never driven on the left hand side before.

Slowly the bumper to bumper city traffic faded away and the towns became smaller and more picturesque with every passing kilometre. We stopped for lunch and wandered up to a lighthouse, before watching in awe as the ocean exploded through a blow hole at the picture-perfect town of Kiama.

On our return to the car Nik announced it was my turn to drive. Reluctantly I climbed in and spent a while faffing around with the seat and mirrors, until I could not delay the inevitable any longer. It was an awkward start but I picked it up quickly. My main error was constantly turning on the windscreen wipers instead of the indicators, an easy mistake that made me look repeatedly dumb.

Before we entered the national park we stopped off for food and booze. It was a simple culinary affair consisting of bread,

Nutella, jam and Doritos as we had no cooking equipment. Upon arrival, I stopped to take in the scene. The camp site was a beautiful haven nestled in amongst the trees. We pitched Nik's tent while kangaroos hopped past and brightly coloured parrots noisily swooped above our heads. The beach was a thirty second walk from camp and seeing it made my heart rise. Before me lay perfect white sand with lapping, crystal clear water and not another soul in sight. Paradise.

That evening we sat on the sand eating our snacks and enjoying a bottle of wine. The sunset left a rainbow of colours in the sky, and I felt every inch of tension leave my body as we lay looking up at the stars while our tiny speakers played music in the background. We talked for hours and I couldn't believe the level of knowledge Nik had achieved in his twenty-one years and of course all this discussed for him in a foreign language. His English was almost perfect and having learnt a vast amount of it in Australia, he had developed an Aussie twang. Mixed with his German accent, his English sounded somewhat Canadian.

That night we crawled into the tent bringing the Nutella and bread for an evening snack. After twenty minutes of our continued chatter I heard a noise. At first it didn't even interest me. After my trip on the Great Ocean Road, I was well used to rustling in the night, but then I realised that something was trying to claw its way into our tent. A brief flash of panic crossed through me, but after a quick pause I came to my senses and opened the zipper. My eyes caught a glimpse of a cheeky possum running away, closely followed by a camera wielding, naked Nik desperate to get a snap of the native creature.

The following day we strolled hand in hand along the beaches. The sun shone down from a clear blue sky and the scenery around us could have come straight from the Caribbean. I could feel the pureness of the white grainy sand as it slipped between my toes, but I had to watch my step as among the traditional beachside landscape was a rather unusual feature. An abundance of large onions had washed up on the shore, presumably from a cargo ship, which had lost its load, adding a little randomness to the otherwise perfect surroundings.

After a leisurely stroll we decided to take a break and walked to the end of a rocky jetty, before sitting back enjoying the sun as it warmed our lazy bodies. Before long, a large white pelican with a pale pink beak flew down and began to fish. I smiled and watched curiously, it was the first time I had seen one of the birds up close. Soon after, Nik pointed into the aqua blue water. A few metres from our perch, as if on cue, a large pod of dolphins were jumping through the water. Sold as a package holiday this experience would have cost a fortune. For us it had simply taken a three day car hire, $12 park fee and a $7 tent. It goes to show you don't need to spend vast amounts of money to enjoy a taste of heaven.

After a refreshing swim, we headed back to camp, packed up the tent and jumped in the car for the short drive to Hyams Beach. There was a reason I was so keen to see this particular strip of sand. Hyams is officially the whitest sand in the world. It is even in the Guinness book of records. Indeed it was very white, although I couldn't see much difference between the sand beneath me then and that of our morning walk.

Our second camp site was at Cave Beach where we again enjoyed our food at the water's edge. It came as no surprise to see the beach had two large caves which we eagerly explored. I loved the simplicity of Australian place names. Some towns, villages, streets and areas were named after those who discovered them, their friends or relatives. For example, the Sturt Highway running through the centre of the country was named after the first white explorer to cross Australia from south to north, while Sydney was called so in tribute to a British home secretary from the 1700s. Many places had been given Aboriginal names, which again often described the location, but conjured up beautiful fairy-tale images in my English mind. Wagga Wagga, Woolloomooloo, Bunyip, Yarra and Kangy Angy are all real places around Australia. British street names are another favourite especially in Sydney where settlers were trying to create a home away from home. Familiar names such as Oxford Street, Liverpool Street and Kings Cross triggered memories of London, while Ashford, Canterbury and Hastings reminded me of my birth county Kent. But I guess some explorers must have been lacking inspiring friends or Aboriginal connections, resulting in obvious names such as Duck Creek, the said Cave Beach and even The Bay of Plenty Lodges. As for Cockburn in South Australia I'll leave that one to the imagination.

Having finished our adventures around the caves we ate on the shore, washing the food down with vodka, as Nik's iPod played Latino rhythms into the night. Eventually the conversation came around to our future. I knew Nik needed to work and I had already booked a flight to Melbourne but I wasn't ready for us to separate. So I was surprised to find that we were going to continue our journey as a couple after all. Nik confessed to having arranged a flight to Melbourne. He had wanted to tell me when the time was right. He had sensed this was more than a quick fling and I was grateful for his intuition.

Many vodkas later and a little worse for wear, we staggered back to the tent long after dark had fallen. Once again we could hear the wildlife running around outside, and once again we were curious to see what was making the noise. Trying to entice the noisy creature, I put a piece of bread outside the tent flap. I sat waiting, camera poised until a shuffle outside made us both jump. Cautiously unzipping the tent, we were amazed to not only find a possum but also a large kangaroo. Both of which were engaging in a tug of war with the slice of bread between them (note to future travellers: I have since learnt that you should not feed local wildlife. I'll be getting some kangaroo carb karma for that).

Our elation didn't last long. The weather had cooled and a breeze picked up. We cuddled together for warmth but soon, against all forecasts, we heard the distinct patter of rain. Nik had picked the tent up for a bargain price so we already knew there was no chance of it being waterproof. At surf camp he had strung a tarpaulin between the trees to keep the rain at bay. We had the tarp with us, but it was currently stowed in the car, a ten minute walk away.

Nik, ever the hero, made a break for it through the now torrential rain, while I stayed inside trying to fight the seeping water with towels. He returned and pegged the tarp around us before returning to bed, soaking wet. We tried to fall asleep but the wind was strong, and the tarpaulin had to be constantly repegged as the rain battered our shelter.

Finally the weather calmed and the drizzle reduced to a patter. I drifted off, thankful for sleep to finally take me. But my rest didn't last long. After what felt like five minutes, Nik awoke me once more. 'Don't panic,' he told me, as my mind automatically ran wild. 'I think there is something in the tent.' He was right and I swiftly shot my legs up to my chest as a brown furry rodent scuttled past my foot. I flew out into the rain while Nik scared, what I hoped was, a large mouse out of the tent. Sleeping with food inside obviously hadn't been a good idea. The mouse had chewed its way through, in an attempt at stealing our bread, leaving a fair sized hole in the side of our tent. Poor Nik had to spend the rest of the night trying to stop an army of rodents doing the same thing. Even leaving the bread outside didn't make a difference. Oh the joys of camping.

*

The next morning it was unanimously decided that the tent was finished, and we would treat ourselves to a nice warm, comfortable hotel room for our last night away from the city. Hopefully we would be safe from rodents, rain and all other sleep related problems. Having binned the tent we drove up to a different beach to eat breakfast, before heading to Wollongong a few hours up the coast, to look for a place to stay. Luck was on our side and we found a reasonably cheap room, complete with a Jacuzzi bath. What luxury.

After a very long, much needed soak, we dressed in our best and headed out for dinner. After days of bread and Nutella we gorged on a beautiful meal, washed down by a bottle of wine, followed by a blissfully uninterrupted night of sleep. The perfect end to a wonderful few days.

RACING FOR GOLD

By the time we flew to Melbourne Nik had already been offered a job. Sadly for me it was on a farm located four hours from the city. He would have to start the following day, but there was no other option. He needed to fund the rest of his trip. We said our goodbyes once more and I promised to visit once my sightseeing had been completed. I had no schedule or solid plans, so when he had settled in, I would go to rural Victoria and work things out from there.

Melbourne is known for its food, music, arts and cultural diversity. Heavily influenced by various European nationalities it was an interesting city to explore. I booked a hostel and spent the first few days wandering the markets, gardens and cafes. I even boarded a tour to visit the set from *Neighbours*—the cheesy Aussie TV series that I had been glued to during my pre-teen years. The show still ran in the UK, but Australians never took as much interest, preferring its rival *Home and Away*.

The day started badly, with me getting lost and nearly missing the bus, but I finally arrived puffing and panting, to meet our *Neighbours* 'celebrity' who was signing autographs. Having not watched the show for the last ten years, I had no idea who she was but dutifully held out my Ramsey Street postcard for the tall middle aged brunette and asked someone to take our photo. Perhaps one of my Facebook friends could ID her.

My group piled into a mini bus while old *Neighbours* tapes played on the overhead TV. The tour guide tried to make the drive exciting and kept our small group of twelve entertained with facts about the show. I had paid a little bit extra to go on the VIP tour which involved seeing some of the actual set, as well as the famous Ramsey Street. I'd expected to see inside the studios and was disappointed to find we were only visiting the outdoor locations. Most I had never seen as they were from the more updated episodes, but I instantly recognised Lassiter's Lake and a few other older landmarks.

Then we drove to the street where the series is based. In reality it is called Pin Oak Road and is a lot smaller than it appears on TV. I took photos and wandered about while security prohibited access to the houses which are actually inhabited by local residents. It was a nice way to pass the day, but for me I think the trip would have been far better appreciated had I taken it a decade earlier.

*

Another tourist attraction saw me hopping on a coach for the second time in a few days. This time I was destined for Ballarat. Victoria's largest inland city boomed after the discovery of gold there in 1851. Within a year 20,000 diggers had arrived all searching for their fortune. Now the mines were run by corporate companies, but a tribute to the miners of past still stood. Sovereign Hill brought the old mining town back to life, with costumed locals, replicas of shops, houses and even a stream in which guests could try their hand at panning for gold.

After jumping off the huge air-conditioned bus, I made my way eagerly through reception and out onto the streets of Sovereign Hill. A horse and cart rattled past and groups of women, clad in black dresses and frilly caps wandered about clutching woven baskets and gossiping. I peered into shops, firstly at the fully functioning bakery and then into the black-smith's, who true to character was hammering away at his anvil.

It didn't take me long to find the gold rush stream and after a quick demonstration from one of the costumed panners, I was sieving away looking for my million dollar nugget. Imagine my excitement when in my first pan, I struck gold! Admittedly it was the tiniest sliver that could only be seen when held up to the sun, but I was as proud as punch. I stuck it to my fingertip where it sat like an ant on a mountain, before I dropped it into a little, glass, water filled bottle that I had purchased from the gift shop. Enthused, I continued my hunt until there were five or six pieces floating in the bottle.

One of the 'locals' came over to see how I was going. Mark was easy to talk to and within a few seconds his role had been forgotten and we were chatting away. He had been working at 'Sovy Hill' as he called it, for three years and loved it. He examined my find which I showed off with pride.

Now, I'm not completely stupid (well I guess that's debatable), and I had a feeling that after all these years there was not much hope of gold naturally being found in this stream, but it didn't stop the disappointment dropping through my stomach, when Mark kindly informed me that the staff sprayed about $250 worth of gold flakes into the water every morning. Although we were now talking like friends, I felt he could have kept up the act and made me feel a little special about my now, not so impressive achievement.

On the bright side I guess if I was to return to the river early one morning there was a good chance of me emptying it and leaving the place a few bucks richer. Thank god I have some sort of a life and therefore not enough time for such pathetic, but rewarding schemes.

It was a great day out: I had explored a mine; watched Mark (who had changed into an army officer costume) lead a firing squad up the main street; and seen a gold bar being liquefied and then solidified under extreme temperatures. I had also gained a wonderful insight into an industry which had created a huge colonial boom; bringing nationalities from around the globe to this unforgiving, yet vibrant land. An industry which still today creates fortunes, jobs and an awful lot of controversy throughout Australia.

*

Finally the time arrived for my big Melbourne event, a day at the Grand Prix. I had been looking for friends to join me, but unfortunately everyone at my hostel seemed rather uptight and sat in small groups ignoring any outsiders. Then I met Serge, a German speaking Swiss man who had character and charm. At over six foot with a shaved head and a huge smile I couldn't help but be warmed by him. We met over dinner one night, as he commented on my salad which stood out from the continuous stream of pasta and spag bol that most travellers lived on. Having established that I was trying to be healthy and he was trying to be cheap, our talk continued and a friendship based on a general loathing of everyone around us, blossomed wonderfully. Serge also found the place very unsocial and fortunately for me not only was he looking for a friend but also someone to accompany him to the Grand Prix that weekend. It seemed fate had leant me a hand once more.

*

That Saturday we jumped on the tram, Melbourne's ground level version of the metro, and headed off towards Albert Park. The crowd buzzed excitedly and groups of mates wandered about looking at various cars, old and new. Engines revved constantly throughout the numerous displays and demonstrations that were dotted about. The track was separated from the crowd by huge metal fences which were patrolled by wardens. Crash barriers lined the edge and crowds gathered on grassy verges to watch the action. It was my first Formula One race, so I had no idea what to expect.

Having taken advice from friends, I had bought my ear plugs normally used to block out the sound of hostel snorers. I was glad to have them. The cars roared past, the sound so loud I winced. Serge proved to be great fun and took photos of me trying to 'hitch a ride' from one of the whizzing cars. They flew past at such speed that the first few shots were of empty track. Thank god for digital devices or we would have gone through a whole box of film trying to catch one on camera.

In between the warm up and race we explored the stalls. After much persuasion from Serge, a kind man let me sit in a race car before we walked across a bridge to 'ride' display motorbikes and watch a tyre changing competition. I even got to pose on a podium holding a wreath, winner's cup and champagne. Sadly they were all fakes, otherwise the champagne, at least, may have mysteriously disappeared. Someone must have already tried to make off with the replicas because even they were tied to the stand by strings.

Serge may have been tall and manly, but he was a child at heart and liked to cause trouble. The queues for food were miles long and a gap had formed to let passers-by walk through. Serge decided to stop in the gap and pretend to push in the line. I giggled as the woman behind him became outraged. Five minutes later we were crossing a floating bridge on the lake. Scores of people were lined up with cameras taking shots of the city. Serge bounced and rocked all the way along, no doubt blurring people's shots as he went, and within seconds I was joining in. Later he stole the pass out stamp that allowed people to return to the venue later in the day. Chasing me down the street he covered me in chequered flags. Security hunted him down to retrieve the stamp but while the ink on my arm was still wet, I pressed it against those of some teenagers who were desperately trying to get a glimpse of the cars over the fence. They were all overjoyed as they ran in the entrance for a free day out.

During the race break a huge jet flew over. The roar even dwarfed the sound of the Formula One cars. The plane flew at such a speed that the sound was heard a split second after it had passed. Royal Australian Air force pilots looped and chased each other through the skies in displays that made me fear for a crash. Between you and me, I found the planes more exciting than the cars, but I didn't dare mention it aloud around all the diehard race fans.

For the qualifying race we found a spot in front of a big screen. It was far easier to follow when you had a visual of the full track rather than just a flash of colour whizzing past. By this point I had also managed to educate myself slightly on the teams and drivers. The Australian's were very competitive when it came to sport, VERY competitive. Therefore imagine my delight to find that Jenson Button, an English driver, had won the race. Webber, the Australian representative had not only crashed his car but also put legend Lewis Hamilton out of the race in the process. Finally I had a retort to use next time I was abused for bad cricket or 'lame' English football.

The day was certainly an experience, although if you really want to see the race it's far easier to follow on TV, but then again where's the fun in that. Serge had been a great companion, but I was sad to find that he was leaving for Sydney the following day. Such is the friendship of a backpacker abroad: take what you can, when you can and just enjoy the moment.

WORK! WHAT A LOAD OF SHIT

Before long it was time for me to move on, reunite with Nik and begin a whole new adventure. I had come to realise that Australia was a country I wished to explore in-depth. I wanted to get to know the people, traverse the land while truly living the experiences. A year would no longer be enough.

I remembered what I'd been told by the Kings Cross backpackers when I first arrived nearly five months ago. I could apply for a second year working holiday visa, but in order to obtain that visa I would have to undergo three months of farm work! THREE MONTHS! For a girl whose experience of farm life had so far been to feed baby lambs in front of my grandparent's video camera, it was sure to be an interesting time. Nik was already working in a very small village called Maffra, so my plan was to join him and try to find work.

I had been advised that it would severely increase my chances of finding a job if I had a car. As you may remember, back in Sydney I had pined over the cars advertised on the noticeboard. With another 18 months, down under, ahead of me, I thought I could finally justify buying one. I would be able to join the millions of other backpackers driving barely, if at all, legal cars around Australia, camping and exploring along the way. Previously, the idea had seemed expensive and pointless as I was alone on my trip, but now a car would be useful in job hunting, taking Nik and I around the country, plus I could finally buy as many clothes as I wanted. My new vehicle would double as a portable wardrobe, fantastic!

I started looking online and decided that camper vans were not for me. I would eventually have to spend a fair bit of time, in and around cities, hopefully getting a job and earning some extra travel money. To be honest I struggle to park a car, let alone a van. Plus they ate fuel like crazy. Then it was on to the traditional backpacker station wagon, these cars reminded me of a hearse and had enough room to put a mattress in the back to sleep on. Again not a good choice, if there was mattress in the boot where would I store all my newly purchased luggage. So after considering petrol costs, storage and parking abilities, I decided a small five door car would be fine. Hopefully there would be just enough room for Nik and I, plus luggage, tents and camping equipment. Which bought me to another exciting realisation, I would get to go shopping for that too!

After spending hours pouring through backpacker sales ads, I finally ended up at a car auction with a new found local friend whom I had met at the Grand Prix. At the auction, after days of careful planning, everything went out the window, and before I had the chance to comprehend what was going on, my friend had bid for and won me a Ford Festiva. It was a bit scary and everything happened very fast. I hadn't had time to do all my pros and cons, and as a Virgo, the whole rushed, unplanned experience left me feeling as if I'd been run over by, well, a Ford Festiva. However, it was a really cute colour which helped ease my doubts.

I was now the proud owner of a five door, greeny, blue car with a 1.3 litre engine. Most people would describe it as a run around. This was the vessel which would transport me through miles and miles of desert, rainforest and mountains.

Once everything had sunk in, excitement bubbled and I spent ages pinking it up with fluffy accessories. It was my first car as I had made it through the last twenty-seven years by foot, moped and company vehicles. I loved that Ford with pride and care, I even took the time to change the light bulb in the boot. I wanted everything to be perfect. If only I had known what the future held.

*

I finally arrived in Maffra, a tiny, beautiful little township consisting of a pub, petrol stations and a handful of shops, which took up no more than one street. Surrounded by green fields and of course farms, it was the typical country town. There was only one hostel, which had been opened to accommodate other farming backpackers like ourselves. I spent my first week there relaxing, loving my car and desperately trying to think of more things I needed to buy for a road trip, until I realised it was time to get a job.

Nik and I had a private room in the hostel, which was a luxury we could afford as a couple. Thankfully everyone staying in the dorms seemed nice too. I started to talk to the other residents to help me fathom what to do next. There were a few other girls who were working in packing factories. This was supposed to be the best work as it wasn't too physically demanding. All I could think was BORING! Boredom is one of my biggest fears and I'm sure my constant need for entertainment drives a lot of people mad. Packing factories were not going to suit me. The boys however, were working on dairy farms, milking cows. They came home stinking and dirty but normally with a smile. Well, as they say, a smile is worth a million dollars, and so I decided milking was for me.

Alex, a warm-hearted Scot staying at the hostel, agreed to take me to his work and show me the ropes. I rose, cold and sleepy at 5 a.m. and begrudgingly followed him up to the farm. It was dark and misty but I could hear the cows mooing among the shadows.

Inside the large tin shed we got to work. The basic idea was to attach milking cups to the cow's udders while the cow seemingly tried to piss, shit and kick, all at the same time. The cups were long sliver tubes with pulsators in the ends which mechanically milked the animals. Attaching the cups, I was stood directly under the cows arse … oh, you can imagine.

Just to make it more exciting, the cows were on an elevated platform which constantly rotated. This meant that the cow I was attaching cups onto, was constantly moving away. And of course for newbies like me, if you're weren't fast enough, you got dragged around trying to keep up with the moving udder, dropping the cups, tripping over and getting a literal pat on the head.

I also discovered, that if by some miracle I managed to avoid these problems and cup the cow, just as I paused for a second to breathe, the spinning rotary would no doubt be making the most of my lapse in attention and bring a shitting cow directly in line with my head.

Impossible as it seems, I loved it. At least it wasn't boring and I had definitely found a challenge. It seemed ironic that this career which was based entirely on multitasking was dominated by men. (Now, now boys, research has proven that us girls rock at the MT), I guess boys never lose that childhood urge to come home covered in filth.

*

After my training was complete I drove out to another farm. I had been given the manager's number by someone from the hostel and had been invited to work a trial. Just to confuse things, this dairy had a different system.

At the new farm the cows were stood in two opposite rows. The milkers worked in a lower alley between them, allowing a pleasant view of cow's udders on either side. This time the cows didn't move automatically so it was easier to attach the cups. The cows walked in, were cupped and milked before being let out and allowing the next crowd through. However, while I was attempting to cup the four bloated teats in front of me, the cow behind had the advantage of being able to lift its tail (the giveaway that they are about to dump a load) and shit on my head before I'd had the chance to move out of the way.

It was good work experience to learn the *herring bone* system, but the farm needed someone long-term and I couldn't provide that. Nik's visa expired in June, and I had made him promise that if I came to Maffra, he would help me drive the car up to Darwin before he left the country. That meant that we only had a couple of weeks before we would set off on our road trip. So with no job on offer I had now been crapped, pissed and leaked on, twice in one day for zero pay.

Thankfully my training didn't go to waste, and I eventually got a job at a farm just down the road from us. The people there were very friendly, in fact so were all the farmers I had met. The country Aussies really had time for people. They actually seemed to enjoy teaching me, and even if I was only there for a few weeks, they made sure I understood how to do everything. The farm manager always told me, 'Well, it doesn't matter too much now, but you might need to know this if you milk somewhere else in future.'

I thanked him and listened carefully while praying that this was far, far away from any eventual career path I might find myself on. Short-term it was fun, but I had a feeling the novelty would wear off before long. The farm staff wanted me to learn as much as possible even if it meant making their shift longer and harder. It was incredible to experience the display of human spirit that I thought was long extinct.

After a few days, I was doing the afternoon milking alone. I was more confident and no longer afraid of the cows, which had several advantages. If I jumped when they kicked, they got scared and kicked more, this nervousness between us had also made them shit a lot more too. It was nice to relax and enjoy the work. It had been a lot of pressure to know my tension was being passed on to five hundred animals, twice a day. I was also advised not to wash my clothes, so that the animals got used to my smell. Putting on dung stained trackies every morning certainly didn't add to the pleasure, although to be honest the washing machine didn't do much to ease the thick coating of shit on my overalls anyway. Washing detergent adverts would be much more impressive if the subject had just come out of a dairy. Red wine had nothing on those beasts.

I learnt how to inject antibiotics into udders and put sick cows on a special milking bucket so that the bad milk didn't go in with the good. All in all I was getting quite good at it. However, I still had to be alert at all times, as cows are sneaky creatures. If

I kept them waiting too long, they would knock the grain feeder out, which meant I had to climb under the rotary to fix it, sliding through mud, urine and excrement as I went. So every milking I rushed to beat them to the tin shed.

Once each beast had completed a full turn on the rotary, during which they were simultaneously fed and milked, the cups automatically dropped off and the cow walked into the yard, leaving their slot on the wheel free for the next cow to get on. Somehow they had worked out that by not getting off they could get a second load of grain and would occasionally try to stay on the wheel for a free ride. The idea (and in my mind it was only an idea, as I found it almost impossible to achieve) was to keep an eye on the cows getting off, at the same time as fixing cups to the cows getting on while also avoiding shit and piss and trying not to lose my sanity. Despite my best efforts sometimes they managed to stay on or even worse, get off while I was watching and then turn around and run back on as soon as I looked down at the cups. Cows are not as stupid as they would have you believe.

The herd consisted of 500 females, which were milked at 5.15 a.m. and 3.15 p.m. every day. That meant I was cupping 4,000 teats a day! The herd appeared to have some form of social conduct and normally arrived roughly in the same order every milking. It was certainly the same few cows first and last every day. I began to recognise a few of them by their distinct markings, habits and numbered tags. This helped warn me as to who was likely to kick, cheat or literally give me the shits. To get the naughty ones off the rotary I had to squirt them in the face with a hose. I thought this was quite funny, the cows stood out in the rain all day and night no problem but a little jet from a well-aimed nozzle scared the crap out of them. Power is glory.

The farm, Maffra and their surroundings were lovingly picturesque. The scenery reminded me of the English countryside, very green and lush, but here a backdrop of silhouetted mountains lined the horizon. Regardless of the setting, I struggled with the milking hours and the subsequent sleeping pattern. I had to get up at 4.30 a.m., which during Victoria's April, was foggy, dark and cold. Every day, I somehow managed to avoid a head on collision with the overconfident farmers, who flew down the narrow roads at ridiculous speeds, appearing out of the mist in their utes and Land Cruisers, like giant monsters, with full fog lights blaring. I would take a second to be thankful for a safe arrival, before having to leave the warmth of the car, which of course had only gotten hot during the last two minutes of my journey. Wandering out into the icy darkness, I flexed my hand until my frozen fingers finally recovered enough movement to turn on the light switch. I had to get the dairy set up as quickly as possible before the cows arrived and started causing havoc in return for inconvenience to their schedule if there was even a minute's delay.

After milking all 500 cows, I had to clean the impossibly vast mess they had made in the yard. I swear they had some secret stash of laxative that they would intentionally digest just before heading down to me. Finally I would arrive home at 8.30 a.m. and go back to sleep, before repeating the entire process again in the afternoon. It always felt as if I had worked two days instead of one. All this said and done, it was one hell of an experience and I would definitely do it again. Well, if it was short-term, with constipated cows, had more sociable milking hours and lived in a much warmer climate. Oh yes and preferably with much higher pay.

CHAPTER 5

UPSIDE DOWN OUTBACK

FINALLY THE TIME came for Nik and I to head off on our big road trip through the outback. Packing up the car I felt simultaneously nervous and excited. We had all my newly purchased gear and many thousands of miles ahead of us. I couldn't wait to get up north because in Victoria, temperatures can drop below zero in winter, something that I was not keen to experience.

We headed for the Great Alpine Road stopping on the way at the Buchan Caves. They were intensely stunning with magnificent coloured stalagmites and stalactites, surrounded by pools of water, lit up by well-placed spotlights. There were even some sparkly rocks, which combined with the lighting and atmosphere, created a rather magical effect. I almost expected to see little fairies flying amongst them.

Upwards and onwards, the Festiva headed into 'the Alps'. The inverted commas are there for a reason. They weren't quite the Alps that us Europeans are used to, rather a sequence of large hills, but still very pleasant to visit. We arrived at our very first campground after dark. Not a great start, but—and here's where my shopping paid off—having purchased my own pop-up tent, within three minutes we had a nice warm tent complete with doona (here's another new Australian word, doona = duvet) and self-inflating air mat. It was definitely a more comfortable set up than our Jervis Bay experience. Unfortunately the altitude had turned the air icy cold, but we snuggled up tight and were soon warm enough to sleep. One day down, four weeks on the road to go.

*

The next morning, invigorated by a chilly welcome to the world, we packed up quickly and continued on. Heading across the Alps I began to realise what an intensely varied and vast country Australia is. The scenery constantly changed. One side of the mountain formed rolling grassy hills, then as we drove through the clouds and across the top, out of nowhere appeared a ski resort. There was currently no snow on the slopes, but we saw the lifts and the empty hotels. I had never associated Australia with snow before, I guess there was a lot to learn and I planned to enjoy every second. As we began our descent down the other side of the mountain, the land became a tropical forest with waterfalls, tall woody trees and a rich floor of ferns and greenery. Diverse was an understatement.

*

That night Nik impressed me no end by managing to start a fire when everything in the forest was wet. He was certainly a very useful man to have around. We camped at the base of Victoria's highest mountain, Mt Bogong. The plan had been to climb it the following day, but you'd be amazed how easy it is to change your mind after a bottle of Amaretto, followed by a night in a cold damp tent. Anyhow, we had found a new mission.

The plan was to drive across to Mount Kosciuszko, Australia's highest mountain, and climb that instead. So after a lot more driving—there was always a lot of driving on that trip (I don't think you can have any idea how big Australia is until you have driven around it)—we arrived in the Snowy Mountains, New South Wales. I thoroughly enjoyed climbing the mountain, although I guess the use of the word 'climbing' could be debatable. Nik hiked up the first bit, which would be the steep and ragged part, while I paid $30 to ride the ski lift.

We united at the top, me raring to go and Nik looking a bit puffed out to say the least. Then it was a 13 km round trip across a metal walkway to the peak. The boardwalk-style trail was mostly flat, and certainly not what I considered a mountain climb. I must say though, it was bloody cold. Really cold. Hat, scarf and gloves cold. The wind chill had taken the air temperature down to a frosty minus 1°C. No one has ever seen me walk as fast as I did that day. I guess a cold climate could be good for my calorie burning. In hindsight I wish I had hiked from the base, but Nik was an experienced climber, 21 years old and fit. Whereas I was ... well, how can I put this without hurting my own feelings? Let's just say that I wasn't quite in the same league. Having taken this into consideration, I didn't think I would be able to keep up with the young German but I raced ahead during our walk to the peak. Maybe my fitness wasn't quite as washed up as I thought.

*

Next on the Festiva stop list was Canberra ... enough said! Australians and fellow down under travellers will understand my humour, but for the rest of you I had better explain. Canberra is the capital of Australia—not Sydney, as many people, including myself for many years, think. The problem with Canberra is that the city was built just for that reason. Sydney and Melbourne were competing to be the nation's capital and when no one would back down, they simply built a city between the two. In fact during my travels, I constantly met with the Sydney/Melbourne debate. All the Australian's have a preferred favourite and love to talk about it. For example, I would just mention to a Victorian that on my arrival I flew into Sydney and it would quickly be followed by something along the lines of: 'I'm not a fan of Sydney. Melbourne's got all the restaurants, art and culture, Sydney just can't compare …'

Or I could start saying that I went to see the Grand Prix in Melbourne, only to be suddenly interrupted by: 'Melbourne's got a few things going for it but the weather's terrible, very cold and unreliable, plus there are no good beaches nearby. Sydney on the other hand …'

And so it went on. It's very similar to the UK debate on how to pronounce the word 'scone', there is no firm conclusion that can be reached but millions of people seem to enjoy arguing over it, time and time again. Anyhow, Canberra was built as a midway point to finish the argument and became the capital of this vast country.

Mostly known for politics and museums, Canberra generally has a reputation for being boring. I always feel sorry for people from Canberra. Naturally after being introduced to someone at a dinner party etc., etc., conversation generally comes around to discussing home towns. For a Canberrian I guess this is where the awkwardness begins. The poor soul must admit, albeit as quietly as possible, 'I'm from Canberra.' After which the discussion surely falls into silence and occasionally a tumbleweed might roll past. Finally someone will take a deep breath and pipe up, 'Well I was driving through Melbourne last week …' and everything carries on as normal, the capital of this great nation having been quickly sidestepped.

On the plus side, the Australian Capital Territory, which

basically encompasses Canberra and its surrounding suburbs, forms one of Australia's seven states, so I was happy to tick another one off the list. May it also be said that I have since met a lot of people from Canberra who have become good friends. Sorry guys!

The reason that I am rabbiting on about the city, is that I am trying to distract you from the fact that I have no exciting story to tell. We did spend a few hours in the museum where I jumped at the chance to pretend to be a radio presenter. As you may have noticed I do love the sound of my own voice. Canberra also has an interesting road system, which when viewed on a map, resembles crop circles. Maybe aliens did build it, maybe politicians are in fact from outer space. That would certainly explain a few things. Anyway, now I'm definitely rambling. Swiftly moving on.

*

After a week on the road we finally turned west and headed towards our destination. Yes people, in the name of exploration, this whole time we had been driving further and further away from our final goal of Darwin. Oh well, in Australia, what's an extra few thousand kilometres here and there. Everything began to get smaller and smaller, as towns petered out and we drew closer to the dustiness of the outback.

On our way across inland South Australia we hit a plague of locusts. At first I thought it was funny, as they thudded and squished on the windscreen while I laughed and made videos. It was as if we were under attack. However, after ten minutes of splattering, it became clear that the storm of bugs was going to continue for some time. The novelty soon wore off. Sadly the smell of them cooking, as they smattered themselves over the engine never did, and it lingered inside the Festiva for months to come. If the smell wasn't sickening enough, bits of leg and the odd wing started to come through the air vents too. I began to worry we were about to experience a mobile locust version of the film Arachnophobia, where spiders take over entire houses. By the time we drove out of their airspace, the caked layer of guts was so bad that we couldn't even read the number plate. Later, even after many attempts of cleaning you could still see poo coloured smears, a grotesque memorial to what was once, a fine work of nature.

*

Flying squadrons excepted, the outback really was as barren as you'd expect. Nothing but dirt, red dust and blue sky, stretched as far as our eyes could see, with the odd bush, tumbleweed or kangaroo punctuating the landscape. Until now we had been camping in the beautiful forests in the national parks. However, now with not so much as a lone tree in sight, I dreaded having to sleep next to the highway or pay for an equally barren camp site. There was a small park on the map, so we headed towards it thinking that it would be a nice place to spend the night. It was however, also a 100 km trip away from the road we needed to be on and a very bumpy dusty journey at that.

*

Upon arrival the drive was instantly justified. Families of kangaroos lined the roadside, bounding gracefully away from the car or maybe fleeing in terror, but you get the gist. The sun created beautiful pastel colours on the horizon as it set, and we began to spot wild pigs and their babies, or 'Piggies!' as I declared excitedly, disappearing into the thickening bush. Sadly the piggies were very photo shy and didn't want to stay around for any cuddles either, such a shame.

Upon reaching a cluster of trees and purpose-built fireplaces, we pitched the tent and cooked a delicious meal over the flames. That day was one of the only times we had been organised enough to pick up some fresh fruit and veg after already crossing a fruit fly exclusion zone. These zones are designed to stop the spread of the fruit flies across Australia. All fresh produce has to be disposed of in designated bins before crossing the zones. Just in case the threat of an entire country's ecosystem wasn't enough to stop us, big signs warning of two thousand dollar fines dominated the roadside.

We only ever came across one that was actually manned but something about the way the officer looked at us made me feel nervous. His manner was very dominant, as if we were trying to smuggle cocaine across from Mexico or something. Even with the security in place, I have no idea what's to stop the fly from actually flying over this invisible line. The zones seemed to pop up everywhere, normally just after an expensive, health inspired, fruit spending spree in an overpriced local shop.

But that night in our bush haven camp we happily gorged on fresh vegetable kebabs and corn cobs, before lying back on my pink flowery picnic rug, staring at the stars. Various wildlife rustled in the brush and there was something very liberating to know we were the only humans for miles around.

*

The next day we set off on the not so exciting track back to the highway. I would have to try and drive on a dirt track at some point, so with direction from Nik I took the wheel. The car bounced everywhere, slipping and sliding around. However, I learnt how to correct it without losing control and it was quite fun once I got the hang of it. Finally we made it back on the highway, although it wasn't a sealed road. Some main roads in regional Australia are just dirt with no tarmac but fairly smooth thanks to regular grading. The road we had to take stretched for 250 kms, so off I went.

*

And this is where it all went wrong and a chain of events, changed my attitude towards driving forever. I had been at the wheel for over an hour and no dramas had unfolded. The speed limit was 100 kph and I was trying to keep at a minimum of 80 kph. We had a lot of ground to cover.

I had just taken a corner, when the car suddenly slipped on some dirt. As we were already on a bend, the wheels flew out sharply. I was so relaxed, having been driving for so long, that the jolt made me jump. Then the worst happened. As I jumped, I tried to correct the wheel but must have oversteered. Realising my error I turned the wheel back the other way, producing an even bigger skid. My reflex saw me jerk the wheel in the opposite direction once more before everything went hazy. We went hurtling out of control and as Nik had instructed on my practice drives, I didn't touch the brakes.

To be honest I really thought it was going to be fine. I really believed that I was going to regain control just as I had on the small road earlier. This had happened before on my practice drive and was easily fixed. Normally I would just wait for the car to naturally slow and regain control. However this time, we were on a bigger highway, speed was faster and due to the turn in the road, it was a totally different situation.

I am now thankful that I had no idea of what was about to happen as we flew up the bank. I didn't realise what was going on at the time, but the back wheels over took the front, and as the car turned, it was sent off balance and flipped 360 degrees. The entire body of the car was in the air except the rear slant of the back windscreen which rolled down the bank. We then slammed with extreme force, back onto the road facing the direction from which we had come. The next thing I knew, I was sitting motionless in the driver's seat still clinging to the wheel with a vague notion that I had just been upside down.

I hadn't even had a chance to work out what was going on, when Nik asked me if I was ok. I replied with a simple 'Yes,' and he told me to get out of the car. Finding I couldn't open my door, he instructed me to crawl out of his side. The whole time my face remained blank and I could not speak, my brain was still trying to catch up with what had happened.

The car looked a mess covered in dust, with the tyres flat, metal crushed and a surrounding of shattered glass. Our equipment and possessions were scattered all over the road in among the thick red sand. A cloud of orange dust filled the air. Nik asked me to help gather everything up. Bless him, I couldn't do anything. I was just picking stuff up, putting it down somewhere, then moving it back again and generally walking round in circles. Nik knew this, but he had worked as ambulance crew back in Germany and was just trying to distract me to stop me from going into shock.

Within a few minutes a man approached in an ute, and upon seeing us and the wrecked car, offered to drive and find an area with phone signal to call a tow truck. He asked me when the accident had occurred and when I answered, 'About five minutes ago,' He replied:

'Well that explains why you're still struggling to breathe.'

I hadn't even realised. As we waited for the tow truck, the enormity of the accident hit me. I was seriously pissed off with myself and how much cash I had just smashed up. All that money spent on the car: the registration, the paper work but only third party insurance. I was just wondering if I could get the rego money back, when I realised I could have killed us. I could have killed Nik. I had been pacing up and down, but as this thought struck, I stopped midstep, tears exploded from my eyes and I crumpled to the ground. On cue Nik jumped up and wrapped me in his arms.

Everything in the car, including ourselves, were miraculously unharmed. I know for sure that the seat belts saved our lives; we were the only thing still in the vehicle. Our windows had been open allowing everything to fly out and even my driving glasses were halfway up the bank. Luckily they hadn't broken; neither had the iPod, computer, video camera or anything else. The red sand of the dessert seemed to have saved us all. I took another look at the Festiva. The two tyres that took the landing impact had come off, the driver's side was dented and the back was a mess. The rear windscreen and a window were smashed and the impact bars caved in. We had also lost a wing mirror. But somehow we got away with more than our lives that day, as the car's roof was untouched and the engine actually started. Not that we had any intention of driving it anywhere.

The tow truck finally arrived and after the owner popped our tires back on, the Festiva was able to drive onto the truck. In the cab I became bewildered as I realised not only had I just been in a major car crash but less than an hour later, I was in another vehicle with no seat belt available. The next town was 100 kms away.

It was a horrible drive. My usual ability to make conversation with anyone about anything completely abandoned me, and it was one of those awkward moments, except that it lasted an hour. I did manage to ask about the driver's work and how regularly this kind of thing happened, maybe to reassure myself I wasn't the only one capable of such a catastrophic error. He explained that it occurred fairly often, which prompted me to enquire about injuries people had sustained. He told me that one guy had been killed but that he must have been dead before the car stopped rolling because his head had …. At this point I interrupted, this was a sentence I didn't need to hear finished.

We arrived in the town, which was as run-down and smashed up as my car. Shortly after our arrival some Aboriginals drove past us shouting at us from their open window in an aggressive manner. I couldn't hear what they were saying, but this was not somewhere we wanted to stay. The car was inspected and after charging us a hefty fee, the lanky, buck-toothed, blank looking, tow truck owner, announced everything looked mechanically sound. He also said it would be irresponsible of him to officially tell us to drive, however he couldn't help us any further and our best bet was Broken Hill, 250 kms away. There, we would find a few mechanics and scrapyards.

Broken Hill was a long drive, but we didn't see any point in hanging around. Our saviour had told us that there was nowhere to stay but the pub, and that it was not a good place for tourists. Before we left, I popped into the police station as we had been advised to inform them of the incident and check that no one had reported us as stranded. A few cars had passed by during our wait for the tow, and Nik had spoken to the drivers reassuring them that help was on its way. He had even let them presume he was responsible for the crash to save me from extra trauma.

That done, we dubiously set off. Needless to say Nik drove; I just wasn't up to it. Fortunately the lights were working, as were the signals, radio and air con. Our luck, or fate must have been blessed that day. It was a stressful journey and I occupied my mind trying to work out what to do about the car. Nik was insistent that the car was a write-off, but as we were currently driving it, I couldn't justify this belief. I couldn't throw away all that money when straight after the crash we were back on the road. Typically with no back windscreen, in country that is dry and arid for most of the year, it started to drizzle.

We eventually arrived at a Broken Hill camp site and got a spot for the night. I had decided that we would have the car looked over again, and if all was well, then a scrapyard was our best bet for repairs. Thankfully my USB modem had a signal and I emailed my father some pictures as he had plenty of experience in car repairs. Half an hour later I had a phone call and my reply. After patiently hearing my story, he lovingly managed to listen, advise and counsel without becoming overbearingly worried or patronizing; a feat in itself for any parent. On top of this he agreed that another safety check and a scrapyard were our best options. The body work on the back would be impossible to fix without spending thousands, but that was the least of my worries.

*

The following day the camp site receptionist recommended a mechanic, who assessed the internal running of the car and with a bemused look on his face, announced that it appeared to be fine, with the exception of one wheel which was bent. He didn't charge us a cent. More determined than ever, off we went to the scrapyard and by some miracle they had a Ford Festiva two years older than mine. For $250 they agreed to change a bent wheel, put on a new boot door, replace the broken window and the smashed wing mirror. The mirror would have to be from a different car as their Festiva was also missing the one we needed, but for once having things matching and colour coordinated didn't interest me in the slightest.

Four hours later, we still had a crunched up rear but also a slightly different coloured boot with the glass intact. The dents down one side were now joined by a puny looking mirror that had been screwed into the driver's door. Plus we had gained a whole new appreciation for the fact that we were alive. Everything was good to go.

It was agreed that I should drive to get over the fear. For the most part I was fine, although every time we went round a corner on the side that the car had rolled on, I had the feeling it was going to tip. Emotionally I had been ok considering the circumstances. As usual I had just wanted to get things done and make progress. I wondered a lot about the crash. What if I had braked? What if I had let Nik drive? What if I had killed him? But in the end I had to admit that I was just driving myself crazy (pardon the terrible pun) and just acknowledged that although it wasn't a nice experience, we were very, very lucky.

We kept our mood positive, determined not to dwell on it and headed to our next bit of sightseeing, the Flying Doctor Museum. The Flying Doctor Service is an air ambulance/mobile clinic for people who live in the outback on cattle stations or in remote settlements and can't drive hundreds of kilometres to see a doctor or dentist. It was a really interesting experience, however we had to watch a film which involved emergency calls to car crashes and it may have been a little soon for me to be dealing with these kind of images. A tear or two escaped me, but compared to those on the screen we had escaped lightly, so by the time the lights went up I had forced myself back to full composure.

We had a tour of the building and saw the planes. Each cattle station is given a big box full of numbered medicines, plus a body chart. This allows them to call the doctor and describe the pain location using the numbered chart and in return the doctor can tell the patient which medicine to use and what to do until the plane arrives. Shockingly, even though this is the only health system available for people living in isolated areas, the government only partly funds it. The rest comes from donations. The organisation isn't charging its patients, even foreign tourists, fees. From that day on if I ever saw a donation box I would drop our change into it while hoping we would never have to use the service.

Then it was on to Silverton, a deserted mining town famous for, you guessed it, silver. Silverton's story was similar to that of many small towns in Australia. The valuable mineral was discovered, everyone rushed to mine it, then once the resource ran low or bigger quantities were found elsewhere, everyone promptly upped and left. In this case even taking their houses with them, pulled along by camels! Over forty-four movies had been filmed in

Silverton. Most of them Wild West films, but much to Nik's excitement, also *Mad Max*. I hadn't seen the film, I was more excited by the wild horses and gift shop but we took pictures of a *Mad Max* replica car and had a walk around.

*

Once more it was time to drive on and we had a couple of days staying at various camp sites, or if we weren't in need of a shower, camping at the rest stops along the roadside. I hated the rest stops but a lot of people camped in them. They were simply lay-bys off the highway and we could hear the trucks passing by in the night. It was a far cry from the national parks that we were used to. Nik, sweet as ever, would hear the trucks coming and put his hands over my ears, in an attempt to stop the roaring rumble from waking me, as they sped past into the night.

When I say trucks, I actually mean road trains. Seeing is believing. Lorries that pull not one trailer, not two, but three or sometimes even four. My first thought was, wow that's dangerous, but Nik in his infinite wisdom commented that it was far better for the environment. Australia didn't have much of a train system compared to Europe, certainly not sufficient enough to carry all that cargo and stopping at the necessary places along the way. The huge road trains seemed to provide a good service in place of a busy rail network.

The alternative to rest stops were official camp sites which would charge around $20 to camp in pretty much the same situation, a small space of earth surrounded by motor homes and growling generators, but with the added bonus of showers and laundry rooms. As we headed deeper into the South Australian outback, the towns became no more than a road house, serving food, beer and increasingly expensive petrol. Occasionally they had a camping area attached to the side or rear of the property. There was not much to see, but the overwhelming experience of driving across this barren land was excitement in itself. Well, at least for the first 500 kms!

*

The next stop off was Coober Pedy. Famous for its opal mines. However, that morning when we tried to start the car, it failed to get running. It had now been some time and many kilometres since the crash, so it was presumed we were safe from any car trouble. Luckily we were still at a campground near a petrol station. My first thought was, 'We need someone who knows about cars.' This was naturally followed by, 'Truck people know about cars' and finally, 'Truck drivers stop at petrol stations.' Simple but effective thinking I tell you. So we pushed the car to the fuel station and while Nik examined it, I kept my eye out for 'people who know about cars'. I can't really say exactly what they look like, just that I know them when I see them. After 10 minutes of only seeing 'fat, hairy and possibly drunk men', I went looking for 'someone sane' and finally, 'what the hell', to the cash desk, to ask where the nearest mechanic was.

As luck would have it he lived just around the corner, so off we went. Sadly he wasn't in. In fact there was a queue. Two Aussie guys who needed to weld their tow bar were also waiting. We explained our problem and chatted away, but after twenty minutes it became clear that this guy could be out all day, or all week for that matter. I went to the road house again to ask if anyone had his number. I only managed to get the house phone but thought that maybe he would have an answer phone and that that might have his mobile number on it, or divert to it at least. Things were becoming more and more desperate.

By the time I returned to the car, our new found friends had come over to help Nik. It was decided that there was some sort of problem with the fuel, be it dirty or blocked. After a lot of blowing through pipes while I turned the key at just the wrong time, squirting petrol into the nice man's mouth, they finally managed to make it start. The men guessed it was dirt in the fuel, but who cared, we were free to go.

*

The most alluring feature of Coober Pedy, aside from its mines, was the opportunity to sleep underground. Most of the houses were dug into the hills, or should I say mounds of dirt. This maintained a constant temperature the whole year round, avoiding the heat of summer and the cold of desert nights. We chose to stay in a private room at the underground hostel. It wasn't cheap but I was excited by the cave-style idea. As it turned out, the highlight was the world's most comfortable bed, or maybe we had just spent too much time in the tent. The walls were carved out of the dirt and a door had been fitted into a hole cut for the entrance. The guidebook promised that if you turned out the lights it would become pitch-black, however due to the lights in the hallway this was disappointingly not the case.

*

After a wonderful night's sleep we headed out for a mine tour. It was a small opal mine, but we learnt about mining techniques both past and present. I thought it sounded like a lot of hard work for a potluck chance of finding anything, but who was I to shatter their dreams.

There was no doubt that the best part was 'the blower', and not just because of the funny name. Yes, I still have the mentality of a twelve-year-old! It was a big machine used to clear rocks out of the mine and was essentially a giant vacuum cleaner. We got to play with it and held up big rocks for the machine to suck out of our hands.

The operator said that if I held my hair under it, it would suck that up too, but I wasn't secure enough about the strength of my roots. Imagine if a girl with extensions was actually stupid enough to attempt it. I must admit that it would be extremely funny to watch, preferably if it happened to one of those annoyingly perfect looking girls who funded their beauty via daddy's wallet. But I guess those women tended not to visit dirty towns in the middle of a scorching, dust filled desert and certainly wouldn't embark on dodgy mine tours with bearded country men.

After the demonstration we got to play in a sandpit. Sorry, I mean we sat and fossicked for opal. This involved sitting in a box which resembled a child's sandpit but was actually full of small rocks. The rocks were cast-offs from the mines and were cut from around discovered opal. They could still contain traces of the gem. There were stories of tourists who had discovered thousands of dollars' worth which had been overlooked by the professional miners. But as I would later learn, every mining town came with stories of a big find. I guess it's what kept the diggers out among the dust.

We picked up the smallest stones in a handful and dipped them in water. We then held them up to the light, hoping to see opal shining back at us. We only found small pieces but it was nice to sit back and relax in the sun.

During the afternoon we wandered by the shops. I had decided I wanted a piece of opal, set in some sort of jewellery to remind me of our trip. There were lots of little shops. Most were owned by Greeks, but hey that's Australia for you. So many immigrants over the years colonising and populating wherever there was a dollar to be made. A lot of the opal for sale seemed rather expensive, but I didn't have a clue how to value the stuff. I found a cute pair of earrings and a necklace that were a very good price and extremely beautiful. Ever the bargain hunter, I wanted to shop around and ended up going home to our cave empty-handed.

*

The next morning we got up and packed the car. It made a nice change not having to take the tent down. In need of petrol we pulled up at the local BP, fuelled up and started the car again. Except it didn't actually start. Not again! This could not be happening. After much repeated blowing into pipes, etc., etc., trying and failing to re-enact the previous day's method, then failing to find any help, we called for roadside assistance. Following our previous issues I had purchased a package online.

Our rescuer came in the form of a tall, well-built South African immigrant named Ash, who managed to reach us pretty quickly considering it was a Sunday. He then embarked on a drawn out inspection of the car. He wore the look of a man who has no idea what he is doing but figures if he stares at something for long enough, the universe will suddenly reveal all the answers. I was feeling increasingly nervous, when finally Ash raised his head and declared that we needed a new fuel pump. It was what we had expected, due to our previous fuel issues and tip-offs from several passers-by.

I will now put in another word for the Australian people. During the short time we had been waiting at the BP garage, one man had gone to get his mechanic friend, who was sadly out of town. A second passer-by, having noted our situation, drove around looking for someone to help us, before he finally came back with a mechanics number, just as Ash had arrived. They really did want to help, it was a refreshing change. I had been all but ready to give up on acts of random kindness.

Anyhow, back to the story. So it was a Sunday, in Coober Pedy, in the middle of nowhere and there was no chance of a fuel pump being found locally. Ash would have to order one and have it delivered from Adelaide around 850 kms away! He couldn't order it until the next day, as everything was closed on a Sunday. Even once it had been ordered, we had no idea how long it would take to arrive in Coober Pedy. Things were not looking good.

Ash decided to tow my car to his friend's house. This friend was not an official mechanic, but Ash had great faith in him and so we had to hope it was well founded. We would be getting cheap labour, but I hoped that the saying, 'you get what you pay for', would be disproved and that our car would be returned safe and not fall to bits halfway down the road.

*

Having parted with the Festiva, Ash kindly drove us to a camp site. I mentioned to Nik that we could go and look at the underground churches the next day. Overhearing us, in true outback spirit, Ash offered to drive us there himself. Right then and there. He obviously didn't have much to do on a Sunday afternoon, or maybe he was just hoping to catch a late service and pray for our car. Once again I was dumbfounded by the generosity of a stranger. Sadly the actual church was damp and cold and although unique, I found it a tad depressing.

Despite dingy churches, car break downs and dodgy mechanics, I was still in high spirits as Ash pulled up to the local camp site. We planned to pitch up and spend the day chilling by the pool. Well it certainly beat breaking down back in the UK and having to stand next to the M25 in the rain.

The camp site was perfect, but the occupants gave us some very funny looks. As I travelled further around Australia by car, I began to realise there were thousands of people driving exactly the same route and they were not all backpackers. Known to locals as the grey nomads or the grey plague, on these roads they by far outnumbered us foreign travellers. Aged 50+ they invested their retirement funds in luxury caravans, motor homes and shiny new four-wheel drives in which they travelled the land in a seemingly endless manner. Equipped with satellite television, home-made cake and a year's supply of incontinence pads, they headed off around the country with vehicles that could conquer mountains but never actually made it past the cafe/toilet block or heaven forbid, off the tarmac. Some of the motor homes were so big that owners actually used the van to tow the four-wheel drive. Many had stickers or spare wheel covers joking or maybe stating, that they were driving their kid's inheritance.

The nomads may sound like a slightly loopy but boring bunch of crazy old grannies, but if you had the patience to get past the *oooing* and *awwing* over their grandkids, they often turned out to be extremely entertaining company. They certainly spoke to us a lot more than the other backpackers did, and we were often offered cups of coffee and travel tales of old. I think they felt sorry for us in our tiny tent, overshadowed by the mansions on wheels and let's face it if there's free cake to be had, I was more than happy to be a charity case.

I actually thought it was great idea to spend your retirement exploring the land. It certainly beat a weekly stroll to collect a pension from the local post office. Although on the down side, the plague members drove *soooo* bloody slowly, while producing enough pollution to melt Titanic's iceberg, as they dragged their wheeled lives across the country.

Anyhow, this particular campground/tourist park was rather upmarket and a little on the snobby side. It also contained an entire clan of well equipped grey nomads and some of the largest privately owned vehicles I had ever seen. While the grey plague were contentedly enjoying a glass of wine in front of their 'homes', with the compulsory monster car parked meekly alongside, we were plodding through on foot, carrying our little tent, sleeping mats and tiny gas stove, with not even my mangled car to show for ourselves.

*

After a night of much needed rest, we woke up and went back into town for a walk, having decided that after Ash's kindness it would not be fair to chase up the car so early. I ended up back in the opal shop with the pretty necklace and chatted to the owner who, surprise, surprise was Greek. I bought the chain and matching earrings and we talked for a while. I explained what had happened to our car and once again was pleased to receive a kind offer.

He felt bad for us stuck in Coober Pedy with nothing to do. He lived in an old miner's house and the gravel in the yard consisted of stones thrown away after big opal finds. He said there were still lots of small pieces of opal left around if we wanted to come by the next day and fossick while he was at work. After taking his address, we thanked him and decided it would be fun way to pass the time. In normal circumstances I would have felt down and annoyed due to the car problems and delays to our trip, but instead I was just feeling happier and happier, ever amazed by the generosity of all these incredible people.

We had decided to call about the car at 10 a.m., but Ash beat us to it. I braced myself to find out how long we would had to wait for the new pump, only to be told that our car was fixed and ready to go. Our man had a connection with the BP garage manager, who knew a lot of truck drivers. One of the drivers had driven around Adelaide on Sunday night and had managed not only to get our pump but had driven up to Coober Pedy with it overnight. Ash's mystery friend had then got straight to work that morning and had fixed the car which was now ready to go.

I nearly fell over, it seemed so impossible. People may laugh about the little 'backward' outback towns and the people who choose to stay there but with organisation and community spirit like that, I had a new found respect for them. If we had been in the city, it probably would have taken longer than that just to get someone to look over the car.

Ten minutes later, my Festiva rolled—thankfully not literally this time—into the camp site on the back of Ashes tow truck. I looked around at the nomads meaningfully. See, we do have a car! I had to pay the cost of the pump at the BP garage, and then we were free to go on with our journey. The labour was either included in my roadside recovery policy or Ash's' mate was actually a real life angel. I certainly wasn't going to push the subject of money. It really was the best day and added another chapter to my ever increasing faith in human nature.

*

So once again we hit the road, maybe slightly poorer but with broad grins glued to our faces. However, in true adventurous, slightly crazy, Julia style, half an hour later we were bumping my Ford down a four wheel drive track—bouncing around like a speedboat against the waves. This task wasn't simply for the purpose of seeing how quickly we could wreck the car again, in fact it was for something much more important and monumental.

Much to my excitement we were heading towards the world's longest fence! Yes, the famous dog fence, built to stop the dingoes, which are wild, ginger coloured dogs, from spreading into other parts of the country where they had become a pest. First erected in 1941, the fence was currently 5,300 kms long, but it used to be 9,600 kms. I have no idea why they shortened it. I wondered what had happened to the leftover 4,300 kms; maybe they had sold it on eBay.

We took some pictures, including one of me pretending to be a dog, before driving back through The Breakaways: big sandy looking rocks and mounds which tower above the desert. They were somewhat impressive and there are even two called salt and pepper due to their colouring.

*

Further along the main road we came upon a sign for an arts centre. Intrigued, we took the turn off. Among the roadside brush, lay a smattering of rusty, dented, car wrecks. This was not unusual for the outback highway, I guess not all crashes and break downs ended as happily as ours, but here there were an unusually high number of vehicles.

Nik thought we were probably heading towards an Aboriginal arts community and I was looking forward to seeing one. So far, I had only witnessed the drunken Aboriginals around the towns and felt these individuals were giving me an unfair impression of their people.

What I actually saw came as a bit of a shock. Kids were playing and running around in the road, followed by small packs of ragged looking dogs. Most of the children were naked and those who weren't, appeared to be wearing dirty, tattered clothes. None acknowledged the moving vehicle. Even the adults who walked along the middle of the street didn't move for us to pass. We had to slow to walking pace for fear of running someone over.

There were broken, rusty cars lining the streets and smashed windows on the houses, which resembled squats. It looked run-down and dirty. It certainly shattered my illusions of peaceful traditional communities living out in the desert and I wasn't sure how to react. I felt a little threatened and uneasy. No one did anything to make me feel that way, I guess I was just out of my comfort zone and taken aback by the reality. We decided it was best to keep driving and headed back towards the highway.

From that point on, the road became very boring to say the least, and we spent several days driving constantly and camping in the dreaded rest stops.

Rocks and Crocs

Our next stop was the famous Ayers Rock or Uluru to use the Aboriginal name. It is a long drive to Ayers Rock from anywhere. Even Alice Springs, which I had presumed was close by, is located over 300 kms away. Nik was at the helm of the Festiva while I was reading out loud from the guidebook. My current paragraph mentioned that Mount Conner, a nearby mountain, is often mistaken for Uluru. Mount Conner could apparently be seen on the road that leads up to Ayers Rock. We had a good laugh about the idiotic tourists who apparently got confused and overexcitedly took pictures of Conner before happening on the rock itself.

Twenty minutes later the large burnt orange rock of Uluru came into view. Stretching out of the window I tried to capture it on camera as the spectacle rose out of the desert. The pair of us *oowed* and *awwed* over the infamous landmark. I felt a great sense of achievement to have finally reached it. Pilgrimage completed!

A few kilometres later we realised our embarrassing error. I wonder if there were bonus points for being stupid enough to make the prementioned mistake, having already been warned. Of course, the first rock, as predicted had been Mount Conner and Uluru was actually just appearing on the horizon. How did we even make it this far?

After our laughter had subsided, we sat back and experienced the intensity of seeing the real thing for the very first time. Also predicted by the guidebook, Uluru was not flat as I had imagined but full of bumps and gaps which we could see from afar. We purchased our three day pass and headed into the national park which of course was dry, dusty and red. As we drew closer, the rock became more and more detailed. There were small caves and an array of overhanging or leaning rocks in different shapes, sizes and shades of colour. After scanning over the booklet, we decided to do the base walk to see everything in detail.

Our chosen track went around the bottom of the rock, but there was also a very dangerous looking steep climb. It was closed during the days we were there, due to wind, but we didn't want to climb anyway. A sign explained that the local Aboriginals asked visitors not to climb Uluru, as it was disrespectful to their culture. They believe that it's a sacred place and should not be clambered over. I guess it would be the European equivalent of climbing all over the Vatican.

A lot of people had even died during the climb, by falling or due to bad health and lack of fitness. In fact, two weeks before, halfway up the climb a man suffered a heart attack. The rangers had put themselves in danger to help him, but it was too late. A park worker informed us that the Aboriginals found it upsetting if someone perished on their land, but still the climb was usually open and the issues around it were being heavily debated. I must say that, beliefs aside, had we been in the UK, I'm sure Health and Safety would have closed it down in an instant. I was certainly a long way from home.

So off we set, safely on the ground and around the base. Uluru is beautifully stunning and we took the free guided tour which explained more about the culture of the local indigenous Australians. It was then that I began to understand a little more about the people I had seen in the Aboriginal community. As a race they had been struggling, not only with everyday life changes as their land was being colonised, but also, to understand the thought patterns of the settled Australians. People of the ancient culture, we were told, were very intelligent, managing to live in unforgiving climates and surroundings for longer than any other civilisation on earth. They survived in a land that took the Europeans years to cross, even with advanced technology. The Aboriginals had been travelling the country for longer than we could even imagine, while many Caucasian people perished in the outback after only a few days.

However, previously the Aboriginal life had been simplistic in other ways. I listened as the ranger explained that the local people didn't count in large numbers but simply had, one, two and many, (although I have since heard that this is incorrect, but I'll let you do your own research, I can't do all the work). In fact, he told us their mentality was entirely different, with unique social and survival skills. They were very spiritual people who had the ability to tune into their environment with sharp, almost animal-like senses.

Foreign men had then come to their land, took it away and vastly changed the country. The Aboriginals were forced to live in a white man's world and by the white man's law, but even then they were only allowed to be second class citizens. Their children were taken and their lands destroyed. They were told to forget their languages and customs, and that they would need something called money to survive in this new world. All this happened within a few generations, and it was impossible for the majority to acclimatise so quickly. Combined with the introduction of alcohol it became disastrous, as many Aboriginals began to use drink as a way to deal with the disruption in their lives.

Thankfully, our guide informed us, things had improved over the years, some land rights had been returned and on February 13th 2008, the Prime Minister, Kevin Rudd officially apologised for the terrible way in which the Aboriginals had been treated. Sadly for many families it did little to take away the hurt of the past. Vast numbers of Aboriginal people are now living and working alongside the rest of Australia's multicultural society; but many are still lost, having no link to their traditional roots and do not feel at home in this installed world either. I was surprised to hear that one of the local men who worked at Uluru could still remember seeing his first white man; so this was only a recent happening. No wonder some individuals struggled to find the means and interest to live in those houses or a reason to go out and work.

Although the stories saddened me, I enjoyed learning about the past, culture and geology of the rock, and I felt it was important to understand some of the history of this unforgiving land. I stood and imagined the place before the tours and buses. I tried to envisage the ceremonies and events of years gone by, when Aboriginals had created the beautiful paintings on the rock.

I also discovered some additional features that don't get so much world press—flies! Millions of them, no sorry, squillions. The base walk was a fantastic experience, I just wished I didn't have to share it with my personal winged army, determined to buzz around, crawl, and occasionally enter, every inch of me. I learnt my lesson and swore to avoid them the following day. That night, despite Nik's threats to disown me, I purchased an unattractive green floppy hat with a sanity saving fly net attached. To add to the overall effect, I purchased a tacky Ayers Rock badge and pinned it to the front. Nik shook his head and walked away.

Once my headwear had been organised, we addressed a more important issue. We currently had nowhere to stay. Among some upmarket looking buildings was a camp site belonging to the Ayers Rock resort, but it was way out of our budget. Logically, our money needed to be saved for important things like beer and ice cream. After a quick map check, it was decided that we should head to the nearest rest stop about 40 kms away.

Upon arrival it was dark, and I couldn't see much but gravel and tarmac. It looked dull, cold and eerie in the desert night, but it would have to do. We were about to choose a spot when Nik noticed smoke rising from behind the grass verge. Looking over, my heart soared as I took in the cluster of vans, cars and tents surrounded by blazing fires, accompanied by soft music that floated up into the air. A rebel camp! I loved it, all of us too tight, poor or clever to pay the resort fees.

*

Before heading to camp we had taken in the sunset alongside Uluru and over the next few days we religiously repeated the experience from various viewpoints. We watched silently as Uluru transformed from light pink to various shades of glowing orange which all too soon deepened into a rich red wine, just as the sun slid out of view behind us.

Much to Nik's objection, we also rose each morning at 5.30 a.m., packing up the tent with perfected efficiency before dashing to join the queue for park entry at 6 a.m. We then stood in the bitter cold and wind of the desert to watch the whole spectacle in reverse. Complaints and stiff joints aside, Nik had to admit that it was worth the early start, with the golden orb of the sun making a slow but steady appearance from behind the infamous landmark. This time it was silhouetted against a vibrant backdrop of dusky orange, yellow, and grey, before finally revealing the wondrous art of nature framed by a warm blue sky.

It was an experience that I would never forget and suddenly I understood why millions of people from all over the world, travelled hundreds, if not thousands of kilometres through the unforgiving outback to see what is essentially a large rock. Knowing I would never willingly drive this seemingly endless highway again, I insisted we watched every sunrise and sunset during our three day visit. As a result we have so many photographs that if we stapled them together they would probably recreate the whole event flicker book style.

Sadly, although the scenery was awe-inspiring, I didn't experience the intense spiritual feeling that so many people talk of. The drive through the almost empty, vast desert did make our journey feel like a pilgrimage; but on arrival I had been surprised to find a highway running around Uluru itself which took away some of the natural ambience. Swarming the points of interest were busloads of people queuing to take their snapshots, before jumping back into their air-conditioned coaches which waited in the car parks ready to whip them off to the next photo opportunity. In fact, things became so busy at sunrise one morning that we gave up on Uluru and took pictures of the crazed tourists desperately pushing and shoving on the viewing platform.

I couldn't help but wonder if this unique natural creation would be more alluring if it was only possible to view from a distance, allowing the imagination to envisage clans of Aboriginals roaming the surrounding land and practicing their traditional ceremonies around the base. We tried to escape the masses as much as possible and were even informed by a guide that this was actually a pretty quiet week!

*

Mixed among the walks, sunrises, sunsets and coffee breaks, we visited the Olga's thirty-six almost glowing, rich, brick red/orange rocky domes, which rose out of the desert. This time I was well equipped for walking, proudly wearing my new fly net hat and feeling rather smug—knowing that no matter how stupid I looked, I would be protected from the squadrons of insects. Nik wouldn't think it was such a bad idea once the little buggers set out en masse to explore his inner ear drum, while I would grin triumphantly from behind my netting.

The disappointing reality was that the flies were one step ahead of me and were nowhere to be seen or even heard. Obviously their battle techniques were far superior to mine. They must have based their attacks on the element of surprise and had clearly moved on to invade some other unsuspecting tourist areas. This provided

Nik with no end of satisfaction. Just to be stubborn I wore my hat for the entire day under the pretence that I liked it.

I thought the Olgas were just as beautiful as Uluru, and we set off for an early morning stroll around them, magically managing to escape the bus loads of people. Finally, peace and undisturbed tranquillity. The sun shone brightly, lighting up the vast valleys filled with forests that could easily have been the set for Jurassic Park. How strange this country was. Here in the middle of a red desert, hidden behind a pile of massive round rocks was a sea of green shrubbery. We sat for a while looking down at the view while I imagined triceratops and T-Rexes roaming the oasis of trees and grass below. I felt dwarfed by the gigantic boulders and couldn't get over the intensity of the burnt orange rock.

As we were reluctantly heading back to the car, a large group of retirement age Americans came wandering down the track, like a flock of sheep, herded by their very loud and annoying tour guide, complete with what looked like an actual shepherd's staff clasped in his hand. As we dodged our way through them, trying not to get caught up in the many camera straps and knapsacks, I couldn't help but think to myself, 'Ha ha, we beat you.' For a few short hours we had been alone with the spirit of the outback.

*

Close to Ayers Rock lay Kings Canyon, well when I say close, I am of course speaking in Australian terms, i.e. 300 kms away. The Canyon offered a walk around the top which begun with a steep climb. Although I found it very challenging in the heat—which became extremely intense during the day and vanished like an apparition at night—the hike was worth every struggling, sweating, step. The Canyon was huge, although I think perhaps to truly appreciate its vastness you needed to see it from the air. Lots of helicopters buzzed around in the skies like curious wasps, but chopper rides were most definitely out of our budget. However, being grounded was still fun, and I was more than happy to explore the crevices and rock ledges, and we even relaxed by a waterhole hidden among them.

The camp site, as at Uluru, was also expensive, but a shower was definitely due and even we backpackers had to draw a line somewhere. So we pitched up at Kings Canyon Resort and sat back to enjoy our camp food after our hard days walk.

As we started to eat, a dingo casually strolled past, stopping for a split second to check us out or maybe to observe what was smelling so bad—we had been too hungry to grab that shower yet—before continuing on past. It was the size of a large domestic dog, and a dusty, sandy colour with a pointed face which reminded me of a fox. I had never seen one before so I was intrigued. A few minutes later it scampered back past, this time with a packet of cheese gripped between clenched jaws. Someone, despite all the warning signs dotted about, must have left food out.

Ten minutes later, clearly not satisfied with its stash of cheddar, the cheeky mutt trotted back into the camp site again. His passing was soon followed by angry shouting, as a man staying nearby came running across to chase it out of his tent. I asked if he was missing any cheese, this was answered with a polite nod before he dashed into the tent and a few seconds later began some loud cursing.

*

Alice Springs was our next destination. I found it an interesting town where you could really see a mix of Aboriginals and settled Australians milling about. Sadly Alice provides another example of the cultural clashes between the races. The Aboriginals I saw were drinking heavily and hanging around in the streets hoping for the tourists to drop them a few coins; a far cry from the generation who helped to lead white men through the unforgiving landscape.

We had a look around the town and planned to go out for a few drinks that night. However, despite all our wonderful adventures, I had been feeling more and more tense. Luckily Nik, who again showed that he was far wiser than his twenty-one years, had picked up on my change in energy. He sat me down and set about trying to discover what was causing my unease. What could be wrong? We were sharing all these incredible experiences and getting on like a house on fire, even enjoying the constant jokes and jibes we made at one another.

The truth was that sleeping in the tent every night was taking its toll; I was finding it hard to sleep at all and the packing up, travelling all day and constant sightseeing, although fun, was exhausting. So once again he became my little angel, swiftly calling a motel in the area and making a booking. He then announced that we would have two days' time out in Alice, staying in a room not only with a bed but an en-suite bathroom and a TV!

Oh to lie in bed until you wanted to get up, not because the tent had got so hot and sweaty you couldn't take anymore. To be able to wash every day! To pee in a real toilet, and to be able to laze in front of the telly, laughing at cheesy local ads. Heaven is a place on earth and sometimes when you are living the dream full-time, reality is all it takes.

That night refreshed, revived and with me forever grateful for Nik's intuition and support, we headed into town for a few jugs of beer in a local pub. The venue itself was decked out with old boots, a live snake, saddles as bar stools and a fantastic atmosphere. It was just what we needed.

*

The following day we visited the Alice Springs School of the Air. Known as the world's largest classroom, they used a unique set up to teach children who lived in isolated areas of the outback. In years gone by teachers had conducted lessons over the radio, but modern technology had vastly improved this system. Now the children had lessons via the internet using webcams. The teaching method had worked so well that they had seen results which competed with those of the top schools in the Australian education system.

The school itself had been visited by Queen Elizabeth II, Prince Charles and Princess Diana. Charles and Di had signed the wall along with many other well-known icons. The Queen however, had left her scrawl on a piece of paper which was framed and displayed. Apparently if a Monarch signed a building it became protected by law and had to be maintained in the current condition with no modifications.

*

The main Red Centre attractions, seen, photographed and imprinted on our memories forever, we started our final leg of the journey to Darwin. There was really very little along the way. The drives got longer and the endless scenery of dust, dirt, road houses and rest stops could have been a recorded landscape on repeat.

We stopped for a night at the famous Daly Waters pub, firstly checking into the campground before checking out the bar. Filled with signed bras, underpants and a million business cards, donated by visitors from all over the world, it had amazing character and charm. The pub was also known for serving an amazing dish of steak and barra. Barramundi or 'barra' is a fish that lives in the Australian waterways and most famously in the Northern Territory.

Once, on the terrace of the pub, we sat near what I can only describe as a thong gazebo; thong, as in flip-flop, not G-string. It was a wooden sunshade, but nailed to it were various thongs, some in pairs, some odd and most signed and dated by guests from years gone by. A man on a small stage sang some interesting versions of popular songs including the Beatle's hits, with the chorus sung loudly and enthusiastically but with most of the verses skipped. The grey plague were out in full force with some of the more lively ones hitting the dance floor.

As we had started up our little gas stove an hour earlier, I asked Nik if he would prefer to eat in the bar. He had decided that camp food would be fine, and tonight's exotic menu had consisted of veggie omelette, which we tucked into before heading off for our drinks. However, now having seen and smelt the food, it was not long before Nik had forgotten his eggs and was ordering a burger which came served almost the size of a fully grown cow.

*

Another highlight along the road to Darwin was a stop at Devil's Marbles, a group of large round rocks that were, surprisingly enough, in the shape of marbles. After enjoying an exquisite breakfast of baked beans on toast (we never did tire of them), we had a walk around. I took great delight in having my photo taken, pretending to lift a rock that had one side a metre or so off the ground. There were even boulders which had split in two, that I squeezed in-between as if the sheer brute force of my strength had broken them apart.

*

We drove on and on before suddenly, after weeks of being in the desert, the landscape and the weather changed dramatically. In the outback it had been chilly in the evenings, too cold to sit outside for long, well at least not without the heat of a fire. Now, as we drove further north it became humid, hot and sticky, so warm, that even the thought of getting in the tent made me sweat. On the plus side, our surroundings became green, lush and tropical.

The North of Australia doesn't have the usual winter and summer, instead it has more of a wet and dry season. The wet, full of torrential rain and thunderstorms, accompanied by a thick, unmoving, humidity. The dry, sees the water slowly evaporating, leaving behind a barren, unforgiving land of dust, rough scrub and rock. I had intentionally chosen to arrive in June which was the start of the dry season. The heat would normally be a bearable 30°C and the sweltering humidity gone, but there would still be enough water left to keep the rivers and waterfalls flowing. Unfortunately, no one had informed Mother Nature of my impending arrival and the wet season's humidity had run unusually late.

At Mataranka National Park we pulled over to have a look at the map on the information board. It seemed an attractive place to stay, and there were even hot springs which we visited later in the day. I was relieved to find that contrary to the name, the spring's water was only tepid, certainly warmer than a normal river, but not hot enough to make the sweaty air any more unbearable. I was still uncomfortable floating about in them, but it had nothing to do with the heat.

Being from the UK I don't normally swim in rivers. I grew up fishing in them and after seeing what comes out, I really didn't want to go in. Also back home in the Medway, there was often a rusty shopping trolley or worse, hiding under the surface. So the whole experience of swimming in the wild was totally new to me. Going into the clear water of the springs was not too terrifying, apart from the very large spiders lurking in the webs above our heads, but the river, which we were camping next to, was a very different story.

We walked to some small waterfalls where Nik stripped off and dived in. As I looked into the murky green waters and at the slimy mud on the bank, I just couldn't bear to get in—no matter how much the heat was making me crave the relief of a swim. These were not the beautiful clear waterfalls that you see in shampoo ads but a torrent of opaque angry water flowing down a wide river. However, I still had some fun.

As I bravely held one foot in the passing water, Nik climbed out and sat next to me. He didn't have his swimming shorts with him, and not wanting to get his torn off jeans wet, he had dived in naked. Upon hearing some other walkers approaching, he sunk chest deep into the chilly water to hide his modesty. Rather than call out a brief hello as the walkers passed, I mischievously started to chat to the elderly couple who approached from the bush, and they came right over to talk to us. I tried to keep a straight face as a shivering Nik had to stay in the river, politely holding a conversation while hoping the pair would leave, so he could finally get out.

*

That afternoon we sat on floating pontoons, sunning ourselves, engrossed in our books. Nik jumped in and out of the water to cool off. I bravely managed to get half my body in, all the time clinging onto the ladder and trying not to think how many horrible scaly fish could be swimming by my legs.

*

In the evening we camped in the national park, each obligingly putting the $6.60 charge into an envelope and posting it into the self-service check-in box. I made a fire, my first attempt since my Girl Guide days. Nik and I had settled into the stereotypical and rather old-fashioned roles of man making fire, woman cooking dinner. So naturally I was proud of my first fire attempt. Sadly it was so hot already, my effort became pointless and my wonderful achievement only made the heat more excruciatingly intense.

We loved the park so much that we decided to stay a second day and relax by the river for an entire afternoon. By a miracle, I managed to not only get into the water but to swim out to a floating platform in the middle. Firstly, clinging onto Nik's back so he could scare the fish away, then returning all by myself. I went to bed full of pride for this monumental achievement.

*

On our way out of the park we stopped in the 'town' of Mataranka, i.e. three overpriced petrol stations, a supermarket and their own tacky claim to fame, 'The Giant Talking Termite Mound'. Ironically, this man-made model did not seem much bigger than the towering authentic ones that lined the roadside. I guess that's why they had to make it talk so they were not outdone by an insect; anything to get the tourists to stop, take photos and hopefully spend some money. During our stop, which was for fuel not the termite mound, we noticed an advert for a rodeo. It was taking place in Katherine, our next destination, so we headed on northwards excited by the chance to see one of Australia's cowboy traditions.

*

Katherine was a small but pleasant town, with more not too hot, hot springs that provided us with a relaxing evening swim. In the morning, we headed off to the showgrounds where the day would start with some horse races. With the rodeo image in mind, I decided my denim cut offs, straw hat and a t-shirt would be fine for the whole day. Nik had lived on a cattle station earlier on his trip and been to these events before. Upon seeing my attire he quickly advised me to change.

Prewarned and saved, I arrived at the races in my best summer dress—pulled crumpled from my spare bag which had been buried in the Festiva's boot. All the local girls were dressed to impress, it was like a mini, country town version of Ascot. Ridiculous feathers and oversized hats were worn by women who, no matter how hard they tried could not escape the heat. Many had streaks of foundation dripping down their once perfectly made-up faces.

Fuelled on by alcohol and a lick of mascara, I placed a few dangerously large bets of $5 and had a wonderful time losing it all. Unfortunately, I failed to keep up my ladylike image, shunning glasses of champagne (but let's face it, it was cheap fizzy wine anyway) for cans of beer.

For the evening we scooted/staggered across to the camp site to finally change into my denim shorts, vest top and boots, the look completed by my cowboy-style hat; before heading over to the rodeo where my attire would finally fit in. It was an eventful evening which began with horses being ridden around barrels, the idea being that the fastest time won. It was great to see the community in action and a variety of ages took part, from children being helped by their parents, to the professionals who competed for a living.

Then it was onto men riding bulls. Nik told me that they got the bulls to buck by tying a rope around their testicles. Being an animal loving vegetarian this didn't impress me too much. However, I did wonder if next time I wanted some real action from a man in the bedroom, this technique might be worth a shot.

It was a great evening and thrilling, yet scary to watch. Irritatingly, they only seemed to have five songs available to use as background music, and these were played on repeat for the entire night. As much as I chuckled the first time I heard the speakers sing out, 'Save a horse, ride a cowboy!' Seventeen repetitions later the novelty had well and truly worn off. We could hardly hear what the commentator was saying, and I've no idea who won. It certainly wasn't as electrifying as I had imagined, but Nik advised me to see another rodeo if I had the chance, which would hopefully have more atmosphere. As always I still had a ball; even getting drunk enough to do some guilt free shopping, as I hazily purchased a cute pink cowgirl-style shirt that I still haven't worn to this day.

*

Katherine was also famous for its gorge and usually you could canoe down it and swim. However, due to the late wet season, the park staff hadn't finished the crocodile checks and the river was still closed. We were now in the heart of the Northern Territory, full of waterways which were brimming with real life, human eating, saltwater crocodiles. There were also plenty of freshwater ones which were apparently harmless, but the salties were a whole different story. They could launch themselves out of the water within a split second to attack people on the bank, or if you entered the river they would take you directly to a toothy, watery grave.

The lovely park ranger explained, probably for the millionth time that week, that a team went out every night checking the water for crocs. Their eyes lit up in the shine of the torches and the rangers could then see if it was a freshy or a salty. There were also traps in place. The crocs were territorial, so if they hadn't relocated during the floods of the wet they were unlikely to move that season. We saw safety signs, which announced there were measures in place to stop the crocodiles, but warned they may move into the area undetected.

I was secretly pleased I didn't have to face another river swimming trauma, although I guess brushing up against a fish would be most pleasurable compared to this new found fear. However, there were still plenty of gorge walks we could take, and one we were told about had a swimming hole safely out of reach from crocodiles. Enthused by the idea of a refreshing swim, we set off.

I can't put the intensity of the heat and the humidity of that day into words. The sweat poured down us and the simple 8 km walk seemed ten times harder than climbing the mountain back in New South Wales. If I had known how much strength it would take to complete the 'moderate' walk I would have stayed in the air-conditioned cafe enjoying ice cream and a magazine. Unfortunately it was too late and I suddenly appreciated the danger of Australia's heat. As advised we were equipped with hats and water, but they did little to ease the fiercely beating rays of the sun.

Spurred on by the promise of a swim, after what felt like hours, we finally made it to our destination; a disgusting, green, puddle of water, only a couple of metres wide and less than a metre deep. By this point we were too hot to care and simply needed relief from the weather. I resentfully slipped into the pool until the various pond bugs skimming round me, drove us out.

The return walk was just as exhausting, and upon reaching the visitors centre, I was relieved to finally enjoy that well-earned ice cream; whilst Nik, the little diamond, went to get the car which was still another fifteen minutes up the road.

*

Later that afternoon we arrived at Edith Falls. With no time for a longer walk before dark, we had a look round the bottom of the falls. It was a large slimy pond with big dirty looking fish lurking around the edge. People were swimming and even snorkelling. Why you would want to swim in that water, let alone know what was sharing it with you, was beyond me. I was resigned to yet again sitting out of the swimming sessions. So imagine my joy the next day when after a short hike, we reached the top of the falls and found crystal clear water sitting in rock pools of various depths, and not a fish in sight. There was a big waterfall to swim up to, with plenty of smaller streams in which to relax and receive a free massage from the passing current.

Nik took immense pleasure in seeing me swim for enjoyment and minus the look of horror that had been previously plastered onto my face. We spent the morning there soaking up the sun, laying on the rocks, reading and relaxing, before we took on an adventurous 7 km circuit. It passed through some challenging forest, rocks and grass. Luckily Nik was paying attention, as I missed the path markers several times and would have been another statistic; one more tourist lost to the bush.

*

En route to our next stop we played real life wacky races with an old camper van. Much to Nik's annoyance it was doing about 80 kilometres per hour on a 130 kph road. Eventually, after fifteen minutes of bends and oncoming traffic he managed to overtake; but by the time we reached Pine Creek, we had to stop for petrol and of course the compulsory ice cream break.

Once back on the road we caught up a line of traffic. It wasn't just any old traffic. Five caravans, no doubt being driven by very cautious grey nomads, were bobbing along; and proudly holding up the front of this snake-like convoy was the slow camper we had already passed. We weren't running late for anything. We had nowhere to be and nothing to do. But this didn't pacify Nik in the slightest.

Half an hour and a lot of frustration later, we finally made it past them all. However, not long after, with a look of sorrow on my face, I was forced to turn to Nik and declare, 'I need to pee.' Much swearing ensued. Needless to say, no matter how quick I tried to be as I dashed to the loo, the infuriating little van had managed to sneak past once more. As we caught up with it for the third time, I got out the video camera to capture the confused look on the occupants faces as we flew past once again. Surprisingly they were young backpackers and not the golden oldies we had imagined. I guess they were already doing the top speed of their battered old van.

Just to add to the irritation, Nik's iPod was starting to drive us both mad, and I think we had listened to every decent song at least 200 times. So as a refreshing change, I decided to DJ with a difference. I enthusiastically chose the cheesiest songs ever known to man. Highlights included, 'YMCA' and 'Barbie Girl'—which scarily, Nik actually enjoyed—MC Hammer and of course, Men at Work's 'Down Under'. It was certainly a drive to remember or in Nik's case, desperately wishing he could forget.

DESTINATION DARWIN

There were two very popular national parks near Darwin, Litchfield and Kakadu. We were due to spend a couple of days in Litchfield and I would visit Kakadu after Nik's impending departure. As our destination drew closer we tried not to let our emotions run too high, but we were both very aware that our time together was nearly over.

We had agreed to stay in touch but there was not much more we could do. Nik had to go to Germany to study and carve out a career. I wanted to stay in Australia for at least another year and was certainly not ready to move to Germany.

We tried not to talk about it too often, but the closer we got to Darwin the more real the situation felt. Nik wanted to get to the city so we could relax and chill out a bit before his big flight across the globe. I was in denial, if the trip carried on longer Nik wouldn't be going. However, like it or not, Litchfield was our last camping stop.

Once again we enjoyed crystal clear waterfalls, streams and walks. We even saw some enormous termite mounds, much bigger than any of the previous ones. Foolishly, but not without pleasure, with the fuel station many kilometres away, we used all but the emergency petrol to get ice creams and cold drinks. Consequently, we did not have enough to drive to Litchfield's old tin mines. I guess that's how you know when it's time to return to the 'real world'. When everyday things become novelties and sightseeing spots seem less and less enticing.

*

To break up our final drive into Darwin, we stopped to take the famous jumping crocodile cruise. After boarding the two levelled boat, we set off up the muddy brown river. It wasn't long before hungry saltwater crocodiles came out to see us. They were used to the boat and knew that the sound of the engine meant feeding time. Two women dangled bits of pork—or to be more graphic, parts of a chopped up pigs head—into the water. These were attached to a pole by a long piece of string. When the croc came over, they whisked the meat upwards and the croc jumped in an attempt to catch it. Well to be technical they couldn't jump but used their tails to propel themselves out of the water. Either way it was eerily thrilling to watch. There was a running commentary from a man with a very Aussie accent who, in dedication to the part, was wearing Crocodile Dundee style get up.

The biggest croc was five metres long and it certainly brought home the truth behind all the warning signs. I was glad we saw this after my swimming experiences, not before, or Nik would have been lucky to get me in the park, let alone the river. For future reference, if you are attacked, the general advice is to poke the enormous toothy beast in the eyes. I'd say, just stay the hell away from the water. Crocodiles can stay completely hidden, only one inch under, and can attack at lightening speeds. So fast in fact, that you'd need to be at least three metres from the water's edge, to stand a chance of glimpsing the toothy jaws before they snapped you up. Hearing all this made the underwater shopping trolleys back home seem a little less threatening.

*

My heart was in my throat as we drove the final leg of our journey and into Darwin. As we approached it looked as if the whole city was on fire, with smoke and flames on each side of the road.

The Australian's didn't bat an eyelid, so we carried on as normal presuming these were controlled bush fires—burnt to rejuvenate the scrub and reduce the threat of wild fires. However, the flames weren't the cause of my distress. Nik and I only had a week left together. We had booked a room in the city and aside from my sadness, I couldn't wait for a real bed and a good shower.

The hostel was nice, with a pool and spa, and I absolutely loved Darwin's atmosphere. It was much more relaxed than Sydney, Melbourne and Brisbane. Backpackers milled about in shorts and thongs, and the locals weren't dressed much differently. From Mindil Beach we watched the sun setting directly down into the ocean; quite a spectacle having just spent the last month in the desert. Hundreds of people gathered twice a day to do the same thing before exploring the stands and entertainment at the night market. There were food stalls selling cuisine from all over the world, street performers, mixing comedy with fire and even a drum and bass didgeridoo duo.

I visited the markets numerous times during my stay, enticed by the food and atmosphere. Each time I saw the same group of Aborigines who sat at the top of the beach playing a guitar, banging sticks together and singing with a mat placed in front, for passers-by to drop change onto. One evening I saw them being asked to move from within the actual market as they didn't have a permit, but they were allowed to play down on the sand. It felt strangely ironic as I heard the famous 'Down Under' song playing loudly from a recording in the market, drowning out the voices of the three indigenous men. Among the crowded stalls, white didgeridoo players mixed up the traditional instrument with dance beats while the local clansmen played an imported guitar. It was certainly a sign of how the country had changed.

*

Nik and I spent an evening at a sprint car race which I found to be just as exciting as the Grand Prix. I could see the entire track from where we sat on the grass verge, watching as the cars crashed and flipped. Some of the drivers even had a fist fight. I loved it. Unfortunately, we were the only people who hadn't realised the cars would produce a huge cloud of dust and dirt, that would encase the audience. Unlike the other 4,998 people there, we had no glasses or goggles for protection, and I swear I still have red dust in my ears to this day.

The beaches in Darwin were stunning but rugged. The weather was picture-perfect, but we couldn't swim due to the pre-mentioned crocs and now a new danger. The box jellyfish, or the Portuguese man-of-war as it is commonly called, delivers one of the most painful toxins known to man via its long, evil tentacles. There were warning signs explaining which months the jellyfish were present. In the dry season, swimming was permitted, but we were advised to be cautious. I however, wasn't prepared to risk one of the nasty little blobs getting their dates mixed up and causing me so much pain; it supposedly leaves victims begging for death. Judging by the empty waters, everyone else felt the same. It was a beautiful coastline to walk along, even without the swimming, and we meandered around the beaches, streets and parks.

*

In the town we saw adverts for fishing excursions. I grew up lake fishing and seeing all the pictures around Darwin finally got the better of me and we booked a trip. I had always wanted to try sea fishing so I could experience having a really big catch on the line. Entering a booking shop we were told there was a trip leaving that evening. I mentioned that I wanted to fish in the open sea, not just the harbour, even if it was the biggest harbour in Australia. Darwin's harbour is much larger than Sydney's, although it certainly doesn't have the same style or fame. Big as it may be, I wanted the freedom of the ocean. The shop owners enthused that this wouldn't be a problem, and furthermore some Sprint car drivers from Saturday's race were also booked on.

Neither of those things turned out to be true. The boat stayed in the harbour and the race car drivers turned out to be fans. I was slightly annoyed at having been conned, but our new fishing buddies were friendly so it didn't matter what they did for a living. As we headed out, the sun was setting and I felt an immense sense of peace and relaxation; maybe something to do with the three beers I had drank before we left the bank.

The night started with Nik catching something very, very small, but we took the obligatory photos before returning the tiddler to the water. Then the real action started as my rod twitched, the line pulled and no word of a lie, I hooked a shark! Ok, so maybe the word 'action' might be slightly overplayed. In all honesty I could hardly feel it on the line. I thought I must have lost it. The poor frightened fish was only 30 centimetres long. Anyway that bit is just our little secret, and everyone else can hereby know me as 'Julia the Shark Hunter'.

Photographically there was a way around this inadequate size issue. The crew showed me how to hold the fish, with my finger hooked under its gill, out towards the camera. Its closeness to the lens made it look far bigger in relation to my body in the background. The shark also went back into the water. I prayed that he wasn't good with faces. I didn't want any surprise ocean reunions when the bugger had grown up and decided to seek revenge for his traumatic childhood experience.

In terms of catch, the rest of the trip didn't get much better. I managed to hook one small fish that was just about large enough to cook, and the closest we got to seeing anything bigger, was watching the fish as dots teasing us from the radar screen. With a few beers, a striking sunset and a lot of atmosphere, it was still a great evening, albeit an expensive one.

*

Eventually the day came for Nik and I to go our separate ways. After a beautiful meal in a restaurant overlooking the water, I drove him to the airport. We had shared enough tears over the past week or so, although admittedly most had been cried by me when drunk; so we had agreed it was best to make the separation as swift and painless as possible. I dropped him off at the tiny departures building; we shared a tight hug, said goodbye and after sneakily watching him disappear up the escalator I drove away before the pain could catch up with me.

Keeping my mind blank for the drive back to the hostel, I held it together, but upon reaching what was 'our room' I promptly burst into tears. Over the last few months we had bonded and shared each other's journeys, both literal and emotional. He had treated me like a princess and in return I had cared deeply for him, but now, far too suddenly, I was alone. I felt empty and isolated.

I guess when you are far from family and friends it is easy to achieve much more, in a far shorter space of time. The four months we had together, felt like a year, but in my heart I knew that if it was meant to last, we would have done more to secure a future together. Tears aside, and as much as I would miss him, I realised that in the long run I would be fine. Life goes on and as sad as the situation was, it was just a pitfall of travel adventure.

Deep down inside I knew I hadn't missed out on a partner but gained a friend for life. Through the events of our trip we had formed an everlasting connection and shared moments and memories that neither of us would ever forget.

CHAPTER 6

MOVING ON

AFTER NIK'S DEPARTURE I took some time for myself but didn't mope around. I couldn't let myself get down, there was so much more to see and do. Nik wanted me to enjoy my trip, and although I missed him, I had to keep moving forward emotionally and physically.

Kakadu National Park was next on my list. I didn't want to travel alone, so I made signs advertising for people to join me and put them up in local hostels. I planned to go for three days and tours were expensive, so my little car would make a great alternative for thrifty travellers.

It was common for people to put up ads, but it was my first, I was nervous and intrigued to see who would call. It was one thing to make friends in a hostel, but on this trip I would be spending 24 hours a day, for three days solid, with people I knew nothing about. I was praying I didn't attract the local weirdo, one per car was enough and I didn't need any competition. With all the camping equipment and luggage, I only had room for two more people; I just prayed someone would answer.

The first to get in touch was Michelle from Switzerland. Then another call came from a Dutch girl, Lei. I arranged for the three of us to meet for a drink in town. I felt nervous, it was like going on a blind date or to an audition. What if they hated me and didn't want to come? What if I ended up having to go alone because no one liked me? I had no idea where my usual over the top confidence had run off to, maybe it had jumped on the plane with Nik. I just hoped it would come back soon. Luckily all went well and I organised to pick the girls up the following day.

*

We met early on a Sunday morning. I had warned them that my car had 'a lot of character', as it still had a dented side, doors which could only be opened if you did so in the correct sequence, crumpled rear impact bars and a very dodgy wing mirror. I casually mentioned some dents, while trying to make sure they didn't run for the hills. It was a fine line between prewarning and scaring the crap out of them before we had even left the city. If they were worried they hid it well.

The first day was spent food shopping and driving to the park, but we did arrive in time for the sunset at a viewpoint. We all climbed to the top of a huge rock which overlooked a sea of long, vivid green grass that stretched for miles. A couple of giraffes and lions wouldn't have looked out of place. There were also random large stacks of rock, every few kilometres or so, resembling Aztec temples in a jungle. Again Australia was offering up a completely new landscape.

The downfall to watching the sunset was having to head for the campground in the dark; always a bad scenario especially in national parks. Firstly, because setting up in the dark is a nightmare and secondly, because kangaroos go on nocturnal hop about suicide missions and have a tendency to jump in front of cars. I had enough trouble driving bendy roads, let alone in the pitch-black, while avoiding moving obstacles.

Thankfully, we arrived safely and Lei suggested we use the headlights to help us see in the darkness. Unfortunately, not only did this light up our camp but it also attracted approximately forty thousand mosquitoes, moths and anything else that could fly, bite or buzz.

Tents constructed, we had planned to enjoy a relaxing meal, cooked under the stars. Instead, we were forced to take shelter in the larger tent to escape the plague of insects and satisfy ourselves with bread and jam; so much for bonding around the campfire.

*

The next morning it was off to explore the billabongs (the Aboriginal word for water hole), rock paintings and to watch presentations from park rangers. We took a river cruise and saw huge crocodiles basking lazily in the sun, before we briefly stepped onto Arnhem Land. The guide told us this was the only land in Australia where Aboriginals still lived in the full traditional way. Out of respect for their land, access was limited, but everything has its price and for a few hundred dollars (which we didn't have) you could go on a tour or buy a visitation permit.

That night we had more success with our camping, building a fire and enjoying a cooked meal of veggie sausages washed down with beers (I had to make up for the lack of meat somehow). Fortunately the humidity of the late wet season had finally lifted and we sat up playing cards by candle light. I soaked up the tropical Kakadu vibe and it was refreshing to be in female company after so long alone with Nik.

After a good night's sleep, the girls got to experience my

reversing skills first hand as I backed over a concrete slab. The car got stuck and they both had to jump out and help push it off. It was a bad day to witness such a display of my road skills as we were preparing to drive an unsealed, ungraded track— another exciting challenge for my little car. Several of the roads in Kakadu were closed due to bad conditions and the only waterfalls currently accessible were Gunlom Falls. Normally the road was passable for any car but due to late rains it was now listed as four-wheel drive only.

Once again my determined spirit kicked in. Where there's a will, there's a way and my Festiva was very willing to try and find that way. I was desperate to visit a least one of Kakadu's famous falls, but despite my external confidence I was a little shaky underneath. The accident hadn't been that long ago and I no longer had the luxury of Nik's reassurance.

We hit the 35 km track and it was a bumpy start. The car bounced around and the vibrations visibly ran through the steering wheel and down my arms. I smiled and reassured the girls, praying we wouldn't come upon an impassable piece of road halfway down, or worse still, get stuck or break down. Keeping the speed steady but safe, I enviously stared into the dust clouds as four-wheel drives flew past.

Luckily my optimism paid off and we were all relieved to finally pull into the campground. It had been a very uncomfortable ride. The car was good, we were happy, and a carton of eggs was the only thing to suffer any physical damage from our adventure. The tiny Festiva certainly raised some eyebrows as it hobbled into a field full of four wheeled monsters.

We set up the tents and I got a lovely man from the neighbouring camp to check my tyres. He agreed to top up the air for my piece of mind while his wife confided he'd being dying to try out his new compressor. Tents pitched and tyres full, we set off on foot to the top of the falls.

I thought by this time that nothing could impress me. I truly believed I had seen every variation of waterfall, viewpoint and landscape this country could possibly provide. But I was wrong and happy to be so.

The water flowed peacefully through various rock pools before tumbling over a sheer drop into the lake below. The view overlooked the park, continuing for as far as the eye could see. The tropical landscape shone a dense, green, lushness, made brighter by the golden sunlight that filtered down from a pure blue sky.

I live for those moments, when the physical scene is so impressive and intense that it somehow transforms into emotion. The energy rushed through me and I felt vitalised, elated and alive. Literally spine tingling. Australia made me fall more and more in love with her every day.

We spent the whole afternoon lounging on the edge of the fall, bathing in the clear water, taking in the view and soaking up the perfect weather. It was paradise and we stayed until the fading light forced us down the steep hill to camp.

That night there was a short presentation from a ranger. Grey nomads, families and travellers crowded round on the grass, blankets and camp chairs, as she explained the history and future of the park. It was a beautiful way to spend the evening and a perfect end to a perfect day.

*

The next morning we regretfully set off. I was not looking forward to the return drive, but we were breaking it up by stopping for more walks. Once again we were rewarded by refreshing crystal clear waters in which we took a swim before returning safely to Darwin.

On our arrival in the city, I said goodbye to Michelle who was leaving on a flight to Cairns and I promised to catch up with Lei sometime soon. Exhausted, I crashed onto a hostel bunk and prayed no one would disturb my well-earned sleep.

A Friend to Share the Miles

The next leg of my adventure was another major one, Darwin to Cairns, a 2,770 km drive. I drew up more posters, hoping once again to find companions for my journey. My heart sank as I pinned them to the boards, they were littered with ride-share ads. Every person with a car could give at least two people a lift. This made it a very good market for anyone looking for a ride but not for those of us offering. I tried to make my ads appealing, even mentioning the case of beer I had stowed in my boot. This may have been a bad idea as I began to receive calls from older, Aussie guys, who thought travelling with a young, beer drinking, British girl would be a great experience. Otherwise, the phone stayed quiet, and I had to stop myself from running around taking other people's adverts down.

As it turned out I wasn't going to be alone after all, Lei was happy to endure a second round of my never tiring talk. I honestly think I could find something to talk about 24 hours a day. I'm surprised Nik managed 4,000 kms without losing his mind. Poor Lei, she had no idea what she was in for, but I guess it was the perfect way to improve her English listening skills.

During the Kakadu trip she had come across as a nice, quiet girl. She was tall and slim, with an athletic figure and a short crop of light brown hair. With my new best friend in the passenger seat, I hit the road and set off in the direction of Queensland.

*

The drive took us back due south along the Stuart Highway. I had already covered this route with Nik, but as Lei hadn't seen it, I agreed to stop at the main attractions again. She had also found a place in her guidebook that I had never heard of. My book had been ditched some time ago. I'd hardly used it over the last few months, only to read up about Uluru or other tourist spots. My road map had taken its place as it had all the camp sites and rest stops marked. I found the best sightseeing advice came from other travellers and for accommodation, bookings were easier online. However, I was glad Lei's was leading us to new places, beginning with Robin falls.

After another dubious drive along a stony track, we walked up a rocky footpath and came across a small waterfall. I had seen a fair few falls by now but I was most excited by this one as you could stand underneath it. I got to fulfil a lifelong dream as I stood under the wall of water while Lei took my photo.

I was going for seductive, tropical goddess, gazing dreamily out from under a plummeting torrent of misty water. The reality was, more drowned rat in soggy clothes, half chocking on the water and sliding around on the moss ridden rocks like an uncoordinated skater. However, I believe it's what's on the inside that counts and I felt like an angel from paradise; well, until I started to shiver.

Anyway, I was pleased to try out my new toy, a drop proof, waterproof and hopefully Julia proof camera. The last two cameras I had bought had lasted less than nine months (remember the sandboarding incident) as apparently digital technology, sand and water are not a good mix.

Just down the road were the Douglas Hot Springs, and as we walked towards them I noticed warning signs with a picture of a thermometer—maybe these hot springs would actually be hot.

They were very hot. In fact so hot, it caused physical pain if you got in where the water bubbled from the ground. A cold stream ran alongside and the two currents merged further downstream. It was like a mixer tap on a bath and we moved up or down as it became too hot or cold.

For the past week I had been run-down with a cold and this was now being accompanied by stomach pains. As I lay back in the clear, warm, running water, it soothed my sickness away. I loved it and passed some time talking to a couple of grey nomads. I continuously jumped as the small, but not scary, fish nibbled me. The fish were tiny and pretty, not at all like the big, ugly, slimy ones from previous lakes and rivers. The couple informed me that the fish were probably trying to clean small cuts on my legs. Sure enough, as I watched, they repeatedly went to my scratched mosquito bites, tickling me with their tiny mouths.

*

The drive continued on towards Katherine and the two of us discussed farm work. We knew we could find voluntary work on farms in exchange for accommodation and food. There would be no pay but the hours were much shorter than at paid jobs, and it would still help with my second year visa application.

Lei and I had previously talked about volunteering along the way and there was a place up in Katherine that sounded good. I had already called the woman, who said they had a lot of workers but could squeeze us in a cabin. I liked the idea of staying in Katherine, with access to the gorge, hot springs and Edith Falls. I called the woman to confirm our arrival, only to be told that the farm wasn't anywhere near the town and that the accommodation was full. We would have to camp. This was all a long way from the image she had created during our last phone conversation.

I followed her directions but we started to get further and further away from town and even the road, as it turned to a barely visible line in the dust. Darkness began to fall, and Lei and I agreed that this wasn't what we had signed up for. I was also becoming more and more run down with the cold/flu. It was not a good time to be starting work. In the end I called the farm to cancel.

We were not far from Edith Falls, so the new plan was to camp there, but it was getting darker and darker. Lei took her turn at the wheel and got to see her first snake; unfortunately it was only for a brief second before she tragically ran it over. I wanted to turn the car around and have look, but poor Lei was traumatised. I didn't want to make her feel worse by viewing the corpse.

By the time we arrived at the camp site, it was dark and the ground was closed. A barrier was across the road with a 'Camping full!' sign attached. In front of the ground was a car park with another sign declaring 'No Camping!' It was dark and our options had just run out.

I knew there was most likely space on-site for our little tents. Undeterred, I dragged a concerned looking Lei past the barrier for a walk round the grounds and I decided, yes there was room for us. There was also a gap between the trees by the gate just the right size for a Ford Festiva to squeeze through. I'm not sure Lei thought it was a good idea; well to be honest, I know she didn't as she was telling me quite loudly, while I set off on my ram raid break-in. But as she soon discovered, nothing stops me when I'm on a mission, and before long we were setting up next to a couple in a camper van who were happy to help us break the rules.

*

The next morning the camp site manager wasn't so pleased, but I sleepily passed him some cash and he left us in peace. After our impromptu wake-up, we ate breakfast before I enthusiastically led the hike to revisit my favourite falls. This time I only managed a quick swim as it was still early morning and cold to say the least, but it was certainly an invigorating start to the day.

Refreshed we drove into town. I was looking forward to arriving in Katherine and trying the gorge again. On my last visit, the ranger had assured me the croc checks would be finished by the time I returned. After the previous sweaty and painful walk up the gorge, I couldn't wait to canoe along the river. Unfortunately, Lady Luck was in a bad mood and the river was still closed to the public. The rangers informed us there had been even more rain, and as the water had risen up again, the croc checks had to be restarted in case any had come up the river with the floods.

Not one to be beaten, I figured we could still climb the gorge and at least it wasn't humid this time around. However, my cold was driving me crazy and the stomach cramps were becoming increasingly bad. Lei decided to take a 6 km butterfly walk, but even in sickness I couldn't bear to be left behind. As the Aussies say I would just have to 'suck it up'.

I tried sucking it up as hard as I could but inside it was agony. We had to stop constantly so I could rest, regardless of the stunning scenery. I just couldn't wait for it to be over so I could lie down. Katherine Gorge was cursed and I was doomed never to enjoy it.

On return to the car I relaxed while Lei drove and after some painkillers, I started to feel better. I hoped the worst was over.

*

Further down the Stuart Highway we turned off to visit an Aboriginal community which was recommended in Lei's guidebook. After driving up yet another dirt track, we came upon a little green village. There were a few small houses, a large coach and a group of tourists throwing spears. As we were walking down to watch the activities, an indigenous man approached us asking if we would like to join in. He redirected us to the white tour guide who announced that we could partake for $80. Having seen the Aboriginal community en route to Darwin, with its run-down houses and streets full of people, I found this perfect grassy area with two quaint houses a striking contrast. Confused and broke, we declined.

*

On the journey back to the highway Lei and I pulled over to take photos sitting on a rusty car wreck. We thought they would be funny to post online, pretending it was our little car. But after all my troubles I secretly hoped we weren't tempting fate.

We were only a few kilometres down the road when my speedometer stopped working. I knew it! Not too concerned I asked for help at a local garage. They said it would take forever to get parts and that we should wait until our arrival in Cairns. In the car we worked out that providing we were in fifth gear (which was most of the time when driving through 2,000 kms of desert) we could use the revs per minute to judge the speed. I had noticed that many people in the outback had little respect for speed limits anyway. Still, I had no desire to put my car through a second roll over test.

Overhearing our conversation, an obese hairy man took it upon himself to intervene. He jumped out of his large vehicle, and came over to inform us that the Northern Territory limit was 130 kph, and that my bucket of rust wouldn't stand a chance of reaching that. Put out by his rudeness, I informed him it certainly could and had. He was clearly not used to being answered back and responded by making crude comments about the state of the admittedly crushed Festiva, and the incompetence of female drivers in general. I pulled away before I lost my self-control and decided that being fat, rude and ugly, he had to put others down in order to make himself feel good. I guess with a beer belly that size, he needed a big ute to take his weight.

*

Mataranka National Park was the next place to revisit. Having finally admitted that my health wasn't in great shape, I left Lei to sightsee while I rested. Dropping her at the top of a walking track, I continued down to the camp site where she would meet me. I pitched our tents, gathered the firewood and took my book down to the river for some much needed chill time.

A few hours had passed and there was still no sign of Lei. It was only a 6 km walk, so I was getting worried. I started to prepare dinner and decided if she wasn't back by sunset, then I would drive to the roadhouse and start a manhunt.

Just as the sun was about to disappear, a breathless, ragged looking Lei hobbled up to the car from the wrong direction. The poor or stupid girl, depending on how you see it, had headed up the river instead of down. There was a large map displayed where I had dropped her off, and I had even shouted, 'Turn right at the river!' as my parting words. But no, she had gone left, walking through mud, water and trees in her increasingly soggy sneakers.

Once she had made the 6 kms in the wrong direction to the roadhouse, the mistake was realised. I would have bat my eyelashes and hitched a ride back down; but being athletic, Lei had jogged, this time along the road, desperately trying to beat the sunset. It was at that point she had had a standoff with a dingo. She had stopped in her tracks upon seeing the creature, frightened due to my stories of them attacking people on Fraser Island. Unknown to her this was only because tourists had been feeding them on the island and that it was not common behaviour.

Without this latter knowledge the wild dog must have seemed terrifying. Fortunately, the dog had stared at her for a few seconds, before padding into the bush. I felt sorry for her but relieved I didn't have to call a search party and then finally, I couldn't stop laughing as I took in the state of her soaked jeans and feet.

We went to bed agreeing that if Lei awoke early she would walk to Mataranka Falls, where Nik had taken his naked swim, and I would continue to rest.

*

At 7 a.m. I got up to find the other tent empty, and so packed everything away so we could set off on Lei's return. A man from the neighbouring camp came over and asked if it was fair that I was doing all the work on my own, both morning and night. I laughed and told him I was the lazy one resting, while my friend literally ran round the park. Everything away, I sat on the picnic rug enjoying the sun and organising breakfast.

This time the wanderer returned from the right direction but with a limp and only one shoe. I couldn't hold back and was in hysterics before she had even reached me. You couldn't leave the girl on her own for five minutes without a disaster.

Halfway through the walk her thong had snapped and she had cut the bottom of her foot. Her thongs were broken, her sneakers were sodden with mud and her foot was bleeding. I had the curse of Katherine Gorge, but Lei the curse of Mataranka. At least there was one shop in town where we were able to buy replacement thongs and plasters (or Band-Aids to Australians).

*

The national parks over, we headed into the outback. I should have told Lei to keep her broken thong as we stopped briefly at the Daly Waters pub, with the thong gazebo and random wall decorations. Then once again I found myself driving through a whole lot of nothing as we turned onto Australia's very own route 66, the Barkly Highway.

That night, we pitched up at a rest stop right on the edge of the desert to escape the caravans and motor homes. Men from other camps kept wandering past, in hindsight I realise they probably just needed to pee, but at the time, the full moon and high winds made it seem rather spooky. I felt a little frightened and for some stupid reason this inspired me to tell Lei the tales I knew of missing or murdered backpackers. I am obviously very good at storytelling because I scared myself so much I couldn't sleep and every rustle frightened the life out of me.

*

The next day I awoke to find that neither of us had been murdered, and we drove an impressive 800 kms which was to be my record (a great achievement by European standards, but laughable to hardened Aussies). During the drive we passed through Mount Isa, a large industrial town in the middle of the outback. A mine dominated the town which was otherwise vast, grey and depressing. It seemed crazy that this vast place, filled with mines, factories and a McDonalds could exist in the desert, when all other towns for miles around were no more than a petrol station. It was Australia's very own Las Vegas, minus the grandeur and fun.

We also had a fuel crisis. After filling up the tank we saw a sign saying, 'Last fuel 260 kms'. This was not a problem as my car had always managed around 400 kms per tank. However, as we drove, the petrol gauge seemed to be dropping down very quickly. It dawned on me that when Nik and I had passed from 110 kph to 130 kph we had gone through a lot more fuel, but wary from the crash we had never exceeded 120 kph. Lei was going full pelt and I also noticed the hole between the crushed rear and boot felt breezier than usual. Lei pulled over and my fears were confirmed. The boot had been open, seriously reducing our fuel economy.

With only 40 kms to go, the fuel light came on. We slowed down hoping to make it. I carried a spare petrol tank but only used it for water. I had checked the maps and thought with good planning spare water would be more useful than fuel. We held our fingers crossed, then I crossed my legs and feet too, as we headed across a narrow bridge where there would be no room to pull over. Thankfully the Festiva surprised me once more and we must have made it running on fumes.

*

A couple of hours later I was unsettled again, when we were stopped by police. It was just a routine breathalyser but Lei was driving and she only had a Dutch license, not an international one. I also had no idea what legal repercussions the damage on my car might have. I dealt with the situation in the only way I knew how. I started to talk and didn't stop.

Never having experienced a 'breatho' before, I thought it would take a few minutes to get the results. I jumped out and began to talk to the officers while trying to hide the damage by leaning over it. To the cops, I probably looked as if I was attempting and failing to seductively drape myself across the car. Combined with my desperate talk, they no doubt concluded I was trying to snag myself a man in uniform or sleep my way out of a fine. I'm surprised they didn't test me for drugs.

After ten minutes of me talking complete crap, they looked slightly unnerved while informing me that they had to get back to work. We were clear to go. The results had come through in an instant. The police had been waiting for me to shut my mouth long enough to tell me so.

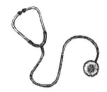

TRAVEL SICKNESS

That evening we camped alongside the highway. Lei stayed up talking to some friendly members of the grey plague, but I felt ill and went to bed early. I had now been full of flu for a long time and the pain in my stomach was so bad I couldn't sleep. When we got up the next morning, it was decided that I needed a doctor.

Previously, I had been excited to see my namesake town of Julia Creek, but in these circumstances I barely even noticed the signs. The doctor was based in a tiny hospital. He saw me within minutes and after I had been poked and prodded, I peed in a cup and had an unnecessary, but still daunting pregnancy test. The kindly man finally informed me that I had a chest and urine infection but was thankfully child free. I was administrated antibiotics and banished to bed rest.

Lei was an absolute star. She had no problem with the delay to our trip and insisted we stay in Julia Creek, a town that offered her absolutely no entertainment, until I was well enough to continue. She did all my washing from the sweat filled nights and bought me several bags of food supplies. We stayed in a campground, me in a box cabin and Lei in the tent.

It drove me mad to stay indoors. The first day I slept and the second I watched TV, took a well needed shower and resisted the urge to go out. The antibiotics were helping my fever, but the pain in my stomach had gotten worse. I couldn't eat and I was starting to vomit too. I desperately tried to eat an apple, taking thirty minutes and still only managing half.

The next morning I was no better. The claustrophobia of the cabin was getting to me, and ill or not, I wanted out. I asked Lei if she could drive me to the next sizable town, Charters Towers. It had a bigger hospital and I hoped they might be able to give me some painkillers. She agreed, but insisted we stopped for a photo with the Julia Creek sign, as before the illness I had been looking forward to seeing 'my town'. It's amazing how happy I look in the picture, by the fixed grin on my face you would never know how much pain lay behind the smile.

It was a Sunday and so we had to wait in the emergency department. After two hours I was looked over by a nurse and another two hours later the doctor saw me. Again, Lei insisted on waiting with me and showed amazing patience (no pun intended).

The waiting in pain drove me insane, but it was worthwhile as the doctor was wonderful. He was from an Indian background and younger than me. It was the first time I had been older than my doctor, age was creeping up on me very quickly. He professionally looked me over and did the normal poking around before handing me the urine cup.

I'd experienced similar pains over the years and had long suspected kidney stones. The doctor came to the same conclusion; but as he couldn't rule out appendicitis, I would need to go to a town with better equipment to be examined more thoroughly. After feeling sick for so long, in all, eleven days, having had no sleep and sitting for hours in a cold waiting room, only to be told I needed an ambulance and possibly surgery, I became overwhelmed. I apologised, as tears poured down my cheeks.

Fortunately this outburst worked to my advantage, as the kind doctor decided to administer strong painkilling and antinausea injections. A nurse told us that the ambulance would take at least another hour to arrive, so we were advised to drive.

Off we went to hospital number three, this time in Townsville. Once again it was a check over by the nurse, followed by a two hour wait. Thankfully, I had applied for a Medicare card and my expenses were covered by the Australian health care system. By this time the injections had worked their magic and I was actually feeling rather good.

On the downside, I am very squeamish and found sitting in accident and emergency a bit traumatic to say the least. I needed the bathroom but decided to hold it in. I hadn't even been able to drink much and was sure someone would request another urine cup to be filled soon.

Eventually, I was seen by a doctor from South Africa with a harsh bedside manner and little interest in communication. I tried to show him my transfer letter from Charters Towers, requesting a scan, but he had no interest and just plunged a needle into my arm. I had to get off the bed and wait for my blood test results in reception, as others were waiting to be seen. Just as I was about to sit down he walked past and put a cup in my hand. I think I peed in more pots than toilets during those few days.

*

By this time I had well and truly had enough. The injections had worked a treat. I was feeling good again and just wanted to get out of hospitals. We eventually got the results, my blood was fine and my infections gone. To get the kidney stone scan I would have to find a doctor to refer me before making an appointment. The process would take around six weeks.

Having experienced the pains before, I knew they normally passed after a few days. I wanted to make the most of feeling well and eat a well-earned meal. I'd worry about everything else when and if, the pain returned. We left the hospital and shamelessly feasted on a McDonalds. Lei laughed at the sudden change in me, those injections had been worth the two days of hospitals.

*

In Townsville we booked a double room at a hostel and the next day I woke up feeling good. Recovery seemed well on its way, and over being stuck indoors, we went to look round the town. Obviously I took it easy, but it was great to finally be out in the fresh air. It was the first time we had seen the Queensland coast and I marvelled at the green tropical islands sitting offshore in a sparkling ocean. This was just what the doctor ordered, well not literally, but my strength was definitely returning. However, my energy levels were seriously low, so I spent the afternoon chilling on the beach.

There was also a lookout with views across town, out to sea and inland to the hills. It was a long steep drive to the top, and I felt we had cheated, as I drove past a line of runners steadily jogging up the slope.

We once again began to plan our journey by tourist spots, not hospitals, and I was looking forward to the rest of the trip. I had experienced a few twinges of pain but kept quiet and hoped it was on its way out. If Lei had known she would have taken me straight back to A & E, and I just couldn't take anymore hospitals, no matter how good her intentions.

*

One thing I hated and had never become accustomed to during my trip were hostel kitchens. I find trying to cook in a room full of people but lacking in pans, cutlery and plates, a stressful event. I'm sure you have experienced it at home. There you are trying to prepare a meal and your flatmate/boyfriend/parent comes in to grab a drink, sandwich or whatever. You end up tripping over each other and then as you turn round with a scolding hot pan, they open the cupboard door in to your face. It's very irritating.

Now imagine that scenario, but with 20 people. You don't know them and you can't scream at them to move out of your *f-ing* way. You must simply smile politely and try to avoid their pasta sauce which is currently dripping down your leg. Infuriating. Plus all twenty of them are also trying to cook in the longest, most awkward way possible, using all the pans and hobs that you need. It drove me crazy!

So in an attempt to escape the madness, we grabbed the gas stove and headed to the beach. We settled upon a nice spot, very popular with evening joggers who streamed past in a sickeningly healthy manner. They gave us curious stares as we hauled our box of tricks down to the sand and set up a portable kitchen on a laid out sarong. It was getting towards sunset and from our perch we had a view of the ocean and islands. Lei and I agreed it was a wonderful place to enjoy dinner. Wonderful that is, until we noticed the smell.

Just as we started to cook, the wind changed direction. There is no fancy way to describe this, it was rotting fish guts. Smelly, putrid, disgusting, evil rotting fish guts. No wonder we had been getting funny looks. I don't know where it came from, but I do know it attracted a lot of birds. Birds, that took a large interest in our food. Seagulls to be precise. They inched closer and closer intimidating us into bolting down our meal. Finally as we left, they launched into a noisy battle over pieces of pasta that had dropped into the sand; so much for a peaceful dinner.

*

My body was almost back to full strength, so we drove on heading north towards Cairns. Along the 340 kms drive there were a series of waterfalls. All were beautiful but the weather had changed. Far from the constant blue skies in Darwin, we were now surrounded by a haze of cloud and fog.

We visited a swimming hole at the end of a dirt track. The road was short but filled with deep potholes that only became visible as the front wheel was about to plunge into them. We were bumping along when I caught a whiff of food. The tub containing leftover pasta had bounced around and come open. After losing a box of eggs during the off-road Kakadu experience, we decided they might need some protection. Lei sat in the front seat acting as a personal security guard to both the eggs and pasta.

Upon the safe arrival of both ourselves and dinner, there was a new wildlife encounter waiting at Crystal Creek Falls. A bush turkey; it was the size of a rooster and had a plump black body with a wrinkled yellow neck. The red head looked as if it was balding with a few human-like hairs protruding from it. At its tail end was a huge fan of black feathers. It was indeed a very strange, ugly creature. We were excited by this weird new bird; however, several bush turkeys later, the novelty wore off and like the cockatoos and kookaburras they soon became just another part of the scenery.

*

I thankfully continued to remain pain-free. Who knew the cause of my mystery illness and who cared, there were better things to think about, and I was looking forward to our next destination. In fact, Wallaman falls, Australia's highest sheer drop waterfall, will stay in my memory forever.

After dodging a variety of cows and their excrement on the road, my little car climbed the mountain, up into the tropical rainforest. Slightly concerned about the weather, which was becoming increasingly grey, we headed to a campground. We had just enough time before sunset to stop at the fall's viewpoint.

Nothing prepared me for what I saw. It physically took my

breath away. The viewing platform looked over a lush green gorge and punctuating it was a huge cascade of water, falling from such a height that the flow turned to mist before finally plunging into the pool below. It seemed as if it was flowing in slow motion. A far cry from the smaller falls we had previously swam in, this place captured my spirit. It was so peaceful, powerful and almost magical. I found it hard to turn away from the awesome spectacle.

I wanted to get closer, right down into the gorge and the pool below. There was a walk to the base, but there were also warning signs mentioning steep climbs and the requirement for good fitness. My health was a work in progress, but I decided this would be worth the risk. Lei had been struggling with a painful knee, our bodies certainly weren't making this trip easy; so we decided that the next morning she would take a turn resting while I took the track.

Dusk was falling so we drove to the camping area and set up for the night. I was thrilled to spot a bandicoot. They are similar to possums, a cross between a wallaby and a rat, and I watched in silence as they hopped around in the bush.

The rain was a disappointing surprise, the weather had been so perfect for so long and this was the dry season. Mother Nature obviously hadn't read the guidebook and during the night it started to drizzle and then finally pour. I had fallen asleep with my tent flap open, so when I awoke my sleeping bag was soaked, along with some of my clothes which were outside on a bench. This was the first rain I had seen since the crash, little did I know there was a lot more to come.

In the morning, I rescued my wet clothes, hung the sleeping bag over the Festiva's back seat and was relieved to find the inside of the car dry, despite the numerous dents and holes. Sadly the walking trail to the falls was so steep and now so wet, it would be impassable. It was a pity, but it wouldn't be long until we found another adventure to take its place.

*

As we drove up the Queensland coast the scenery changed. There were miles and miles of sugar cane plantations which created a beautiful roadside effect. The plants had tall green stems leading up to heads of purple seeds and sat in fields that seemed to stretch forever. Little trains pulling cages, transported the cane from the fields to the mill. Due to my nosey nature I was curious to see sugar in its natural form and couldn't resist stealing a bit of cane from a cage. I gave it a lick and although it was sweet, it didn't taste anything like the sugar that you put in tea.

We came to the small town of Tully. There are a few things for which Tully is famous: it is popular for white water rafting; it has a large sugar mill and is officially the wettest town in Australia. In keeping with the national trend, Tully also has something big to mark its place on the tourist map. To match its rainy reputation, Tully is home to the Big Golden Gumboot (that's wellington boot to the British), and we were excited to find out that we could climb up inside and stand at the top.

Another distinctive feature of the town is the sweet, sickly smell, dispersed from the sugar mill. All in all Tully was not a very alluring place and just to top it off I got chatted up by a big scary lesbian with a black eye. She was particularly keen on my boots, which were cowgirl-style and practical for when it was too cold or wet for thongs. Throughout our trip these boots attracted a few interesting characters and I eventually retired them to the car for fear of being chatted up by another undesirable.

I wanted to see inside the sugar mill but Lei wasn't interested, so I took the tour by myself. Once there I was pleased to be given a helmet and goggles, anything for a stupid photo. The guide began by telling us not to touch the raw cane as it was often covered in rat's urine. Oops! We got to taste sugar at different stages of processing and looked into a big furnace. I was surprised at how environmentally friendly the mill was, the big towers only emitted steam, not smoke as I had previously presumed, and all the waste products were recycled.

Unfortunately by the time Lei came to pick me up I was feeling a bit sick. The half-finished sugar had tasted horrible and now the smell in town was making me nauseous. I was glad to finally leave and head back to the highway.

*

On the final drive to Cairns we stopped to view Mission Beach, famous for sky diving, although we both stayed happily on the ground. The beach was beautiful but the drizzle of rain and dreary clouds cancelled any thoughts of a relaxing day on the sand.

There were more waterfalls as we headed inland to travel through the Atherton tablelands, green rolling hills and beautiful country. Full of dairy farms, Atherton reminded me of working back in Maffra.

Unfortunately the rain kept returning and camping was fast losing its appeal. One morning we awoke to a heavy downpour and packed up, deciding to eat breakfast when we found shelter. The picnic areas were few and far between and all the tables were exposed to the wet.

Eventually we gave up and drove to see a fig tree. It was fascinating to look at and very clever too. It had grown around a host tree, strangling it with roots and branches. When the host tree died, it had fallen and wedged against a neighbouring tree at a 45° angle. The end result was a stunning curtain of roots that reached down from the dead tree into the ground.

What excited us even more than the fig tree, was a dry patch of ground in the car park. Overhanging trees had caused a sheltered spot in the disabled parking space. We received some strange looks from visiting tourists as we spread out the picnic rug, cooked eggy bread and enjoyed breakfast in the parking spot.

Chapter 7

Insanity in Paradise

ON OUR ARRIVAL in Cairns we made our way to a hostel recommended by Michelle from the Kakadu trip. I like to travel this way and some of the best experiences have come from taking other people's advice. Unfortunately, this time the system failed.

As we parked outside the aptly named Lunatics (in fact I have renamed the hostel, so if there are any out there now called Lunatics, it is purely coincidence), I nearly ran over a guy in the parking space having a shave. Yes, that's right, having a shave. There he was in a camping chair using a cheap razor and bowl of water, with his face covered in foam.

I got out and apologised for nearly knocking him over. I asked how long he had been staying at the hostel and joked, unless you are living in this parking space. He was. Originally from Canada he had been in Cairns a month, previously having travelled in his four-wheel drive. He was trying to sell the car, but until then, he was living in the car park and hanging out at the hostel.

Check-in took half an hour as we had to sit and wait while the young girl on the desk complained and discussed the hostel problems loudly with other staff. One man told her to remind the guests to lock the doors, as the circus was in town and things had started to go missing. I was beginning to wish I didn't have to hear all of this as she continued to moan about a long list of problems before finally attending to us.

It was by far the dirtiest hostel I have stayed in but certainly an interesting place. The noticeboard proudly displayed a news-paper article. Lunatics, had been featured due to its rowdiness, complaints from neighbours and for causing general public upset. What a great welcome to Cairns.

They at least had a sense of humour and much to my delight when Lei locked herself out, she was forced to wear a sign around her neck declaring, 'I'm a stupid bozo and I locked my key in the room', in big black letters. Underneath, in smaller print someone had written, 'I am special and do it for the attention'. I couldn't stop laughing.

*

Even in our terrible living conditions all was not lost. When trav-elling, it's not always about the place, for instance, the people and the girls in our room were great. Nina was from Germany and Lei was pleased to meet another Dutch girl, Lara. We agreed to go out together that night for our free meal. Free meal ticket giveaways were common practice in the Australian hostels. The pubs gave out food to the backpackers in the hope they would spend money in the bar.

Well their luck was in. I hadn't been out drinking for a while and I was feeling the need to blow off some steam. The meal was a very basic pasta dish, but happy hour was indeed very, very happy. Sometime later we were dancing on the tables in-between watching the World Cup game on the terrace. Germany was playing, so Nina was following the match and I was happy to be part of the atmosphere.

As it got late the girls wanted to go home, but I wanted to stay out and continue the party. The alcohol had obviously affected my judgment. I didn't notice until it was too late, that the atmosphere had changed. The evening had started off as a bit of alcohol induced fun, but after a fair amount of drinking, the men in the pub all appeared to simultaneously transform from social to sleazy. It wasn't just travellers who made up this crowd of testosterone driven drunks, but a mix of backpackers and local guys who hadn't had any luck with the ladies elsewhere. With the girls around me and the distraction of the football game, I had felt very relaxed. Within ten minutes of being alone, I realised I was now a prime target for bad chat-up lines, dodgy dance partners and the occasional grope. Needless to say I left fairly swiftly, wishing I had gone with the others.

*

Lunatics was a fair distance away, but I heard it long before the hostel came into view. It was now 3 a.m. and the party was in full swing. A glow in the dark Frisbee whizzed across the road, a shopping trolley was being raced about and the people were even more obscure. One staff member, drunk and sitting in the road, started telling everyone how much she loved them, 'To all my friends around me. Really deep in my heart I have been touched by you all ....' But when no one would quieten down and listen she began to get angry. Her face turned red with rage and she screamed at them, 'Shut the fuck up!! Don't any of you give a shit! I'm warning you, fucking listen before I....' Then as they fell silent, she attempted to continue her speech about love and destiny. Thirty seconds later the crowd were distracted again and the whole performance was repeated.

Behind me a local Aussie was trying to fight some hostel

guests. Apparently he had been walking past and someone had shouted at him to put a shirt on. Why he had been walking around at night topless who knows, but he didn't take the advice too well. I thought the suggestion was a mild comment considering the state of the surrounding chaos. It certainly wasn't as abusive as you'd expect from a bunch of drunken lunatics, but this man clearly didn't agree and was looking for a punch-up.

I wasn't ready for bed and with all this entertainment around, it seemed a shame to miss out. I sat between the guy who lived in the car and a few others who were all simultaneously singing completely different songs, totally out of tune. The Canadian turned to me and whispered in my ear. He had been the one to shout at the topless Aussie but as he was not wearing a shirt either, he had been the only person not accused.

I sat back enjoying the show, while being grateful I wasn't trying to sleep and did not live in the area. Eventually things calmed down with the agitated Australian, but just as he headed up the road someone shouted, 'Hey mate, put a fucking shirt on!'

*

Cairns was a small town on the seafront, but instead of a beach there were ugly mud flats, although there was also a beautiful esplanade lined with palm trees. The walkway and grassland provided a perfect location for free outdoor aerobic sessions, live music and markets. Lei and I wandered around the town exploring and I partook in my usual shopping spree.

I had noticed a trend in my shopping habits. A particular brand was becoming an increasingly popular choice. Their designers obviously have very similar taste to myself and without intention I now had a bag, hat, bikini, two tops, shoes and shorts, all purchased from the same label. At this rate I would end up looking like a walking advert. I really had to start buying from a different store or maybe stop shopping altogether. Of course one day pigs will fly.

I was slightly embarrassed and miffed as one of the shop assistants commented that she loved my outfit. I was still sporting dirty camp clothes, greasy hair and my cowgirl-style battered boots. Maybe the bedraggled tramp look was finally in fashion. Half an hour later, as we strolled up the road, a man in his seventies passed by. I was shocked as he gave me a lurid look up and down before he growled, 'Nice boots.'

That was it, the boots had previously attracted the black eyed lesbian and now were encouraging creepy old men and random shop assistants. Enough was enough, it was time to go home and put them away. I wondered about all the years I had spent dressing to impress, while the 'backpacker who had literally been rolled through the outback' look got me far more interest.

*

One of the reasons so many people visit Cairns is to explore the waters beyond. A short boat trip from the shore sits the famous Great Barrier Reef. The reef is so vast that it can be seen from outer space, although that's a long way to go when you can simply jump on a tour. It was most definitely on our to-do list, but with the weather still dull and rainy we decided to wait.

In the meantime, I met up with two friends whom I knew from my time living in Tenerife. It was great to catch up and talk about the differences between life in the two countries. We relived old times and I met their beautiful baby girl. They had been a couple for eleven years and travelled through many countries before finally settling in Cairns. Talking to them gave me hope of a secure life at the end of the adventurous travelling rainbow. It also gave me a story to repeat to my grandparents every time they asked when I was going to stop running around and start courting a nice young man.

*

My next priority was to find work and to add more days to my second year visa application. I made phone calls to every East Coast work hostel I could find, which for a weekly fee would provide accommodation and help travellers secure a job. Disappointingly they were all fully booked for the next few months and I repeatedly listened to owners telling me of bad fruit seasons, failed crops and a general lack of work.

I found only one place that had a bed free and it was available in ten days' time. With the other hostels booked up until the apocalypse, it seemed I would have no option. In a cruel twist of fate the hostel was in Tully, the wettest town in Australia, home of the Golden Gumboot and the only town that had ever managed to make me feel physically sick. When I told Lei she couldn't stop laughing and I was continuously subjected to jokes about me marrying someone from the sugar mill and living in Tully forever.

*

Thankfully, I still had plenty of time before claiming my Tully destiny and I would use it to see the famous Cape Tribulation. Cape Trib, as it's known in backpacker circles, is as far north as you can go in a two-wheel drive. It was sold as a perfect paradise of white beaches and rich rainforest. The planned trip would take a few days and once again Lei decided to join me. Lara, the other Dutch girl from our room was also happy to join us.

We squeezed into the car and headed north up a winding road that ran alongside the ocean. The drive was lined by stunning views of the coast and islands. Although we constantly commented on how nice it would be in the sunshine, as sadly the weather was a continuous blanket of grey cloud and scattered rain.

After an hour and a half of winding coastal roads we came

upon the town of Port Douglas, which according to Lei's book was an expensive, but popular holiday destination with a nice beach. To break up the journey we drove in to take a look.

Heading to a viewpoint, my car made an unusual sound as I changed gear on the steep hill. I didn't think much of it and after ten minutes admiring the view, we jumped back into the Festiva. I reversed cautiously out of the parking space, but something didn't feel right. As I changed into first gear, the car made a clunking noise and I hastily pulled over.

The car was now stuck in gear and had a pool of oil forming beneath it. At least this time I had breakdown cover. I popped the bonnet, but couldn't see anything unusual, although, unless it had been signposted with 'This bit is knackered', I wouldn't have had a clue anyway. Everything simply looked very grey, metallic and engine-like.

I called my recovery helpline and while we waited for assistance various people came over to peer into the engine, but none were much help. Someone mentioned the gear box, but I convinced myself that a pipe had come loose and that we would be back on the road in no time. At least I wasn't stranded in the outback this time.

We took a comedy photo of me stressing out by the open bonnet and Lei joked that to save money on the towing, we could roll the car back down the hill. The slope was extremely steep and winding, and we laughed at the thought of me screaming as it free rolled. After 45 minutes of lame joke making, help arrived. I knew we were leaking gearbox oil thanks to one of the men who had popped over for a look, but was still sure that a pipe would simply need replacing and then the oil refilling. How wrong I was.

We were informed there was a big hole in my gearbox. Alarm bells rang; I knew gear boxes didn't come cheap. We at least managed a giggle as Lei's idea became reality and our saviour rolled the car down the hill and almost to the garage without the use of an engine or tow. In return, I had to drive his enormous rescue truck and was terrified but excited to be in charge of such a huge vehicle. We then had to swap as he towed the Ford for the final few hundred metres.

The car was left with the garage for review while we consoled ourselves with coffee. Halfway through my banana bread I received an interesting phone call. Apparently with my breakdown insurance I had benefits. If I was stuck, the insurance company could provide me with accommodation and hire cars. Maybe this mishap could provide a nice little holiday. My mind ran wild with images of spa hotels and swimming pools.

While we waited for the verdict on the car, Lara taught us how to make bracelets on the beach. It was a good distraction and the sun even made a guest appearance.

Several hours later my phone rang once more, sadly the news was not good. I needed a new gearbox and even worse you could no longer buy gearboxes for my model of car. I would need a second hand box from a scrapyard, but the nearest one they could find was in Brisbane nearly 2,000 kms away. By the time they would have transported the box here and fixed it into my car, at least ten days would have passed, by which time I was supposed to be in Tully.

The owner of the garage was away on holiday, but a young guy, Lance, had taken charge and gave me a quote based on a previous job. The total cost would be a devastating $1200. All in all things were not looking good. I called my Tenerife friend whom I had met up with in Cairns. He was a mechanic and confirmed the diagnosis sounded correct, but that maybe we could find a cheaper, closer gearbox. The garage had also recommended I shop around. This was not going to be easy.

First I used my insurance to book us all a room, although the luxury spa was out. I had a limit of $700 and didn't want to blow it all at once. Unfortunately, the insurance didn't cover the cost of repairs. By the time we got to the motel and checked in, all the wreckers were closed, so I couldn't chase up gearboxes until morning. The room was fresh and clean, with one double bed and two singles. We had our own shower, bath, a TV with free DVD hire and even breakfast included. After camping and hostel life, this was like staying at the Ritz. I relaxed and watched a movie in bed trying to forget the stressful day.

*

The next morning I set up an office on our terrace. The garage had told me that the gearbox they had found would cost $600 including transport from Brisbane. I called ten wreckers, finally reaching Norm from Innisfail, who had one for $350. His yard was also a lot closer than Brisbane, a mere 200 kms away. My Festiva was a different year to Norm's but Lance from the garage confirmed that it should work. It would take Norm a few days but he promised to remove it from the wreck and drop it in Cairns where I could collect it with a hire car.

By this time I was sick and tired of car talk and costs, the phone calls alone had taken over two hours. I used my last bit of tolerance to arrange a hire car using my insurance and we collected the camping gear so we could continue to Cape Tribulation as planned. We would return for the gearbox in a couple of days.

I was impressed with the rental car. It was brand new and had only driven 750 kms. It was also the first automatic I had ever driven and left us thinking I should stick to manuals in future. I was just glad to leave Port Douglas and my worries for a few days.

To get to Cape Tribulation we had to take a drive-on ferry. On the other side were more winding roads, short forest walks and of course the famous tropical beaches where rainforest meets the sand. By the roadside, signs warned of cassowaries. As with many Aussie animals, cassowaries reminded me of bizarre creatures from story books or random dreams. They resembled an ostrich, with a black body, a blue head that was topped with a rhino horn and a red dangly bit, like a turkey's, under their chin. According to the guidebook cassowaries were shy creatures by nature, but if threatened could use their vicious claws to slice open a human torso. Sadly these intriguing birds were endangered and were often run over when crossing roads, hence all the signs. We took our time but were disappointed not to see any.

The beaches at Cape Trib had perfect, clean sand, lined by tropical trees with coconuts washing up on the shore. I hate to repeat myself but had there been some sun and the chance of a swim, it would have been total paradise.

*

That night we chose a camp site near the beach and were happy to find it had a bar. The World Cup football was nearing the finishing stages and The Netherlands had made it to the final. Tonight Germany were playing Spain to see who would be joining the Dutch to compete for the cup. Inside the bar, a large crowd were already gathered around the projector screen. They were cheering and shouting but it wasn't European football that had them so enthralled. An AFL game was on, the Australian Football League or Aussie Rules as it's commonly known. I had no idea what it was all about, in fact it looked very similar to rugby to me, but fans would strongly disagree. The Australian's called AFL, footy and our football, soccer. They had little interest in European football and even less so since Australia had got knocked out of the World Cup.

Squeezing through the noisy crowd, we made it to the bar and enquired about the match. It wasn't on until late at night, but we were hoping they might be showing it as it was such an important game. The bar staff had no idea what we were talking about. I guess for the competitive Aussies, it was a case of out of sight, out of mind. Australia was out of the running, so best forget any of it ever existed.

*

The next morning unsurprisingly, yet disappointingly it was raining. I had seen a bat sanctuary advertised and thought it was worth a look; at least it would be dry. The main attraction was well worth the $4 fee. His name was Edward and he was a very cute, injured bat. We got to stroke and feed him. They had reared him from a baby because his wing was broken. I asked if he had been named after the character in the Twilight series, but they hadn't even thought of that, the name had originated from another film, Edward Scissor Hands.

Information on the bats and the local natural environment lined the walls. It was interesting to learn that the coconut trees which made the beach front so exotic were not native. Like many plants and animals in Australia, they had been imported by immigrants to enhance the landscape. Sadly now they were affecting the natural balance and strangling the indigenous forest that had originally crept to the edge of the sand. Cape Tribulation, although scenic, didn't have much more to offer in the rain, so we headed to Cairns to collect the replacement gearbox. En route back to the ferry we all peered through the window as a cassowary and its baby stalked along the roadside, they were stunning creatures and I hoped they would be around for many years to come.

*

By the time we had completed the trip from Cape Tribulation to Cairns and then back to Port Douglas to drop the box at the garage, it was getting late. We were delayed a further ten minutes when I discovered the new gearbox had leaked oil over the boot of the brand new hire car. Fortunately, it wasn't physically visible but the smell was potent and would have to be masked with perfume on the cars return.

We had been trying to decide where to stay. It seemed pointless to pay for a camp site when we were not in need of a shower, well by our standards anyway. I didn't want to use the insurance as I had a limit on how much I could spend and wanted to save it in case there were more delays. Lara had previously travelled in a camper van and never paid for accommodation, often sleeping in the van by the side of the road. Well we didn't have a van, but I did know a very nice place to sleep.

It may not have been entirely legal, so we decided to eat dinner first and then pitch up after dark. It was a perfect place to enjoy a meal with the coconut trees behind us and the ocean stretched out in front. The sun was setting and both joggers and tourists passed by, making the most of the beach.

After dark the mischief started and we dragged the tents down to the sand and pitched them between the coconut groves. I then moved the car to a more discrete location. As we lay on the shore listening to the ocean, we talked, laughed and I really relaxed for the first time in a while. There was nothing to do, nowhere to go and no guidebook to read. We did have a moment of paranoia, when a torch began to shine up and down the beach, moving slowly towards us. Fearing it was some kind of beach inspector, we panicked for 15 minutes before finally, a couple who had no idea of the worry they were causing, walked past enjoying a night time stroll.

Sadly, even with the lapping of the waves and tranquil surroundings, sleep didn't come easily. The rain continued and coconuts thudded on the ground a little too close for comfort. Then a thought struck me. We were still in crocodile country. Although the beach was open for swimming in patrolled areas during the day, it didn't offer me much reassurance now. In Kakadu I had been told the crocs could wander up to 2 kms into the park at night, what was to stop them exploring here. I had also read a story about a croc grabbing a woman from a tent and trying to drag her into the river, she was luckily rescued by her son who used the poke in the eyes technique. My mind swirled toothy thoughts, certainly not the best recipe for sweet dreams.

*

We had agreed to get up early and pack up before our secret camp was discovered. Lei always woke as the sun came up, if not before, so she would be our alarm clock. But for some reason, on the only day it mattered, she slept in. Still the first to wake, Lei opened her tent and came face to face with a smiling man taking photos of our makeshift camp site. Stirred by her calls, I peered out of my mosquito net to see an army of joggers, walkers and tourists parading up and down the front; so much for being discreet. Needless to say we packed up pretty quick. Then there was time to enjoy a cooked breakfast on the sand before once again we attracted strange looks, as we washed dishes in the surf.

The girls were confident the car would be ready, as were the boys in the garage, but I had a niggling feeling that something would go wrong. It did. The gearbox fitted, we were still missing the original brackets to hold it in place. I called Norm; he had the brackets, but was away for a wedding and wouldn't be back for another three days. On his return I would need to hire a car again and drive south past Cairns to Innisfail to pick up the parts and then all the way up to Port Douglas again. This was getting frustrating.

Where I got my cool from I have no idea, but I didn't stress or even hesitate. We had three days to kill and I knew exactly what I wanted to do. I embraced the travel spirit and used the situation to my advantage. I had always wanted to try another form of travel but owning a car had prevented me from doing so. We would hitch-hike.

In the UK I wouldn't have dreamed of getting into a car with a random stranger, but over on the other side of the world, I couldn't wait. We could hitch a ride to Cairns and spend a few days seeing the reef and watching the football before Norm returned.

After writing 'Cairns' on a large piece of cardboard, we set off to find our spot. By the roadside we threw our backpacks into a pile and Lara held up the sign while Lei and I stuck out our thumbs and jumped up and down. I smiled pleadingly at passing drivers. We received a lot of grins and 'sorry' shrugs, but realised it would be better to get on the main highway. Here in the town it was mostly tourists or locals milling about. The highway was 5 kms away, a long way to walk with our heavy bags. We decided to add 'or to the highway' onto the bottom of our sign. I had just gone to retrieve the marker pen, when someone pulled over.

A very attractive, muscly man, around my age, sat at the driver's wheel and all three of us stopped to marvel at this gorgeous hero who had come to our rescue. He probably thought we were all mad, as we stared in silence, mouths hanging open. Unfortunately he wasn't going to Cairns but offered to take us to the highway. He had hitch-hiked before and knew how it felt.

I jumped in mentally planning my wedding but my heart sank as I saw the baby seat in the back of his jeep. The hunk, who was originally from Hungary, was on his way to the gym (all of us enjoyed a quick fantasy of him working out) and had just dropped the baby off to his ex-partner (heart rose into my mouth again). Sadly we only got to spend ten minutes with the gorgeous guy before we were deposited by the main road.

More sign holding and enthusiastic gestures followed. Five minutes later another car stopped. This time it was two ladies, sisters, who were both in their fifties. They were going to visit their mother in Cairns, were both well travelled and entertained us with stories of their adventures.

One time they had been held at gunpoint by a cocaine snorting couple, who'd employed them as childminders. Their bosses were holding a party, there were children present and a full blown cyclone was currently ravaging the town. Heavy drug use did not seem appropriate. The sisters were worried for everyone's safety and mentioned their concerns. The couple did not agree and pulled out a gun, before forcefully pushing and locking the frightened babysitters in a room. The sisters watched through a window, as the parents went outside to dance in the eye of the storm. And I thought my stories were crazy.

*

After being dropped in the city we checked into a new hostel. Funnily enough none of us wanted to return to Lunatics. The new place was much better and we had a room with an ocean view and balcony. There were four beds and by the time I returned from a stroll, the fourth had been filled. Both Lara and Lei had met our new roommate but he had gone out shortly after. Apparently he was from Germany and had just arrived in Australia.

Once again we had been given free meal vouchers, but this time for a different pub. I figured we would all go together and invite the mystery German. When I finally met him, it was lust at first sight. His face was beautiful with glowing blue, green intoxicating eyes. His body, fit and covered with tasteful tattoos in all the right places and to top it off he had a smile that could melt marshmallows (and British backpackers). Jonas was one spectacular view and as we headed out for dinner, I realised he was also a great guy.

It was nice to meet someone who could hold a decent conversation. I had grown very tired of the normal questions. How long are you here for? Where have you been? Where are you from? Of course we covered those too, but they were mixed with a variety of conversation, laughter and debates.

The food portions were much smaller than our previous free meals and we joked that it was just a starter. For Jonas and me it was true, as we followed dinner with several pints of beer, which led to a dessert of several pints more. Gradually a band built up the crowd and everyone else was dancing and singing. Jonas and I were still enthralled with each other's travel tales and relishing having someone else over the age of twenty-five to talk to, Jonas was thirty. It was a heart-warming night that ended in a kiss.

*

The next day, slightly hung-over, the four of us went for coffee, followed by a chill on the esplanade grass. A local reggae band played on a small stage and an old hippy danced around in front with his tambourine. The aged, tie-dyed clad guy was soon joined by a very merry Aboriginal man and the pair of them were as entertaining as the musicians.

Eventually Lara and Lei left, leaving me alone with Jonas. I can't express how much I needed those days in Cairns, after the stress of the car, being ill and the constant travelling. It was the first time I had enjoyed total relaxation for more than a few hours at a time. Jonas and I talked all day before it got too cold and then we headed back to the hostel for a repeat dinner outing.

That night, Lei and I left the party early. We had a big day planned. Finally I was going to see the Great Barrier Reef.

*

The two of us headed down towards the large boat which had been recommended by my friends. The weather wasn't perfect, but the sun was doing its best to shine between the cloud breaks. Lei and I were pleased to realise there was free tea, coffee, biscuits and even muffins available. Lei also observed that it must be in the job description to be hot and buff, as all the male crew members could have doubled as models. Not a bad start to the day.

Fed and watered we arrived at the first reef destination. We had booked a forty minute dive and a talk had been given explaining how to use the equipment. I had dived several times before, but for Lei it was a first.

We went down in groups of four. Lei and I entered the water, me excitedly and her a little nervous. Before the dive we had to show the instructors we could clear water out of our masks and remove and replace the ventilator. Thankfully Lei and I completed the tasks with ease.

We were still clinging to the ladder attached to the boat, but suddenly I felt myself start to sink. I automatically filled my buoyancy jacket with air. Lei had the same problem and copied me. Back at the surface a crew member shouted something at us. I looked up and he asked what we were doing. I replied that I had felt myself sinking.

'Yes' he answered, 'it's called diving.'

I was embarrassed to realise his fellow instructor in the water had released the air from our jackets.

Lei and I would be diving with the instructor and a Chinese couple. The Chinese girl was messing around and couldn't do her procedures properly, so we got off to a late start. The dive itself was a bit of a disappointment. The four of us had to keep our arms linked the entire time. I had been able to swim freely during past dives and found this constraint frustrating. Then the Chinese girl began to freak out. The five of us had to surface after only a few minutes so she could get picked up by a boat. Even below water, disappointment hit me. The sea life was sparse and the coral dull. I had seen more tropical sites back in Tenerife. This was not the colourful Great Barrier Reef I had imagined.

My desire to swim with fish may seem strange, given my phobia. However, for some reason they don't worry me in the ocean. I guess the bright colours and clear waters make them more appealing than their muddy coloured cousins in murky rivers and lakes.

I relaxed under the water. The breathing came naturally once I stopped overthinking it. It was soothing listening to my breath making Darth Vader sounds through the ventilator. Lei later confessed that she'd hated it and had been panicking. She had noticed that there was a slow trail of bubbles coming from my mouthpiece while hers resembled an overexcited Jacuzzi. The more she panicked the crazier the bubbles went. Being her usual strong, trouper self, Lei kept her fears quiet, and I was proud of her for completing the dive and not getting back in the boat with the Chinese woman.

The second reef location was Hastings Bay. My previous experience of Hastings was the town in England which was generally cold and grey with a couple of good fish and chip shops. Hopefully this one would be a little more exciting and with the fish minus the batter. While we were waiting to anchor, a large fish came to the back of the boat. Clearly he was a regular and was affectionately known as Wally. The crew fed him before we all jumped in. I don't know what kind of fish Wally was, but he was huge. At nearly two metres long he was by far the biggest fish I had seen in the wild. I really wanted to swim with him, but by the time I entered the water he had disappeared.

After taking a couple of photos of ourselves on my underwater camera, Lei and I swam towards a lagoon. The tide was going out and the top of the reef stuck out of the ocean. The crew told us to swim to the shallow water and explore. This was a whole new world compared to the emptiness of the first reef. Blue tipped corals housed a multitude of fish and giant clams bigger than my backpack rested on the ocean bed. We saw a trumpet fish and a wide variety of corals and marine life.

I can't put the exact feeling into words, but it was total fascination. I felt a peaceful tranquillity where I was just being, just following whatever caught my eye. Nothing else mattered, it was just me and the reef. It was as if I was entering a new realm, secretly spying on it through my mask. I finally had freedom. I could follow fish or dart off after anything that caught my interest and in between I floated about taking in the intense new world.

After a while a whistle blew to announce the submarine was ready to take us on our next adventure. One of the last to get out of the water, I swam towards the boat. Then as I queued to climb up the ladder, I spotted Wally. He was under the boat and I wondered if I could get him to come closer. I waved my arm around, wiggled my fingers and sure enough I caught his attention. Wally headed towards me, but as he did so, he seemingly became bigger and bigger. His eyes were rolling round on the side of his head and his huge lips surrounded a mouth big enough to take a chomp of human limb. Suddenly I realised that being alone in the water with such a large creature wasn't going to be as fun as I'd thought. My fish fear came back in full force and I shot up the ladder like a rocket, not caring who I knocked over in the process.

*

The submarine more closely resembled a glass panelled boat, but that didn't affect my enjoyment. One of the crew, a big Torres Strait Islander, was our guide. He had dark skin, long frizzy hair and a whole lot of personality. We learnt about global warming and saw some of the effects. He told us that the rise in water temperatures had bleached some of the corals from bright colours to white. Normally the reef was much brighter and varied in colour, but the cold weather and rains had also caused the corals to temporarily turn grey and brown. A turtle swam past and we saw some clown fish, now known as Nemos thanks to the Disney film, hovering amongst the sea anemones.

The day flew past and sadly it was time to head for land. En route we were served cheese and wine, accompanied by our guide's wit, as he entertained us with his voice, guitar and even used a plastic pipe as a didgeridoo. I will never forget that day and it's definitely one of my favourite Australian experiences.

*

We returned to the dorm and went to sleep early, setting our alarms for 3 a.m. We were going get up and watch the World Cup final live. It was kicking off at 4 a.m. Australian time and the only place we could find to watch it were the hostels, as all the pubs would be closed. We had already equipped ourselves with alcohol, wine for Lara and Vodka for Jonas and me. Lei didn't drink much but that never kept her away from a party.

At 3.30 a.m. the four of us trudged downstairs to the TV room. It was strange sipping vodka for breakfast, but after the first, the rest went down a treat. Spain was playing the Netherlands. Although I had spent most of my adult life in Spain, I had also taken a fair amount of competitive stick from the Spanish. One thing was for sure, had England reached the final (we can dream eh?) my Spanish friends would not be cheering for us. Anyway, I was travelling with two Dutch girls and I was more than happy to support them.

We found a place near the front, having to lie down so everyone behind could see. Jonas and I shared vodka, commented on the play and made digs at each other, as we were supporting opposite teams. Spain won. The Dutch were disappointed, but I enjoyed watching the game, taking in the atmosphere and making the most of the company.

After the match the room cleared out, but we stayed up to finish our drinks. Every ten minutes or so someone would pop their head round the door and ask who had won the footy. 'HOLLAND ...Wooooo!' we would all cry, bursting out into laughter as soon as they were out of sight.

Lara's wine had gone but she helped us with the vodka, and we entertained ourselves chatting to the cleaners until well after the sun came up. By this point Lara was a little worse for wear and looked as if she was falling asleep on the floor. Jonas and I had curled up on the sofa with me gazing drunkenly into his eyes. Suddenly the romantic mood was broken as we heard the unmistakable sound of vomiting. Lara was not asleep but currently emptying her stomach contents onto the floor with an unimpressed cleaner watching on.

I ran upstairs to get some water and Lei, who had just headed for bed, came back with me to help the drunkard. By the time I returned Lara had cleaned up her mess and was now ranting about how embarrassed she was. Lei helped her up to bed and shortly after, Jonas and I followed. Sadly it was always to separate bunks. There was a downside to sharing rooms with friends.

*

The next day I had to pick up the gearbox brackets and make my final journey (I hoped) to Port Douglas. Lei had agreed to keep me company, but I was sad to say goodbye to both Lara and Jonas. Since buying the car I had started to enjoy my travels on another level. The road trips had allowed me to get to know the people I travelled with on a deeper level. Sharing both the journey and experiences gave us a bond and the chance to find real friendship. In the backpacker bars and hostels people were friendly, but it rarely went past that one night or day out.

When I travelled by bus and plane, going from hostel to hostel, I never really had more than a few days with each person I met, with the exception of Sydney at the start of my trip. Having a car not only allowed me to see more of the country, but by camping in a tent I managed to gain a feeling of personal space that couldn't be found in a dorm. I considered myself very lucky.

When I first arrived in Sydney, backpacker travel agents had tried to sell me pre-booked bus tickets, excursions and tours. They had advised me to book the whole year in advance. At the time, it appeared to be the only way to see Australia. I spent hours reading brochures and trying to choose trips to fit my budget. Thankfully I didn't book it all up. It might work for those on a time limit or who were afraid to travel alone, but it wasn't for me. Be it fate or luck, I was happy I hadn't missed out on this alternative experience, exploring in my little Festiva and living in a tent.

The downside was that the goodbyes were harder. However, having seen some of this vast country, Europe didn't seem so big any more. There were certainly a few people I would need to visit on my return. Farewell didn't have to be forever.

Lara was going back to Holland in the next few weeks so I wouldn't be seeing her again during this trip. Jonas was going to spend some time in Cairns looking for a camper van and trying to find work, before heading south. We both agreed it would be great to stay in touch and see each other again. I did run into him a few weeks later, but he was with a stunning Italian girl. My heart felt a slap of pain and then quickly got over it. Such is life in the travelling world.

*

The next day Lei and I left to collect the brackets, in another rental car paid for by my insurance. First we headed south to Innisfail, where Norm lived. It was an hour's journey filled with beautiful green countryside and sugar cane. Turning into the drive we saw him coming over to welcome us. Norm was in his sixties, short and wore glasses and a warm smile.

He led us to his garage where he carefully wrapped the brackets so we wouldn't get the car dirty this time around. We then walked through a graveyard of skeletal cars, some were overrun by grass and weeds and some, little more than a heap of rust. Finally, we reached a Festiva. It had been running well, but a tree had fallen onto it during a cyclone and the insurance company had written it off. Norm hunted around to make sure we hadn't missed more vital parts, before inviting us in for coffee.

His family were sitting around having breakfast. A couple from Newcastle, England had flown over for the wedding the previous weekend. I laughed as Lei looked on bemused as they spoke in a dialect she had never heard before and certainly couldn't understand. I translated Geordie into Oxford English and we all discussed accents. With the coffee finished and Lei praying she would never have to try and communicate with any Scottish or Irish in the future, we headed back to the car.

Once again we were treated to a display of Australian hospitality as Norm insisted we take a giant melon from his garden. Then it was retracing our journey once again, back through Cairns and on to Port Douglas.

*

As we pulled in for petrol just outside Cairns I caught a glimpse of some hitch-hikers at the roadside. The usual drizzle was now a torrential downpour. Returning the karma for our lifts, I ran over and rounded them up. The boys were heading to Cape Tribulation. I would take them most of the way, to our previous hitching spot outside Port Douglas.

They were all from Italy, but one had lived in London and spoke perfect English. They were heading north to work on a boat but had previously been looking for work in Tully. It was good to get some info on my future work prospects, although judging from their feedback things weren't going to be easy.

The journey flew past, with our new friends for entertainment, and soon enough we were dropping them off. As Lei and I turned into Port Douglas I hoped and prayed that my car would be finished later that day. It seemed like forever since I had last driven it.

*

We left the brackets with the garage boss, who had returned from his time off, before checking into our motel. I still had money left on the insurance, so it would have been a shame to waste it. Several hours later, I still hadn't heard from the garage. The boss had assured me that the car would be ready by the end of the day. I called reception and was worried to hear that the work was taking longer than expected. It wouldn't be finished until the following morning. I felt stress crawl back into me. I had been quoted for six hours labour, I couldn't afford for it to take any longer.

That evening we returned the hired car and stopped by to check on the Festiva. All the boys were sitting around it, deep in discussion. The boss saw me coming and called out, 'Whoever told you this gearbox would fit was wrong.'

I couldn't believe it. Lance the young stand-in manager had assured me that everything would be fine. The stress gripped me harder. I didn't want to get Lance in trouble as he had tried so hard to help me, but I couldn't take the blame or cost for this error. Fortunately, before I could panic too much, they told me that with some welding and adjusting it would be ok. I noticed Lance looked very sheepish and avoided my eyes, he obviously hadn't told his boss the full story.

*

That night I began to worry over the expense. Lance had clearly messed up and the garage was making no effort to keep me informed. What if they hit me with a huge bill? I would have to fight it; I certainly couldn't pay any more than what was planned.

I had been calm and collected up until now and the idea of a confrontation filled me with dread.

The next morning, finally, the car was supposedly ready and I went to collect the invoice. Upon my arrival the work still wasn't finished and I was told to come back in half an hour. However, it was another two hours and several phone calls later before they managed to get it done.

By this point I was pissed off and stressed out, and that's putting it nicely. I held my breath as the receptionist handed me the final bill. I looked down, the total sum was a fair bit more than I'd been quoted. I saw the boss out the back, called him over and asked if I could have a word. Things were about to get serious.

I told him the events of the past week and that the extra time spent on the car was due to an error by his staff. He argued but I knew I had the upper hand. They had my car, but it was a write-off since its crash and had no market value. I was a poor backpacker and could easily walk out and leave the Festiva behind, along with the bill. I simply could not afford to pay for their errors. The irritated garage owner went off to rethink the amount, and when he returned the bill was a little more agreeable. I paid up. What an absolute nightmare that had been.

I was shaking with stress, but finally the Festiva was mine and with it came the freedom to leave Port Douglas and my troubles behind. It had never felt so good to hit the road. We turned onto the highway with a revitalising breeze of fresh air flowing through my window. I took a deep relaxing breath and didn't look back.

CHAPTER 8

COUNTRY CRAZIES

L EI AND I had spent hours discussing what to do next. I had the hostel booked in Tully but wasn't sure I wanted to stay there. I'd heard so many horror stories of hostel owners taking advantage of backpackers. However, I urgently needed to add more working days to my visa application. Lei wanted to do some voluntary work to experience life with a rural Australian family. The advantage for me would be shorter hours, leaving free time to sightsee or to write my travel diary. I also liked the idea of home cooked meals after enduring months of camp food.

We decided to give it a go. Sitting in a café we called numerous farms, but after an hour we still had no placement. The vast amount of backpackers on the East Coast had made something extraordinary become a reality. We couldn't find jobs, even though we were prepared to work for free. Everywhere was full. Oh well, if you can't plan it, wing it. So that's exactly what we did.

Heading south we decided to drive into any farms we came

across and ask for work. The uncertainty filled me with a strange but pleasant feeling as we headed directly into the unknown. It was getting late and the traffic through Cairns was heavy. We agreed to stop at at least one farm before finding somewhere to camp. Seeing a banana field on the side of the highway, we pulled over to the house a short way down a side road. Lei seemed nervous, but I boldly strolled over to the entrance. There was no front door or bell as such, just an open garage, so I called through it and a man in his thirties came out. Sadly he didn't have any work but he did direct us to the nearest rest stop where we could camp, before continuing our venture the next morning. I was undeterred, there would be plenty more farms along the way.

Night had fallen by the time we reached our destination and visibility was limited. As we parked and jumped out, Lei realised we had driven into boggy grass. Not the best place to camp and more worryingly not a good place for my car. Luckily we were able to reverse out and managed to find somewhere drier to pitch up. I fell asleep with my resolve still strong.

*

We rose at dawn and hit the highway to continue our mission. Stopping at several packing sheds, we were continuously turned away and eventually began to feel disheartened. We came across a quiet spot on the ocean front and took a break to eat breakfast. As we waited for our toast to cook on the stove (yes, we made toast on a frying pan), I wandered down to the water. I called Lei over, as a large pod of dolphins swam past. Even on an ordinary day, job hunting, Australia had given us a special moment.

Having seen a few of the packing sheds, the idea of working in them was becoming less appealing. They were basically factories and the thought of having such a boring repetitive job filled me with dread. I was becoming too fussy for my own good. I had to do something. I was just glad that unlike many backpackers, I was not depending on work for income.

After more failed attempts, we arrived in Innisfail not far from where Norm, the gearbox man, lived. We stopped for a coffee and again sat in a café, calling more farms in a last ditched attempt. Suddenly Lei started to make excited gestures; she had found somewhere! It was near Tully and they had room for us straightaway. No matter how I felt about sickly sweet Tully, it seemed I was destined to spend time there.

I called to cancel the work hostel. I was sure they had a queue of backpackers dying to take my place. We planned to arrive in Tully just before dinner and enjoyed one last day of freedom around the shops of Innisfail.

As we headed towards our new home we began to realise that the farm was a fair way from Tully itself, and with every bend in the winding road more doubts crept into my mind. Turning into the driveway we looked for the house. Instead, there was just a cluster of sheds. Then we came upon an elderly woman sat in the grass. She introduced herself as Dora Harwood, the farm owner (all farms and names in this book have been changed to protect their privacy or in some cases avoid offence).

Dora directed us to the back of a shed that looked overgrown and run-down. As we got closer, to my horror, I realised this wasn't a shed, this was their home. My instant reaction was to turn around and flee, but my desire to obtain the visa was just about strong enough to stop me. Having parked up, we walked back over to Dora who was pulling leaves off vines and putting them into a bowl. She asked us to help and told us they were weeds she was going cook for dinner. I tried to squash the voice in my head as again it cried, 'Run! Run!'

Dora was seventy years of age and rather overweight. She was wearing a home-made floral dress and had a long, thin, grey plait of hair that limply hung down her back. Nothing about her was in any way attractive. She even lacked that warm glow that older people tend to take on and had instead adopted the mean old lady look. Her speech was abrupt, but it was hard to tell if it was intentional or just the way she spoke. We were informed that they had two other volunteers, both boys, who had full-time jobs on other farms. They paid board but helped out on the farm at weekends in return for a rent discount. The boys would be joining us at dinner.

*

As we helped prepare the meal, I tried to ignore the insects crawling in the butter and Dora's constant coughing over the food. Out of the corner of my eye I spotted a prescription lying on the side. The headed paper listed the address of a mental health clinic. Where the bloody hell were we? And more importantly, would we ever escape alive?

Also joining us for dinner was Dora's husband Paul, who was seven years her senior, with a short white beard and hair that resembled a dried dirty paintbrush. In contrast to Dora, he was very slim and frail, maybe she had been stealing his food for the last forty years. Then an even older man appeared. Laurie, we were told was ninety-five years old and had been left in their care after his son moved to China. Laurie was entertainingly senile.

I sat down at the table nervously and he looked me straight in the eyes before shouting with great volume, 'My mother used to force me to drink it!'

My ear drum cringed but I managed to reply with typical English politeness, 'I'm so sorry but what did you have to drink?'

Laurie, in complete disbelief and much to my horror cried, 'Aren't you listening? Cod liver oil!'

'Oh,' I exclaimed cautiously.

Before he continued in his gruff old man's voice, 'I hated it, but my sister, she loved it, she used to put it in her coffee.' He then began to laugh hysterically before turning away.

I made a polite chuckle. Although a little disturbed, I thought I'd better make an effort to bond with my host family and so asked, 'Was your sister older or younger than you?'

To which Laurie turned around and with a look of outrage he asked, 'What on earth are you talking about?'

I sat numb with shock and confusion while Laurie made a *Hmmmph!* noise as his gaze returned to his tea cup and we all continued passing plates around as if nothing had happened.

Thankfully, just at that moment, the other two volunteers arrived in a big ball of energy. One was Dieter from Germany, who was tall and muscular with a crazy mop of frizzy blonde curls on his head. The other, Max, was French but had been adopted and was gifted with beautiful Korean looks and long silky hair worthy of a shampoo ad. Both of them were smiling and joking as they bustled in. It was a relief to see people our own age who seemed to have a sense of humour and an ounce of sanity.

The last to join the table was Kevin. Ginger haired, tall and lanky, he reminded me of the redneck from The Simpsons. Kevin had been fostered by Dora and Paul and lived in one of the caravans outside the 'house' with his dog, Yellow.

At last Paul said grace and we tucked in. After camp food and free pasta dinners, the fresh home-grown, organic vegetables tasted amazing. I complimented Dora on the food and the boys giggled like teenagers at some private joke. They continued to laugh between themselves throughout the whole meal. Ignoring them, I chatted to Paul, who was originally from England. He spoke gently with a kind tone and smiling eyes, a total contrast to Dora's coldness. He was definitely a grandfather figure; in fact, they had five children and twenty-five grandchildren.

We were then served dessert. Mine was accompanied by a live earwig which I did my best to subtly remove. It seemed that creepy crawlies were a common part of the menu. Just as we were clearing away the plates, Laurie made me jump as he announced to the world with all his might, 'My mother used to force me to drink it.'

Incidentally, I later discovered that if I actually tried to start a conversation with him, he would ignore me, not even moving his eyes from whatever task he was currently engaged with.

After Lei and I had washed up we headed over to the workers' part of the house. In fact it wasn't really a house but a large tin roof over an open kitchen, lounge and a second lounge for the volunteers. Only the bedrooms and bathrooms had four walls, all the other rooms were open to the environment and wildlife.

Lei and I had our own room as this was apparently a Christian household, and the Harwoods didn't like the boys and girls to mix too closely. To my horror, but not complete surprise, our room turned out to be well and truly spider infested. I had developed a fear of the eight legged little monsters from childhood. Lei was a lot stronger and removed spiders from around my bed. They were only small, but the vast quantity and my arachnophobia made them seem very creepy and crawly.

There was another dorm-style room for Max, plus a bedroom for Paul and Dora and finally Laurie's room. Dieter lived in one of the caravans outside and there was another empty van for any couples who visited. Best to keep any personal and possibly unmarried intimacy out of this blessed house.

Before bed we sat with the boys in the lounge and they turned out to be my saviours. I soon realised that the giggling and jokes at dinner were their way of making the place bearable.

Dieter spoke very broken English but came with his own Aussie catch phrase, 'Not so bad eh?'

Finding a beetle in his sandwich, he held up the insect and flicked it away, before taking a big bite and with his mouth still full, mumbled, 'Not so bad eh?'

Coming home covered in sweat to a measly sized, sneeze covered dinner, he sneaked out the back and rolled up a joint. Turning to me, filthy, stinking, hungry and grinning, he took a big puff and exhaled, 'Not so bad eh?'

Rather than focus on the grotty house or disgusting toilets, the boys made their own fun and always came home with big smiles despite having endured a hard day at their physically challenging jobs. Laurie shitting himself. Deadly spider in the toilet. Cockroach in their dinner. They laughed at it all. It was an ideal place for them to save money, as the pay was good and due to their extra weekend work the rent very low; although for the amount of labour they contributed, they shouldn't have paid any at all. I think they enjoyed watching our reactions that first night. It certainly explained all the giggles.

Apparently, the previous evening, two French boys had turned up and stayed for dinner, but come morning they had gone, disappearing without a trace. Over the next few weeks it became a game, betting on how long new workers would last, and in turn Lei and I enjoyed seeing the horror on the faces of others as they took in their new home.

Having dusted away the spiders and checked our sleeping bags thoroughly for wildlife, Lei evicted a cockroach and I drifted off to sleep. As I did I wondered what surprises the next day would hold for us and prayed nothing would crawl into my bed during the night.

Work started at 8 a.m., so we were up at 7 a.m. to allow time to eat and dress. The first thing I noticed was a dark shape on the wall. Instantly I knew what it was, a huntsman spider. Suddenly the smaller spiders didn't seem so scary. Normally I would have run out the room screaming, but I didn't think that would help me on this farm. I was determined not to be another terrified fleeing backpacker, so miraculously I stayed calm.

It was a very big spider, about the size of my hand and there was no way I was going to touch it, Lei wasn't too keen either. Running out of time, not sure what to do and not wanting to ask for spider assistance on our first day, we left it where it was. After a breakfast of delicious toasted home-made bread (which as far as I could tell was insect free), all eight legged thoughts had gone as we set off to work.

Jordan was the Harwood's son and was in charge of running the farm. We soon forgot all our worries as we sat on the back of a quad bike riding to work. We laughed and squealed in excitement as we travelled through banana plantations, across a shallow river and finally into a sweet potato field.

Our work was simple and involved moving stray vines back into rows. Totally exposed to the sun, which was making a rare appearance, it had become fairly hot and our backs soon began to ache from constantly bending down. Thankfully we had a distraction, there was another boy working with us. His name was Simon, he was fit and lean with blue twinkling eyes. He was very good-looking and had known the Harwoods for years. His family were Christian missionaries and they all lived in Papa New Guinea, which I found both interesting and disappointing. He probably wouldn't be the type for a quick backpacker fling. Simon was in Australia to do some repairs on the family boat and helping the Harwoods out with the farm, in return for caravan accommodation on their nephew's property.

I was shocked to discover he was only seventeen; he was so mature in the way that he spoke and looked. I listened intently while he told stories about the alternative lifestyle he had grown up with, intrigued by every detail. Finally the working day was finished, well for us anyway. Volunteers were to work four hours a day, six days a week. Not so bad eh?

Lunch was more vegetables and pulses in a stew and after, we relaxed, taking in the beautiful scenery surrounding us whilst waiting for the boys to return home. I watched in awe as a brave Lei managed to put the spider from our room, which miraculously hadn't moved, into a cup and released it into the garden. I had the disturbed feeling that this wouldn't be my last huntsman encounter and began to look out for them on every wall, surface and sleeping bag.

*

In the evenings we played Connect Four and Crazy Sheep, probably called so because one more attempt to solve its puzzle would have knocked us into Laurie-style insanity. I had started to sew, albeit badly, as a hobby to pass the time and was decorating a skirt with beads and patches. It was pure entertainment to sit and listen while stitching, as Dieter and Max talked rubbish, Lei played with the diablo (those things that spin on a rope suspended between two sticks) and old man Laurie wandered around saying things like, 'Yes, we have no bananas.' Lei even took it upon herself to teach him how to play Connect Four one night. After many hilarious attempts to explain the rules, she left him alone to continuously slot the chips into the board while muttering about castor oil.

I also discovered that Kevin, the redneck, had schizophrenia, which had apparently been caused by a generous intake of home-made acid in his teenage years. I guess there wasn't much else to do as way of rebellion in the middle of nowhere. He was on medication and seemed as normal as you could be, living in the current circumstances. However, every now and then he would mention times when he had been in prison or had done something disturbingly crazy. Out of politeness we would all nod and listen as if this was a perfectly natural thing to drop into conversation. One time he had even pretended to hold up the Harwood's nephew and his heavily pregnant wife with a mask and rifle. Firing shots outside their house and holding them hostage for an hour, as a joke!

Kevin also had a friend, Ken, who came by from time to time. At first I thought Ken was just a bit scatty, he had a high-pitched giggle and would come out with the most random and weird things. Then someone told me he also had mental health problems caused by home-made acid. I guess that was the norm around here. I was living in a real life Alice in Wonderland. I began wandering if, in a strange twist, this would end with me realising I was the mental one.

*

Over the next few days the work changed. We had to put the bananas in their 'pyjamas'. Which meant climbing up a ladder and tying plastic bags around the bunches. There was also a lot of weeding which everyone hated. The aim was to remove all the weeds from around the base of the banana trees. As this was an organic farm, no weedkiller or chemicals could be used. Working on the farm, I gained a whole new respect for organic farmers and their produce. It involved a lot of extra work and they must have needed a huge amount of faith and dedication not to take the easy way out.

Armed with machetes and gloves, we set about hacking the weeds away, pulling out the roots by hand. The field stretched as far as the eye could see and it seemed a pointless and impossible task. A strimmer could have completed the entire job in one afternoon. It was as if we were in some form of Amish world where only hard graft was considered real work. Four hours of weeding feels like eight of anything else, my hands were left raw and my arms in agony.

*

Sundays were our day off and we decided to walk to a nearby waterfall with Dieter and Marcel, a new French worker, while Max stayed at home to relax. It was a long but pleasant walk and once we had finally reached the falls, Dieter convinced me to sneak past the barriers and no swimming signs with him. I then shouted encouragement as he jumped off rocks into the deep plunge pool below. It took the whole day for us to walk there and back, but we enjoyed the journey and escaping the farm.

The Harwoods seemed to be giving us a raw deal, the work was hard and dull and the food, although wholesome, was served in tiny portions. Dora wouldn't let us eat anything that they had to pay for. Eggs, milk, veg and home-made bread were fine, as they had cows, chickens and a veggie garden. But the honey and other things she had to buy from the shop were off limits. However, the boys made life fun and as I needed to add days to my visa, I decided to stay for a few more weeks.

For Lei things were different as she was only in Australia for six months and had to continue her journey. But first she planned to try one more placement in Mission Beach, just an hour away and so I agreed to visit on the weekend.

*

During the following weeks other volunteers came and went, but we had a steady group of five: Dieter, Max, Marcel, myself and a new English worker, Dan. Marcel had paid work, so Dan and I were the only full-time volunteers. After several horrendous days of weeding, we finally got our lucky break.

Dora sent us to work for her nephew on his neighbour-ing farm. His name was Dean and he had inherited his father's warm and friendly manner, plus a good work ethic. Dean had real direction and progress in his work, making sure that while helping him we didn't get stuck doing the same tasks day after day. Our jobs included, freeing pine trees from dense grass with machetes, stringing up tomato plants, drowning weeds with soil in the mango field and setting pumpkin runners in line. The last few days of work were spent setting up an irrigation system for the banana field. It may not sound all that exciting but to me it was a chance to experience something completely different.

We also had a tea break every day or as the Aussies call it, smoko. Dean would always sit with us and told us more about farm life. He and his wife had seven children. The kids were all home schooled and very mature for their ages. The eight-year-old son often picked us up on the quad bike for break, while a twelve-year-old served us tea and toast, chatting as if he was twenty.

Dean also taught Dan and myself how to drive the quad and gave us a car, made in the same year that I was born, to drive around the farm in. He treated us like family and it was nice to be working for someone who showed a genuine interest. On Dora's farm we were left alone in the field and only spoken to if they wanted something from us.

Dean's house was also unique; I guess the apple doesn't fall that far from the tree. In fact he hadn't built it yet. Instead they had two old buses with the seats pulled out, which served as bedrooms and those joined on to a living room/kitchen area built under a tin roof. The garden was full of guinea pigs, ducks and chickens (known as chooks in Australia), and two dogs which chased the children as they rode around on their various motorbikes.

I grew to love the farms in a crazy, sanity testing kind of way and I even conquered my fear of spiders. For better or worse, life was definitely changing.

*

One night we were taken to watch a film at Dean's place. There was a big projector screen set up outside, and we sat in the old bus seats, along with family and neighbours; the children snuggled up in their sleeping bags. We enjoyed a Disney film, projected onto the back wall, while Dean served us tea and coffee. It made me feel warm and fuzzy inside, well at least until we returned to the house of doom.

*

Lei was still at Mission Beach, but due to head south very soon; so that Sunday, when we were all off work, I agreed to take the workers to visit her. As mentioned, the Harwoods were strong Christians and there was no swearing, alcohol or smoking allowed in the house. In true rebellion, the first stop was a bottle shop. The boys were also looking forward to finally enjoying a big, bug free meal. Dora's tiny portions always left them hungry.

We found a BYO (bring your own alcohol) cafe and sat down armed with a box of goon. A group hug embraced Lei as she strolled in with stories of her new, clean and friendly home at a different farm. Of course I was driving so I stuck to tea, but just watching the others made me feel drunk. Faces lit up with pleasure as they were served huge plates of fish and chips and I relished every bite of my veggie burger. Everyone was in high spirits and our table was filled with loud voices and laughter.

Several hours later I decided to drive them home so I could enjoy a drink myself. Dora and Paul were out for the evening, so we could continue the party at the farm, and we decided to take Lei with us. She had planned to hitch-hike south that day, but it was getting late and we were sure the Harwoods would let her stay for a night.

The weather had been bad all day and torrential rain flooded the streets, but Dieter hadn't seen the beach yet. Before leaving, we ran through the downpour, down to the sand, laughing and shouting, fuelled by goon and good food.

The drive back was somewhat stressful, well for me anyway. I now had six people squeezed into my little Festiva, four of whom were very drunk and calling out music requests every thirty seconds. The rain was falling so hard that I could hardly see the road and the boys rocked about singing loudly in the back. I was relieved when we finally reached 'home' and I could sit down for a well-earned drink. The party continued well into the night and only two of the three boys made it to the fields the next day.

*

Lei had to leave in the morning to hitch-hike to Airlie Beach. She had found an intriguing advert on the internet and was going to follow it up. On a website that backpackers used to advertise lifts or travel partners, Lei had found a man with his own boat looking for people to sail the Whitsunday Islands with him. The only cost was approximately $20 a day for fuel. He had a kayak and snorkelling gear on board and it sounded amazing. However, I didn't like the idea of Lei going out to sea alone with a man she hardly knew. I suggested she try and find someone to go with her, when it dawned on me that I could go.

I'd been planning to visit the Whitsundays anyway. The boat I'd been looking at would have cost me $600 for three days and have thirty people on board. This would be a much better option, as long as the guy wasn't a total weirdo and I seriously hoped things couldn't get weirder than at my current location. I would find more visa work after the trip.

Lei left by herself and promised to check things out. After a couple of days she called to say she had met with the man. He seemed like a good guy and she was already staying on his boat at Airlie Beach. Still wary, but keen to know more, I agreed to drive down.

That weekend I would have to say goodbye to everyone at the farm and even with all the insanity, I still felt sad to leave. However, there were a few more dramas to come, including Dieter discovering he had head lice. I had watched him scratch away at the almost dreadlocked curls for weeks. Finally pinning him down to check his bleach blonde hair, my fears were confirmed. At first I promised to keep quiet but after he refused to do anything about them, I had to expose him before we all became infested.

I announced his contamination over dinner. He wasn't happy with me but it was bad enough having bugs in my food, I didn't want them in my hair too. According to Dora, the solution was to pour flammable insect repellent, used in oil lamps, onto his head. It was certainly a different approach, but anything to keep the nits away from my long hair. This done, Dora told him to wait an hour before washing it off. What was wrong with using the usual head lice shampoo, I have no idea. At least he smelt nice, although I moved briskly away as he lit up a cigarette while marinating in the highly flammable oil.

Leaving day finally arrived. I would miss the other workers, but they were heading off for hours of weeding and I was relieved not to be joining them. I gave Dieter a big hug, praying the lice were gone. I told him I wished they were coming with me and not going to work. 'It's not so bad eh?' he replied with the usual big grin and another hug.

CHAPTER 9

ALL ABOARD!

DRIVING 400 KMS on the East Coast was very different to driving the same in the outback. The towns were closer together, the speed limit was lower and there was a lot more traffic. Even short drives could take a long time. I felt exhausted as the hardship of farm life finally caught up with me. To counteract this, I continuously filled myself with coffee and energy drinks. I may have overdone it and by the time I reached Airlie Beach, with the tunes blasting out the stereo, I was practically bouncing off the walls.

On arrival in Airlie, Lei introduced me to Mark. He was forty years old, with a shaved head, stocky figure and glowing, green eyes. He seemed friendly enough, considering he was greeting a shaking girl who was talking non-stop. The introductions made, Lei announced that she planned to go ahead with the trip. Well if she was going to be murdered at sea, she might as well have some company, so I agreed to jump on board too (love those bad puns).

I drove them to the local supermarket to stock up on supplies and Mark came across as laid-back and easy-going, as we wandered the aisles. Then the time came to board the vessel which was to become our new home. We jumped into an inflatable dingy parked on the beach and headed off towards *Smooth Sails*, Mark's catamaran (again I have changed the name here so please don't go getting on boats with random strangers. You may enjoy hearing my crazy ideas but it's probably best not to try them). I couldn't believe I was actually going to be sailing around the Whitsundays on a private boat.

Lei had already been taught how to drive the motorised dingy, and Mark said he would teach us how to sail. An ex-racing yacht, *Smooth Sails* was forty feet long, with hollow hulls on both sides, a flat deck in the middle and nets at the front. Mark's bed was in one hull along with the kitchen and ours in the other. It wasn't vastly large or particularly flash, but it was ours for a week.

*

The first day was bliss. We sailed for a few hours, with Lei and I helping to steer and put the sails up and down. The sun was shining in a perfectly blue sky for the first time since our arrival in Queensland almost a month before. I smiled, enjoying the breeze on my face, and listening to the gentle noise from the rippling water and wind.

Mark taught us how to read the radar to see where we were and how deep the water was. He showed us charts that mapped our route, and I began to feel very nautical. Half an hour later he pointed out migrating humpback whales. They jumped high out of the water creating a huge cloud of spray as they hit the ocean surface. It was breathtaking and I had to shake myself to make sure it was real.

Our overnight stop was a bay just off Hook Island. The inlet was filled with crystal clear waters and fringed by green pine forests. Within five minutes of dropping anchor, a pod of dolphins circled the bay. We watched, while sitting on the deck eating cheese and biscuits. This was what living was made for. Lei and I inflated the kayak and took it in turns to paddle around the cove. Then we all jumped in the dingy and motored over to a cave where Aboriginal rock paintings lined the walls.

Returning aboard, the temperature dropped and darkness fell. We went below deck and watched a movie before falling asleep to the gentle rocking of the waves. Not a bad way to spend my first day at sea.

*

We spent nearly ten days around the Islands, snorkelling in tropical waters and relaxing on deserted beaches. There was nowhere to go and nothing to do but enjoy the environment and fascinating sea life around us. The first couple of places were surrounded by forests and emerald green water which reflected the trees. Then after sailing around the headland, we moored up at an island and took a walk up to a lookout.

At the top I couldn't believe my eyes. Stretched before us were miles and miles of pure white sand, surrounded by cobalt blue Ocean which turned bright turquoise in the shallows and inlets. The sun shone down making the water sparkle, and there wasn't a cloud to be seen. It looked like an advert for paradise.

How long we stood there breathing in the view I'm not sure. I tried to soak it into my memory. I wanted to keep this piece of perfection with me forever. But the best news was yet to come, we were going to sail into the bay below and anchor up for a few days.

Lei and I were now taking an active part in sailing the catamaran. The main sail was hoisted up by Mark, as it was too heavy for us, despite my numerous huffing and puffing attempts. Our job was to steer the boat into the wind while Mark heaved the sail to the top of the mast. Located over the nets on the bow, was the front sail and Lei and I were in charge of putting it up and down. I loved being a part of our small crew.

Once the sails had been hoisted, we tidied the ropes and jumped back into the hull seats or relaxed on deck. If the wind was not strong enough we used the motor but nothing beat sailing. The catamaran was light and skimmed across the ocean effortlessly. With the noisy engine off, all we could hear was the movement of the ocean and gentle flap of wind in the sails. Occasionally we would gather to watch more whales as they sprayed bursts of water through their blow holes and I stared transfixed, silently thankful of this incredible opportunity.

We anchored by the famous Whitehaven Beach, 14 kms of pure white, quartz sand, lined by trees and forestry on one side and the gentle lapping ocean on the other. If there had been a couple of Greek godlike hunks, waiting to serve me cocktails, heaven really would be a place on earth. Fortunately, Whitehaven didn't need my secret fantasies to make it unforgettable, although there were a few crew who'd look very fetching in a crown of vines.

Lei and I jumped into the dingy with perfected style and went to explore the island's bush walk. Mark couldn't take part due to a painful knee, and so stayed behind to spend quality time with a few cans of beer. The path led us up to a lookout and then to the opposite side of the island where we found another beach.

It was untouched, well at least so far that day, and ours were the only footprints. After hunting the wash line for treasures (you know the usual, smoothed glass, pretty shells, bits of drift wood or maybe a diamond ring), we wrote messages to people back home in the sand and had our pictures taken with them. Eventually we returned to Whitehaven for a stressful afternoon

sunbathing, and watching the sea planes take off across the sparkling ocean.

*

I was eternally grateful for our position on the catamaran as I
saw excursions drop sightseers on the glowing sand, only for
them to leave an hour later. Mark knew some of the locals working on other boats and one young guy came over to chat. He was
skippering a boat loaded with National Geographic photography
students. After a day of picture taking, they had put down their
cameras and were off to play cricket on the beach. We declined
an invitation to join them as I was currently unable or unwill-
ing to remove myself from the comfy cocoon of the hammock.
Who needed cricket when we could enjoy dinner overlooking
the water, watching turtles pop their heads up.

Lei spotted a whale in the channel between the beach and
another island. Through the binoculars we could see the top fin
and a small piece of its back hovering above the water. It wasn't
moving, which seemed rather unusual and twenty minutes later
it was still in there. Concerned that it might be injured or beached,
Mark asked if we wanted to have a closer look, I wanted to jump
up and down with excitement. It was illegal to get too close to
whales but we were going to keep at the regulated distance with
our motor off. Hopping into the dingy we headed out.

By the time we had crossed the channel, the whale had turned
upside down leaving only the end of its tail standing upright out
of the water. I joked that she should put on more of a show but
as the minutes past all was still. In awe we silently looked on. All
we could hear was a gentle splashing as the wind whipped the
ocean and suspense began to build. Still nothing happened. I was
beginning to wonder what we would do next, and whether we
should give up and return, when patience finally paid off.

Breaking the surface, a baby suddenly appeared alongside

its mother. We assumed that she had either just given birth or had been feeding. I was delighted as the baby repeatedly jumped out of the water, landing with a splash. After ten minutes of this energetic display, side by side mother and baby began to move.

We were a little concerned to see that they were heading our way. Then the mother nosed up and turned downwards, appearing to dive and we waited with anticipation to get a view of her huge tail. Then the unexpected happened. About a hundred metres from our little dingy, the adult whale's barnacled head emerged in a froth of waves. She was massive and as if in slow motion, she rose up out of the water, revealing more and more of her incredible bulk. The black shiny body dwarfed the precariously rocking dingy. We sat frozen, half in awe, half in fear, as the huge mass of mammal, propelled herself further up and into the air, displaying her lined, white belly. The fin on her side must have been larger than our boat, and it shone sleekly in the sunlight as her whole body cleared the water.

And what did I think during this magical and yet dangerous moment? Well I believe I uttered, 'Ohhhhhhhh fuck!' while waiting to be launched into the water. I then felt the drifting spray hit my face as the whale smashed down onto the surface, creating a swirl of foam before disappearing under the water once more. The dingy bounced around, almost tipping us out, before it eventually calmed to a gentle bob in the ocean. Shaking, as adrenaline pumped through me like an electric shock, I looked over at Lei. Her face was fixed with a twisted smile which had distorted as she froze with fear. Finally, I turned to Mark who, ever the Aussie, seemed far too relaxed given the potentially deadly situation.

I wanted to get the hell out of there in case the whale came for the boat. Lei later confessed she had felt the same but hadn't recovered the power of speech. Mark reasoned that we might scare the mother by turning on the motor and so we stayed. With baited breath we sat shaking in our rubber dingy expecting the whale to torpedo towards us.

Eventually the tension left our bodies as mother and baby appeared once again, but this time heading out into the open ocean. Although this incredible encounter had been a little too close for comfort, I felt privileged to have witnessed such a spectacle. It was an event that cannot be done justice on paper but will be embedded in my memory forever. And all this time the National Geographic students had been playing cricket on the beach.

*

For Lei, the whale was the first of several terrifying marine encounters. Throughout the trip we embarked on some amazingly unsuccessful fishing trips.

Sitting in the dingy, armed with beer and rods, we dropped our lines into the ocean. Lei had never been fishing before, so I was pleased to see her get a bite on the line. Dutifully winding it in, she was all smiles until she caught sight of the tiny potato cod on the hook. For some reason the beautiful speckled fish scared the life out of her, and much to my frustration she wouldn't even keep calm enough for a photo. Mark gave up trying to help and returned the cod into the water in an attempt to restore tranquillity. It was the only fish any of us caught during the entire trip, even though we constantly had lines in the water.

When snorkelling one day, Lei got into a panic as a large sea turtle swam by her. I would have been overjoyed to see one up close, but horrified, Lei flapped about trying to scramble out of the water, fearing for her safety. Much laughing ensued as we informed the red-faced Dutch girl that they were completely harmless.

A few days later there were more dramas. Lei had swum over to the beach and on her return I noticed red patches along her arms. The crazy girl had paddled through a mass of jellyfish lining the shore. On her swim over she had managed to avoid most of them and had only suffered mild stings. However, she was still embarrassed from the turtle encounter and thought the pain might be in her imagination. After sitting on the beach, she decided that rather than risk looking stupid and call to be rescued by the dingy, she would dive back in. A second swim through the evil little blobs had doubled her injuries.

Mark handed her a bottle of vinegar to subdue the pain, and it was established that no hospital visit was required, we laughed some more and gave her a lowdown on marine hazards. We stressed that dolphins, which also frightened her, were safe, but sharks were generally best avoided, as long as she didn't confuse the two all would be well.

*

On our last night we moored at an island that was actually inhabited. There was not only a bar, but a full restaurant and freshwater showers! As much as I loved *Smooth Sails*, it was a basic catamaran and there was no shower or even enough freshwater to wash in. My hair was literally stuck to my head, so it was a great luxury to get cleaned up before enjoying jugs of beer and a meal.

Our vessel also had a rather unusual toilet situation. The one on board had broken, so we were forced to do our business in a bucket of water before tipping it overboard. One night my pee even led us to a bizarrely beautiful encounter. As I was pouring the contents of my bladder into the dark ocean, I noticed glowing dots in the water. At first I thought it was my imagination, but on closer inspection they proved to be real. I called the others over and Mark explained that I had disturbed the phosphorescence, making it light up like glow-worms. We all stared in wonder at the beauty created from my discarded urine. Lovely.

*

235

On our last morning at sea, Lei and I strolled around the island's hills and marvelled at blue and black butterflies that fluttered on the sand in vast numbers. On return to the boat we set sail, bound for the mainland. It was time to get back on land full-time. I would miss the rocking of the waves and Mark yelling for his deckhands, although he had kindly promoted us to officers for the last few days.

The Whitsunday Islands were by far the most beautiful natural wonders I had ever seen. I would be forever grateful that I got to explore them on our own little boat with the best crew in the whole world. I was once again sad another adventure was coming to an end, but nevertheless curious to see what life had in store for me next. The endless torrent of crazy and wonderful surprises never ceased to amaze me and I smiled to myself as Airlie Beach came into view.

CHAPTER 10

I WANT TO BE A HIPPY!

TIME WAS TICKING by and no matter how much I wanted to take the batteries out of the clock, I still had farm work to complete. I decided that voluntary placements were the way forward and had searched for possible destinations, emailing my favourites. One of these had been a community near Airlie Beach. Owned by Evie Lark, the description included a temple of love and peace. This I had to see.

Evie had emailed confirming my spot, but when I called her on the day of my arrival she was out of town. She instructed me to go to the market and find a couple, Jo and Nam, who would help me. Mystified at the farming treasure hunt, Lei accompanied me as I scanned the stools for likely candidates. I was told to look for the man selling gems, and it didn't take long to find him. Nam wore rainbow tie-dyed clothes and blonde scraggly dreadlocks swung around his face. In appearance, he was the full stereotypical hippy. Shortly after introducing myself, his girl-friend Jo came over, a little more conservatively dressed, she was also from England and we talked for a while before I followed their directions to the house.

Lei was staying aboard the boat for a few more days before moving on. I wouldn't be seeing her again. I sadly hugged the kind, caring, patient girl who had such an endearing habit of get-ting herself in to trouble, a big heartfelt goodbye. She had been with me all the way from Darwin. Together, we had endured the insect invasion in Kakadu, dived the Great Barrier Reef, survived the Harwoods farm and even sailed the seven seas side by side. She had waited at my bedside in hospitals, helped relieve my stress during car troubles and listened to me drunkenly rave on about boys with beautiful eyes. It was certainly one of the hard-est goodbyes so far, but as with Nik, I had a feeling I would see her again, sometime, somewhere. This girl was too good to lose and we separated with more hugs and promises to keep in touch forever.

*

Nervousness hit me as I headed into the unknown, alone for the first time in months. It was only a short drive to the house and as I pulled up, I noticed once again that it was a home with a differ-ence. A woman in her thirties with long blonde hair and a slen-der but curvy figure, came over to welcome me. Alison had a soft and gentle presence and she took me for a tour of the property. The community area was open with some couches and a kitchen under a large tin roof, joined to it was the temple.

It was beautiful, the floor was decorated with swirled painted patterns in various shades of purple and yellow. To one side was a library of books, everything from spiritual enlighten-ment to Nostradamus' life story and yoga for beginners. Musical instruments were lined up on one side, including guitars, a drum kit, bongos and a keyboard. Beanbags and cushions littered the floor and various works of art adorned the walls. Alison pointed to some stairs which led to an attic room which was rented by Sophie, a young Australian girl and then to the woodland beyond the temple where Jo and Nam camped.

We then followed the path to the main house where Evie lived. My room was a small shed-like structure off to one side. I loved it; it smelt of pinewood, looked newly built and had a chest of drawers and a double bed. The two large windows gave views into the forest which literally came right up to my cabin.

Back at the communal area I met Mel who lived on-site in his large bus. A travelling musician, Mel was in his forties with long curly brown hair, a huge gentle grin and dancing blue eyes. He was certainly a looker and with his kind and gentle manner it made perfect sense when I discovered he had begun a romance with Alison. We sat and talked for some time. I was thrilled to hear that every week they all had a jam session night and that I could join them that evening.

On arriving, the owners of the house gave us a warm welcome and served up food, before Matt played some chords on his guitar. Within seconds he was joined by a drummer, someone on bass, a singer and Alison on her acoustic guitar. Taking it in turns to lead, they followed random rhythms and beats as their heads and feet tapped in time with the music. Occasionally there would be a tune or song that I recognised but it was mostly improvised.

I was encouraged to join in but my musical talent was limited to the odd finger click or out of tune whistle (unless you count my short career playing the triangle when I was ten; I couldn't even handle a recorder). I explained this to the group, but not put off in the slightest, someone pushed a tambourine into my hand. At first I nervously rattled it, not wanting to spoil their sound, but before long my confidence grew and I was banging away like a crazed Abba enthusiast.

I realised that in this environment it was not about musical ability but being a part of the creativity. Having this simple percussion instrument transformed me from spectator, to musician, feeling the rift, rhythm, beats and pulses as they swirled around the small wooden room. The tambourine had been signed by past bearers and one quote caught my attention, 'There are not enough tambourines in rock and roll'. I couldn't have agreed more.

*

That night I went to bed my heart full and head happy. All was at peace with the world, well until I discovered my new roommate, a small huntsman spider. Having adapted to dealing with creepy crawlies, I figured I could handle the situation and would remove him after a quick visit to the bathroom. Unfortunately, as I opened my sliding door, his much larger, uglier, big brother ran straight past me into the room. Unnerved that I was now outnumbered, I began my attempt at being brave. I'm sure they both had a great time laughing at me as I spent the next half an hour chasing the little gits around the cabin, before finally constraining them under a towel. The end of this story is not a happy one, but I'm sure the quick footed, hairy critters are now peacefully relaxing in spider heaven.

*

The next day I helped Mel clear a shed to make room for a worm composting set-up. At one stage he called me across to see a spider that made my previous roommate look like an ant. This time it was a hairy, grey tarantula type creature that was apparently known as a bird-eating spider. I was happy to hear that they usually lived under rocks, not in bedrooms. I moved onto cleaning the house, and as the day went past I began to meet the other members of our little community.

Juan was a tent dwelling, twenty one year old Mexican with a dark beard and frizzy afro. We talked around the fire that evening before being joined by Sophie, a young Australian and the lovable Charlotte from Ireland. They say the Irish have the gift of the gab and Charlotte was a shining example. Staying in a caravan behind the temple, she was both witty and charming. From that first meeting she constantly had me in stitches and we talked for hours, bonding quickly.

Over the next few days I met people from various walks of life who dropped by for cups of tea and a chat. One of these visitors was Alex, an Australian in his late thirties, whom I had met at the jamming session. We got talking about his fishing business. Keen to make up for my past failures I asked if I could join him on his next trip.

*

A few days later I jumped into the Festiva and headed to Alex's, loaded up with a supply of cheese and biscuits to make up for the lack of beer. Sadly we both had to drive, so my fishing tradition of getting plastered would have to be forsaken. Anyway, we wouldn't have time to drink as I would be too busy hauling my enormous catch on board.

Alex had a new boat to test, and we towed it behind his four-wheel drive to a large reservoir. The boat was a simple fiberglass vessel about fifteen metres long. Alex had warned me that the reservoir was a good place to test the boat, not to catch fish. I didn't care, I knew the saying third time lucky and after my failures in Darwin and the Whitsundays this had to be my time to shine.

Also on board were four underwater traps. We were going to plant them in the shallows in an attempt to catch some red claw.

To Australians, the clawed crustaceans were known as yabbies, I knew them as crayfish. We baited the pots with some of my cheese and dropped them into the water. Each was marked by a floating plastic bottle attached to the trap by a rope. We would carry on and fish, returning to the pots on our way back to shore.

The boat sped off across the lake at a scary 50 kph, which felt like 200 in a bouncy fibreglass boat. The weight tank, which held the boat low in the water, had been emptied as a test/totally insane way to discover the effect on sailing ability. I imagined us flipping mid-air as we skimmed across the water almost flying off the lake's surface. I don't know what scared me more, the thought that we could crash and die or that I could end up in with all the fish I was supposed to be catching.

Thankfully before either of those things could happen, Alex slowed down to navigate the half submerged trees. They formed an eerie forest that protruded out of the water like a crowd of wailing banshees. Most of the trees were dead as the flooding of the valley had drowned them, but the tops of their blackened branches stuck out of the water and we used them to anchor while we fished.

Rods in hand, we cast out and reeled in, cast out and reeled in, waiting to feel the bite of a barramundi. Alex moved the boat constantly in search of my trophy fish which I was sure would be waiting in the shallows. He found a good potential fishing spot, but as he leant over the bow to attach the anchor to a branch, the boats rear swung around and hit a tree with a large thud. As it did so, vibrations travelled rapidly through the fibreglass and I turned to see if the vessel had been damaged. I then heard a loud splash and whipping my head back around I saw Alex gasping in the cold water. After a moment of panic he heaved himself out and I exhaled in relief, I wouldn't have to dive into the disgusting water to save him. I politely checked he was ok before unashamedly laughing hysterically at the man who'd graciously invited me here.

Alex hung his clothes on a tree to dry and finished the day fishing in his boxers. Now don't get me wrong, I love the company of half-naked men or fully naked if possible, but Alex didn't come equipped with a great physique. He was tall, lanky and pale and his boxers were a little too tight for comfort. Nevertheless, I averted my eyes and enjoyed his company.

We talked about everything from the weather and travel, to life philosophies and relationships. As the sun began to set, I had long given up on catching a fish, but Alex was somewhat determined. The sun sank lower, lighting up the sky with tones of orange and gold. Then later, the darkness made the sunken trees seem unearthly and their shadows hovered over the water like twisted witches or evil spirits. Eventually I grew tired and cold. The spookiness of the dam and pointless fishing began to get to me and I asked Alex if we could head home.

On the way back to land I felt a flutter of hope, as we searched by torch light for the floating bottles marking our lobster pots. Alex steered the boat past the first trap, as I leaned over, grabbed the float and hauled the pot on board. Inside were about twenty little yabbies! Alex put the bigger ones into a bucket and threw the babies back. The other three pots were also full so our fishing had at least resulted in some success.

Finally, we dragged the boat onto the trailer and drove back to Alex's house. It was a beautiful two story home, set on a hill and the upstairs met with the tops of the trees. Surrounded by forest, it was both peaceful and stunning. Even more impressively, Alex had built the entire thing himself, from the structure, to the electrics and plumbing. The red claw were cooked and Alex wanted me to try a bite. But I couldn't bear to eat those poor little things, even if I had been a co-conspirator to their murder.

I finally headed home happy and exhausted, fish or no fish the day had been a success.

*

Most of my time at the community was spent relaxing on the sofa, chatting and listening to various people play music. Juan, the young Mexican, attempted to teach me the drums. I sounded terrible but no one seemed to care. In this welcoming and friendly place, they just love to see people try. I had also taken to regular sewing, inspired by my bored afternoons in Tully, and one evening, I taught the girls how to make bracelets, just as Lara had taught me the day of my car troubles. Another evening was spent helping Mel with his publicity poster designs. This was definitely a place for the arts.

I finally got to meet Evie who was a huge ball of energy and every inch the hippy with tie-dyed clothes, short dreaded hair and her tiny frame adorned in crystals. One afternoon she began to explain about 2012. I'd heard it mentioned several times and the general notion was that the world would be undergoing a drastic change, possible destruction or that we would live through spirit (this book will not get published until at least 2013, so by the time you read this the truth will be out, which kind of takes the fun out of things).

Evie began to explain a lot very fast, I didn't get all of it, but she mentioned time speeding up and getting ready for this change which she was looking forward to, and then something about living underground. She spoke rapidly and it was an awful lot to try and take in.

There were a few other mysterious conversations that followed, including one with Mel. I asked him about the dam of water in the garden, enquiring if they were going to use it to feed the land or as a haven for wildlife. He casually replied that they needed a water source for when 'they' turned off the taps!

I didn't ask any more, but just nodded knowingly and walked away before I heard anything else which might freak me out. That night I took a book about 'channelling your spirit' to bed and then spent the following week trying to see people's auras. The place was wearing off on me.

*

At our little settlement, the community was working towards a self-sustainable system. There were compost heaps and worm farms, used to create fertiliser to help grow vegetables, plus some unusual toilets. Set on raised platforms, the toilets had no water system but dropped into a big tank. After we finished doing our business, we had to sprinkle some lime and sawdust down the hole to help it all compost. This was much more pleasant than it sounds; there were no toilet brushes, unflushable situations or embarrassing smells. The loos were open air. Yes, outside in the middle of the forest, fortunately with a screen and some trees to protect our modesty.

I remember sitting on the rather too high seat one day, with my feet dangling above the platform, it was dark and all I could see were shadows from the trees. I could hear the sounds of night insects and birds, combined with wafts of music floating over from the temple. It was the most serene toilet experience of my life.

There were two of these systems, one behind the main house, near my room and the other behind the temple. The temple toilet was by far the most flash, with the option of a 'normal' style toilet to sit on (albeit handmade from wood, with a plastic seat glued on top), or if you preferred, there was a squat hole to the left. Steps led up to the platform, but I found them hard to climb as they were too far apart, even for my (if I do say so myself) long legs.

I preferred the toilet on my side of the house which had no steps but was reached via a tree climb. Getting down was the fun part and I normally performed an energetic leap. This feat was assisted by my previously mentioned long legs, but for the likes of Charlotte, who was several feet shorter, the jump became more of a free fall. One day we were discussing the pros and cons of each toilet; a sure sign we had too much time on our hands. Charlotte said that after launching herself back down to earth, she always felt the need to perform a gymnast finish, bending her legs with her feet together and raising her arms above her head, before waiting for imaginary applause from an invisible audience.

*

During my time at Airlie Beach I discovered another of the world's most amazing inventions. In fact, I had seen them many times before but had always passed them off as something for geeks. Rivalling the pop-up tent for sheer genius, I give you the head torch. Yes, they look terrible, and wearing one does cause temporary blindness to anyone you look at, but man are they useful. I borrowed one to go to the loo after mislaying my torch. Once the ugly and uncomfortable thing was affixed to my head, I begrudgingly turned it on and was taken by surprise. Everywhere that I looked, I could see! Simple, but effective. How had I ever lived without one?

As Charlotte pointed out there were a few side effects. Of course insects are attracted to light and as in Charlotte's case, if you have an unprecedented but traumatic fear of moths, the head torch can distress. Needless to say the next day I headed to the dollar shop and bagged one.

*

Charlotte had been working in a bar which she hated with a passion. The boys who worked there ignored her, the bosses kept her tips and she didn't even get free food. I could almost see the cloud of depression growing thicker and thicker every time she left for work. So we were all overjoyed when she came home one day and told us she had quit.

The two of us celebrated in style, spending the following day doing absolutely nothing. Yes, really, twelve hours of nothing. It all started about 10 a.m. as we had a cup of tea together on the couch, then the hours flew by and our breakfast chat moved into lunch. We cooked and made more tea as the others began to arrive back from work. As the sun set they built a fire. Charlotte and I made the ten metres from the couch to sit around it. More chatting ensued until everyone moved into the temple to jam. I made the huge effort of heaving myself another fifteen metres to a bean bag and played my heart out on the tambourine, before finally crashing into bed at 10 p.m.

*

Juan the Mexican worked in a sail shop. The owners had a boat and were competing in the Airlie Beach races. He invited me to go racing with them. I was sleepy and groggy from the previous day's laziness, so when he woke me at 6 a.m. I told him to go without me. Walking out of my room he told me, 'No problem you just miss the experience. You only have this one chance, but its ok stay in bed, your choice …'

I was up in a flash. Damn him and his clever words.

We were running late, which wasn't actually my fault, but either way the boat was sailing out of the harbour and the crew were not impressed as we ran along the jetty shouting for them to stop. Fortunately, they threw us a rope and we pulled the boat close enough to hop on board.

As we sailed towards the starting line the skipper gave me my instructions. I was there to add weight to the boat, which I tried not to take too personally. I would help increase the turning or *tack* speed. I wasn't alone in my weighty task and five of us sat along one side, our feet dangling over the rail. The other crew generally shouted a lot and pulled ropes manically, while we scrambled under the boom to the opposite rail every time someone yelled 'Tack!' in a loud, scary voice.

Everyone on board took it awfully seriously and the whole experience was extremely intense. The monohulled boat leaned almost completely on its side, as I desperately tried to climb to the other rail before I slid overboard, scraping my legs and usually hitting my head on the boom along the way. It was a little too much for me at seven in the morning. Fortunately the wind dropped on the way towards the finish and although the crew were pissed off with the slowness of pace, I enjoyed a leisurely chat with some of my fellow tackers.

We came third in our division, which apparently wasn't our fault. All the boats had handicap scores as they were so different in design. According to the crew, our handicap was so low that we never stood a chance of winning. If that was the case, I thought they should chill out and stop with all the screaming, but some things are best left unsaid.

*

Back at the house I had decided that it was time to do something about the state of my car. Not that there was any chance I was going to get it repaired, but areas which had been damaged during the crash were beginning to rust. Once again I consulted my father for advice, before heading off to purchase anti-rust paint. I tried to find a colour to match the car but its greeny aqua appeared to be unique. In the end I settled for blue.

Back at the house I began to scrub away any existing rust and paint over the metal with the new blue. There were more spots in need of attention than I had imagined, and by the time I had finished, the damaged side looked like a polka dot collage. At the farm in Tully I had stuck some flower stickers to the sides and decided that I needed someone with an artistic flare to blend the whole thing together. Alison had painted the property's rain tank and so I left her with the blue paint and told her to be creative.

On my return I was overjoyed to find that my Festiva now had rolling blue waves down the side and little fish by the wheel. Alison had used marker pen to highlight the fish, and later we found white paint to add foam to the waves and a map of Australia, with my route drawn on. Enthused, I gathered some spray paint to colour my boot pink and the back bumper cream, allowing space for people to write me messages. To finish the piece, Alison signed her name inside the curve of a wave. Charlotte was most impressed and left me a hilarious message/ rhyme about our time together, on the back.

*

The time at Airlie passed quickly and in keeping with my self-imposed limit I would soon be leaving. I wanted to try a variety of farms and lifestyles and not get caught up in one place. To see me off with a bang there was a party being held at Evie's other community in Mackay about 200 kms away. Ok, so it wasn't really a party for me, Evie was actually going away to trek through Nepal for six weeks. Anyway, a party is a party and I was certainly looking forward to this one.

Charlotte and Juan were also coming along. By this time Juan and I had experienced a few run-ins. He was basically a cheap-skate using git, but annoyingly also a nice friendly guy who you couldn't get angry with, well until that Friday. In general Juan ate everyone else's food, used everyone's phone credit, never washed up and constantly took the piss. He wanted a lift in my car to the party. In itself this was not a problem, but knowing how unreliable he was I warned him to be ready at 2 p.m. or be left behind. Getting stuck in Airlie would cause him huge problems as he was due to leave Australia the following day. He had found work on a boat in the Fiji Islands and he had to be in Mackay to catch the flight.

Myself and Charlotte, were ready to go at 1.30 p.m. There was no sign of Juan, and his tent and belongings, which still needed packing, were scattered all over the community. I texted him a warning but heard nothing in reply (no doubt his phone had no credit). At 2 p.m. I called him and was told he had to finish something at his work, but please could I wait for him. I reluctantly agreed, but I was getting frustrated. I didn't want to drive in the dark and it was a few hours to the city. At 2.55 p.m. a breathless Juan jumped out of a car and began to dash around packing things up. I wanted to kill him.

When he was eventually ready, I hugged Mel goodbye and took a couple of photos of us all. Juan had the cheek to ask, in all seriousness, if we could please hurry up! Everyone else burst out laughing, knowing full well that I had been sitting around waiting for over two hours. I snarled at him under a fake smile.

We pulled out onto the road, pleased to be on our way, when a voice from the back seat requested, 'Girls could we just stop by my work ...' He needed to collect his pay, but as the shop was only around the corner we pulled in.

Once again we set off, before he leaned forward and dubiously asked if we could stop at a bookstore. That's why he had wanted me to hurry with my picture taking, to catch the store before it closed. I think I may have turned red with horns sprouting from my forehead, but he told us the book was essential to his trip and they wouldn't let him on the boat without it. Fortunately, the store was the last stop, but I cursed as we tried to find the house in the dark and Juan slept blissfully in the back seat.

Upon arrival I was happy to eject him from my car and told him to make sure he hadn't forgotten anything. The next morning after his departure, I found his waterproof jacket on the seat.

Ants swarmed it and mouldy food sat in the pockets. The ants stayed in my car for weeks and I sincerely hope that Juan spent his trip, shivering, cold and wet without the jacket.

*

The party was a great success. While the adults set up, I played with the children on the rope swing, climbed trees and learnt how to fire twirl. Yes, that's right, children playing with fire. The children had been home schooled and I was witnessing the results. I spoke to one of the parents about the benefits. The children were told to focus, instead of the usual 'no' or 'put that down'. Rather than keeping them away from dangers such as knives and fire, the kids were taught to think before they acted and to understand the risks.

Lei had also met an Aussie family who lived by the same principles. She had looked on with horror as the three-year-old walked past with a kitchen knife and then cooked pancakes on the stove, completely unsupervised. Much to Lei's amazement the young girl successfully cooked breakfast for her family most days.

That night in Mackay, I watched in awe as the eight-year-old boy who had given me the lesson, twirled and threw the fire stick with practiced expertise. He was joined by other children, older and younger, before the adults took their turn, including myself. Even with my clumsy attempts no one singed a hair and the atmosphere was electric. Orbs of fire whizzed around leaving trails of light in their wake and bongos played soothingly in the background. Giant fluorescent flags and various fire bins set the scene, as numerous people played an array of instruments. There was even a comedian who simultaneously played the accordion to fit in with her stories and jokes. Eventually the children went to bed and a few hours later I retired to my tent, but as I fell asleep the sound of electro beats filled the air and the party continued until daybreak.

*

I woke up feeling a little worse for wear. A lack of sleep and half a case of beer most likely the cause, but travel waits for no woman and I still had a visa to earn. Next up, voluntary venue number three! I had decided that each placement must offer a totally different experience, so I would be waking up at a hippy commune and going to bed on an Aussie cattle station.

Chapter 11

The Naked Cowgirl

THE DRIVE TO the cattle station was a long one. It took most of the day and I was forever grateful for the 160GB iPod that I had purchased back in Darwin. Radio stations were constantly in and out of signal and peppered with static. It took longer than planned, darkness fell and my satellite navigation refused to acknowledge the bumpy dirt road which supposedly led to the station. I wondered if I would ever find the place.

Eventually, tired, hungover, exhausted and slightly deranged, I emerged from the Festiva to greet my new hosts at Ducks Meadow station. Shaun and Sarah were both in their forties, well presented, well-spoken people. I had bags under my eyes, my hair was a mess and I was hardly capable of holding a polite conversation. They invited me for dinner, and I tried my best to be friendly before apologising excessively and heading to bed. It was brief and I felt a little rude, but my body needed to rest.

I would be staying in my own room, this time in the homestead.

I opened the door and relaxed upon seeing the neat and tidy room which housed a comfortable double bed.

*

On awakening the next day I realised that Ducks Meadow wasn't what I had expected. I imagined the cattle station to be the epiphany of stereotypical Australian life. In my mind it would be rough and rugged, run by men who were men and didn't take any flack. Where cows were valued by the meat they carried and work was tough. The owners would have a strong Aussie drool, swear a lot and carry a hip flask of whiskey. They would wear jeans, boots and cowboy hats. Stations were places where dust and dirt hovered in the air and every day was a struggle to push the cattle to profit.

In an extreme contrast, Ducks Meadow was actually lush and green, the cows were more chilled out than a hippy in Nimbin and the owners were well dressed, pleasant mannered and very open-minded. This was no ordinary cattle station. Shaun had inherited the farm from his father, it had then been split between three brothers and Shaun had controversially begun to practice bio-dynamic farming.

This was a new concept to me. When first explained, I admit it sounded slightly crazy. But, having seen the reality, I must also admit that they could be onto something. The principles were based upon the work of someone called Steiner. He believed the best way to cultivate land was to use natural products and to avoid man-made chemicals. Using what initially comes from the earth to return the goodness to the soil. However, do not confuse this with organic practices. It gets far more interesting.

I cannot even pretend to understand the basics of bio-dynamics, however, I will tell you what I saw. During my stay we filled 1,200 cows' horns, which came straight from an abattoir and stank of rotting flesh, with cow shit that had been lovingly collected from a field by yours truly. We then buried these in a pit. Apparently, after six months underground, Shaun would dig them up and the poo from inside the horns would have properties which enhanced the land.

Say what you like about bio-dynamics, but Ducks Meadow was in beautiful condition, even the grass was far greener than that of the surrounding land. The cattle looked healthy and strong and Shaun believed in low stress cattle management. No nasty cattle prods on this farm.

On my first day, Shaun took me on the quad bike to show me the station. As I gazed at the passing country he told me all about the land, its history and explained more about the farming. They used a system called cell grazing. The paddocks were much smaller than most stations, but the cattle were moved more regularly. Cell grazing was designed to let the land recover in-between cattle feeding and seemed to be working well. The best part was that the cows were so used to being moved they practically mustered themselves. At the paddock gate the cows rushed to meet us and after a quick drop of the electric fence they trotted past, excited at the prospect of fresh grass. I was most impressed by this, as their good behaviour would be a big help to me.

Shaun and Sarah were going on a trip for a week and leaving me to run the station. I would spend the first morning alone before being joined by Dorothy, an older lady and family friend. Well you all know how my first morning alone went. The beginning of this book should have left you hanging with suspense as the cattle disappeared over the horizon. My first attempt at mustering had been a complete disaster and I dreaded having to tell Shaun.

Short of driving all over the station to round up the herd, there was nothing I could do. Thankfully I was able to fix up the electric tape by disconnecting it and tying it back together.

I then hopped onto the quad and solemnly headed back to the homestead. Begrudgingly, I dialled Shaun's mobile and informed him that after only a few hours in charge, I had lost his herd. Thankfully he chuckled and told me not to worry. The cows were now simply a paddock ahead of schedule. I breathed a sigh of relief and waited for Dorothy to arrive.

She was a character and had plenty of tales to tell from her 72 years. Every day we changed the rugs on Sarah's horses, walked the cattle dogs and moved the herds. Thankfully my second attempt at mustering was a little less dramatic. The rest of the time I had intended to spend writing, but Dorothy and I usually ended up gossiping and sewing around the fire.

Dorothy was witty and interesting, but as the days passed I started to miss the company of people my own age. As her stories ran out, Dorothy began to bitch and moan about all the local people who bitch and moan. She appeared not to notice the irony, but it certainly wasn't lost on me. I had finally met someone who could talk as much as I could and it wasn't fun being on the receiving end. I just hope for the sake of this book that my tales are slightly more entertaining.

On the verge of insanity, a ray of hope appeared in the shape of a telephone call. Shaun rang to tell us that a previous volunteer was returning to show a friend the farm. *Wooo hooo!* It was all I could do to stop myself from jumping for joy, but I kept a straight face so I didn't offend my fellow station sitter.

The next day Dorothy and I headed into town to pick up who would hopefully be my new best friends. Cedric was a skinny, ragged looking Frenchman who was joined by a cute Japanese girl, Aya. I was pleased to learn Cedric knew a lot about the farm and would be happy to show me around the area.

The next morning, I took Aya with me to move the cattle, eager to make the most of the youthful company. There were three mobs on Ducks Meadow: the cows, the weaners and the two-year-olds. The cows were mothers with babies, the weaners had just been separated from the mothers and the two-year-olds would be off to market soon. We were moving the weaners and Aya looked on camera poised, as I gingerly opened the fence. Aya squealed with excitement as the young cows bounded past to fresh grass, mooing loudly as they went. I was thankful not to have lost any more beef.

Over the following days, Aya and Cedric helped me around the farm with the list of jobs Shaun had left me. Dorothy returned to town, presumably to resume her routine of socialising with the people who made her complain so much. A few days later Sarah and Shaun returned to the farm refreshed and relaxed from their break and with some exciting news. They had purchased a mob of seventy cattle, all pregnant or with calves and the herd would be arriving later that day.

That afternoon we heard a rumble coming up the track and raced out to greet our new arrivals. A huge road train appeared, dwarfing my little Festiva as it headed towards the cattle yards. Towed behind the giant cab were two huge trailers with top and bottom decks. Cows peeked from between the gaps, looking around with a nervous curiosity.

Unloading the truck provided us with great entertainment as the cattle wandered down gang planks and into the yards. Some of the more hesitant ones had to be shooed out by the truck driver and Shaun, who looked like tiny ants as they climbed the enormous trailers. The cows were then left in the yard overnight to settle and so mothers could find their babies if any had become separated in the confusion.

*

The following morning I hopped on the back of the quad with Shaun. We were accompanied by three of the dogs. The dogs at

Ducks were working animals and unlike house pets, lived in pens outside and were only let out for walks or work. It was great to finally see them in action. Our task for the day was to move the new cows slowly around the paddocks. This would gently introduce them to the new farm and make sure they didn't give in to their natural homing instinct and head off to their old station. They had come from a place nearly 1,000 kms north, so it would have been a long walk

I watched while the dogs rounded the cattle and chased any stragglers back to the herd. Every ten minutes or so Shaun would instruct the dogs and move the mob across the paddock. This gave me plenty of time to talk to him about the farm, the industry and cattle in general.

I was particularly interested in their behaviour. During my time mustering, I had been very wary of the cows. I knew from my milking days that they tended to be scared of humans, but was also aware that many animals can become aggressive if they feel threatened. I didn't fancy my chances against a charging cow.

Shaun told me cattle were pretty docile as long as you didn't put them under too much pressure. He explained how to apply pressure by moving towards the cows. If the animals moved in the correct direction then I should continue slowly. If they stopped or turned towards me, then I should pause and remove the pressure. Basically cows needed time to think, if they were being forced into a small space, like a gate, it could make them nervous, but they were also wary of the person behind them. The poor things often needed a minute to assess the situation and conclude that it was far safer to stay with the group and move forward, than it was to confront the human behind. However, without this thinking time, they might panic and charge.

Of course after a while the cattle learnt what was best and were very easy to handle. Well, with the exception of my first attempt. Shaun even employed a man to train the cows and once again this was done without cattle prods or aggressive treatment.

Shaun's advice gave me confidence, and I felt happy to muster alone. Occasionally, a curious cow would come over to sniff me and although no longer afraid, I always made a mental note of the nearest fence. It only took a second to duck under the electrified tape. Thankfully I never needed to use this tactic.

Aside from the trampling of the fence the only other incident was a messy one. I'd been rushing to close a fence and as I ran, my gumboot got stuck in the mud/cow shit. My body propelled forward but my boot stayed behind engulfed calf deep in sludge. Tripping, I bellyflopped onto a squelchy landing with Aya and no doubt the cows, laughing hysterically.

*

Ducks Meadow consisted of flat, green fields, punctuated by ragged hills of dense rocky forest. One afternoon Cedric took the ute and drove Aya and I to the bottom of a large mount. We jumped out of the car and set off up into the hills. Previously, the thought of walking without a track would have been unthinkable, but Cedric reassured me that on this farm it was hard to get lost. He encouraged me to pay attention to my surroundings: the way the hills lay, where they joined the paddocks and where the homestead was in relation to the landscape. As we climbed higher, I was pleased that we had such a good guide. Without a path, the scrub was hard to navigate, but Cedric walked ahead looking for an easy route and holding branches out of our way.

Finally, we came upon a rock face which overlooked the station. The view was beautiful and we could see the house, water dams and cows from our private lookout. After a quick breather we ventured around the top, exploring caves, seeing Aboriginal art, and even finding a snake skin which I picked up to keep. On the way back to the house the fun didn't stop, as Aya and I rode in the ute tray as it bounced across the paddocks and kangaroos bounded into the shrubbery.

*

The following evening, Cedric drove us to another hilltop where we would camp overnight, before waking to watch the sunrise over the farm. That night we sat around a fire talking and sharing stories. Aya was fairly quiet, but I was intrigued by the Frenchman.

Cedric had lived an interesting life. He'd been homeless and lived with heroin junkies, but always kept off the drugs. He'd been in political riots and had a very different outlook on life. Even as a backpacker he was travelling in an unconventional manner. Since his arrival in Australia, Cedric had captured two wild camels and tried to train them, with the intention of riding them to India. Sadly, he didn't complete the task and the camels had remained unbroken. But the plan didn't end there. He would now travel to Cambodia and walk to India!

He had also been hitch-hiking through the outback. He had asked one driver to drop him by the side of the road in the middle of nowhere. The concerned truckie reluctantly agreed, leaving Cedric to walk 20 kms from the roadside into the desert. Once there, he camped for a night before trekking back to the road in the blistering heat. Why? I asked. So he could know how it felt to be totally alone. I found it completely insane and intriguing.

I will take a moment, to warn how dangerous this was. It is not something I would recommend to anyone. Many people have lost their lives to the Australian land. During my travels I read *The Lost Boy* by Robert Wainwright. It is about a boy who went missing from his family home next to the desert highway. In an amazing demonstration of community spirit over 1,500 people joined the search for the child, along with the army and a whole squadron of helicopters and planes. They searched for days on end from the air and ground, with dogs, maps and Aboriginal trackers, with a headstrong determination. Sadly, the poor child wasn't found in time. The boy was only eight years old and his body was eventually discovered less than 20 kilometres from his home. Even in an empty desert, close to the highway with an army of searchers, the outback claimed its find.

Cedric's decision was not a safe one, but this man had something different about him. His instincts were almost animal-like. That night as we were sitting around the fire with music playing, he suddenly jumped up. Swiftly running ten metres to a bush, he called for us to join him. Rustling about in the foliage was an echidna. Over the noise of the iPod and our chatter he had heard the creature and more impressively been able to pinpoint its exact location in seconds; remarkable to say the least.

Groggy from our campfire beers, we arose at 5 a.m. to watch the sunrise over the plain. Crawling directly from my tent to the view, it felt incredible to literally wake up with the sun. As the glowing orb crept higher, my sleepiness lifted and a rush of revitalisation washed over me. To heighten the experience, we saw Shaun in the paddock below and watched with delight as the dogs herded the new cattle towards their next field.

*

The next morning, we had more visitors, another French former volunteer, Philip, along with his brother Mathieu and cousin Adrian. I had also driven the Land Cruiser into town to collect two Taiwanese workers, so we had a full house. There would be plenty for us to see and do as it was time to brand our new cattle.

I was a little unsure about the branding. After all, I was an animal loving veggie who hated violence and gore. Images of burning flesh and distressed cattle flashed in my mind, but once again the reality was far from the stereotype.

The cows were herded into the yard where they walked

through a corridor of metal gates. One at a time, they were let into the branding booth where Shaun closed a metal vice around their heads to hold them in place. This caused more trauma than the actual branding, which only took a few seconds and most of the time didn't even cause them to flinch. The whole process took less than ten seconds, and we all took turns in branding, controlling the gates and taking pictures—another great Australian experience.

Philip, Mathieu and Adrian left to continue their trip, and again Shaun and Sarah were going away. Aya and Cedric also had to move on. I would be running the farm once more, but this time with the two Taiwanese.

I tried with the girls I really did, but they had no interest in anything but cooking. I told them everything I knew about the farm, took them mustering and offered a camping trip, but I was met with serious faces and suggestions that we watch a DVD. So it was alone that I set off to conquer Ducks Meadow's highest peak.

In fact, I had no idea if it was even possible, but I would try. I had recalled Cedric mentioning difficult rock faces, so first I circled the base with the quad planning my route. Having picked the safest looking start point, I headed upwards. I tried to ignore the brush scratching at my arms and prayed I wouldn't tread on a snake, as I literally beat around the bush.

At times, I thought it would be impossible and almost turned back. Instead I indulged in the power of positive thought, realising that if I thought it was impossible, it would probably become so. Determination is a wonderful thing and I grasped at it like a life ring as I trekked upwards. By this time my thin trousers had ripped across one leg, then, as I squeezed between a rock and a tree, a branch caught me and tore away their backside. I would be completing my hike wearing a camouflage patterned, pair of arseless chaps.

I knew the rock face was too steep to climb, so I was intending to approach it from one side. This I achieved, but it was still a scramble across boulders with a dangerously steep drop directly below. The view was breathtaking, although I had to force myself to stop looking down until I had safely reached the peak.

Finally, breathless and trembling, I made it. I sat back and relaxed, the sense of pride and achievement was worth every scrape and bruise on my body. The air was fresh, the view intoxicating and my mind felt invigorated and alive. I took a few minutes to catch my breath, when I had an idea.

A few months ago Cedric had been looking after the station by himself and spent a day working in the nude. Why not he had said, no one would be around to see. Channelling his spirit, I stripped off and stepped forward to the cliff edge. The breeze sent tingles through my naked body, and I was filled with a sense of uplifting liberation. The farmland stretched before me, green and endless. The air around me was silent, bar the gentle hum of insects and leaves bristling in the breeze. I was alone with the power of the world. My mind, spirit and body were simultaneously buzzing with electric vibrancy.

After resting and enjoying my very natural experience, I put on my arseless chaps and took the obligatory photos before beginning the steep descent. The sharp drop made me just as anxious as the climb. This time I took a different direction, which was unplanned but I simply had to make progress wherever the land allowed. The bank slipped away so quickly it was hard to stop myself sliding all the way down, bumping off trees and rocks. Somehow I managed to keep control and after what seemed like an eternity I was back on flat ground.

I said a quick thank you to the universe for getting me out

alive, before heading back to the sanctuary of the homestead. On arrival I smiled broadly at the two Taiwanese girls. They looked back warily as they eyed my dirty face, twig filled hair and finally, my bare wobbling buttocks and mud clad G-string as I headed up to the shower.

When Shaun returned a few days later I coolly told him of my achievement. I waited for his surprise and praise but instead he replied, 'Oh! If you go through paddock five, it's an easy stroll to the top of that hill. Then you can just follow a track straight across to the peak, I've taken backpackers there a few times. It's fairly simple …'

Suddenly my adventure seemed a little less bold and a lot more foolish, but nothing could take away my naked moment alone with the world.

CHAPTER 12

A COLLECTION OF GEMS

MY NEXT PLAN of action was a vague one. It was coming up to my 28th birthday, and usually I would organise a day out, followed by dinner and a club, surrounded by all my friends. This year would be very different. I was thousands of miles from anyone I knew, and as much as I loved Ducks Meadow, I didn't want to celebrate by squelching around in mud and cow dung.

Cedric had mentioned a place called Sapphire up in the gem fields which sounded intriguing. He had found over $2,000 worth of gems there and had sent most of them back to France for saving. He had held on to two, which looked like small rocks but when held up to the light became transparent and shiny. In Sapphire it had rained and after, he walked around collecting the stones as they glinted in the light. He had even drawn me a treasure map listing the good hunting spots.

Back in the UK, jewellery catalogues advertised necklaces with different stones for different birthdays. My birthday is September and the stone is a sapphire. It had to be an omen. I decided to go out on a limb and head to the gem fields a couple of days before my birthday. I'd be sure to at least make a few friends.

As it happened, the only time I spent alone was during the drive. By chance, fate or coincidence, Shaun and Sarah had received an email from Philip saying that he had returned to France, but that his brother and cousin had met up with Aya and were heading to Sapphire together. It seemed it was a small country after all. The drive up was relaxing. I had finally come to terms with Aussie distances. Five hours in the car was nothing.

*

Sapphire was small and dusty; it looked desolate except for a run-down petrol station, caravan park and a few small shops selling sapphires. Cedric had mentioned a free camping area and there I would reunite with the others. I found it by the side of the main street. A dirt area inhabited by five or so caravans, it looked like a gypsy camp. I recognised the boy's ancient van, which they had purchased for the measly sum of $500. Parking alongside, I texted them and ten minutes later we were sharing lunch at the picnic table. I was looking forward to hearing about their sapphire search, as they had been out fossicking that morning. Unfortunately their hunt had gone unrewarded.

There were three ways to search for gems. First there was specking, which involved walking around, preferably bent over, looking for the stones as they shone in the light. Cedric had found most of his using this method, aided by the rain which made the glassy stones shine. There was not a cloud in sight, so no rain for us, but there were stories of people simply coming upon stones as they went about their daily lives.

The second method was the most efficient. A sieve could be taken to any public area and used to sort through the dirt. Most people we met, bagged up the gravelly rock and took it to a wash. Again water was used to make the stones visible. Aya and the boys informed me that they had been specking for nearly two hours and had found nothing. They had decided to hire shovels and sieves the next day.

In the meantime they had opted for option number three, which in my opinion was cheating. In the gem shops, mines and caravan parks, it was possible to purchase bags of wash. These were buckets of dirt cleared from the mines. Cedric had warned against them, as most had been checked for big stones and apparently the suppliers added enough small chips to keep the tourists happy. The more you paid for the bag of wash, the bigger the stones inside.

I thought it took all the fun out of the hunt; it would be like fishing in a goldfish bowl. The others had bought a bucket of wash and found a couple of sapphires big enough to cut. This was key. Sapphires only had value if they were large enough to cut and be used in jewellery. I objected to my friends cheating, but they told me they needed help distinguishing the stones.

When sapphires were hidden in the dirt, they basically resembled any other small rock. Included in the price of the bucket was a demonstration of how to find the gems, which they told me was a big help. I listened with interest, but deep down I knew I didn't want to take the easy option. It had no satisfaction. Driven on by Cedric's stories I had a feeling that, like him, if I went specking I would find my fated stone.

*

An hour and a half later, I begrudgingly drove up the road to buy a bucket of wash. The law of attraction had clearly failed me. I must admit, my new travel partners had been right, it did make a difference knowing how to spot them. I first embarked on a mine tour, led by Nigel. He was around my age, which surprised me as I hadn't seen anyone under fifty around town.

I chose my bucket and Nigel showed me how to shake the sieve full of dirt over a wheelbarrow, before dipping the leftovers in water. I then had to pulse the sieve up and down in the water. As sapphires are heavier than dirt, they were supposed to group in the middle. The wet gravel was then tipped onto a mat and sorted through. I was looking for any sign of a sparkle or shine using the aid of the sun that was burning brightly behind me. I was completely useless at the technique, but there were so many small pieces in my bucket, it was impossible not to find some.

I was told that there were fifty-seven colours of sapphire, the Heinz variety of gemstones, so it was not just the famous deep blue I looked for. I picked out anything that was vaguely transparent whether it be blue, yellow or green. After I'd finished, Nigel looked through my finds only to tell me what I had already suspected. I had nothing of value. At least now I understood the technique and would be prepared when we hired our own equipment the following day.

*

We slept at the campground, Aya and I in our tents and the French cousins outside next to the picnic table. They didn't own tents and had no intention of buying them. The boys were travelling cheap and planned to sell the car as it was too expensive on fuel. Trying to keep belongings and cost to a minimum, they slept just in their sleeping bags, ate out of ice cream tubs at dinner and had cornflakes served in plastic cups for breakfast. They owned two forks and one spoon which were currently being shared between three of them. The boys didn't see the point in wasting money on commodities that were not necessary. This was quite a contrast to my full portable kitchen, airbed, self-pitching tent, doona and numerous pillows. Several times I offered them use of my plates or cutlery, but it was always refused.

One day Aya headed off to the paid campground showers,

and I looked on curiously as the French lads went towards the truck wash. They were in for an extreme shower. I enquired why they hadn't gone with Aya. Apparently the camp site charged $5 for a shower, and that was too expensive. Their tightness was worth far more than $5 in entertainment and I watched on laughing as they shivered in the street, shampooing under the cold but powerful hose.

*

The next morning, armed with vast amounts of enthusiasm, we headed to the dry creek bed with our shovels and sieves. The others wanted to sit and dig in the creek in front of the caravan park. For a short time I was happy with this, but after an hour with no success I began to get restless. I started to talk with other diggers who all told me that in order to see the stones, they would have to be wet. I mentioned this to the boys, but they remained uninterested. We didn't have any water or access to a wash. Not to be held back, I found a muddy puddle and lugged my bag of gravel to it. There I stood, ankle deep in mud, sliding around trying to rinse my sieve, before turning it over onto the ground.

Half an hour later still nothing. Screw that, I had a better plan. If all else fails go shopping and it was Sapphire's market day. I made my excuses and went for some retail therapy. Unsurprisingly, the main produce was gemstones. I wandered around chatting to the stall holders, who were more than happy to tell me about their wares and how they had come upon them. I wanted a piece of sapphire jewellery as a birthday present to myself, but nothing took my fancy.

Returning to the creek and my friends, I made a pathetic attempt to look interested in fossicking, but it seemed so fruitless. The others however were hooked, convinced they were about to come upon something of huge worth. But in reality they only found tiny gems that were ten a penny.

We continuously heard stories of valuable finds, but these tales had one thing in common. The people involved were extremely dedicated to their search. Most of them had been there at least six weeks and spent hours upon hours fossicking; not the kind of commitment I was prepared to give. To me this was supposed to be bit of fun and it certainly wasn't living up to Cedric's description. Then again, I didn't share his finely tuned senses, sharp eyes or his patience.

My birthday was the following day, and I announced that it would be my last in Sapphire. After a morning fossicking I would drive to Emerald, a nearby town with more than one pub. The area had been named after the colour of the grass not the gemstone, so no more fossicking but we could hit the bars for some celebrations. The others agreed to join me. Nigel from the mine had recommended a few pubs, one of which had a topless barmaid. It was no doubt the most exciting and controversial thing happening in this rural sandpit, so I had to go. First though, one more morning sitting in the dust.

*

On the day of my 28th birthday I woke up next to a stallion. No really, an actual stallion. A group of horses had wandered into our campground and one was currently licking my flyscreen. I shooed him away and watched laughing as they moved on to sniff around the caravans, scaring the unsuspecting sleepy inhabitants. That wasn't the end of our on-site wildlife and later that day a herd of cows stopped by. There's no place like the country.

It was the last day of our sapphire hunt and I was still frustrated by our tactics. I felt our usual search location was probably a waste of time. Everyone who came to Sapphire fossicked in the creek. It was the tourist area and had been sifted through a million times. Again I voiced my opinion, but no one seemed to care. Cedric's map had our current position marked as 'crap place'. I slipped it into my pocket and set off, driving further along the creek. The others could stay where they were, but this was my birthday and I was on a mission.

Eventually the road stopped by a deserted area of the gravel creek. I first meandered up and down the dusty riverbed enjoying the sun warming my back as I scanned the ground. Having no luck, I returned to the car, collected my sieve and chose a spot near a tree root. These, I had been told, were where stones would often get caught. They would have been washed downstream in the wet seasons over the past centuries and beyond.

I relaxed in the heat, listening to the breeze in the trees and bird song in the air. It was a moment of total tranquillity, just me, the creek and nature. Sapphires were just a bonus, this was a day for inner happiness, and I felt at peace with the world.

After sieving for some time, I left the tree root and moved to a heap of dirt that, for no logical reason, had been attracting my attention. I shook through a couple more sieves as a pastime rather than a search. Then, as I rattled the last little pieces of sand and rock around on the wire mesh, I saw it. A tiny but beautiful gem, it resembled the small pieces of polished glass which wash up on beaches. I cried out in delight. I couldn't believe it. I had long given up on finding anything. Clear pale blue, with streaks of green and transparent in patches, it was too small to be cut, but it didn't matter, to me this was perfection. I had found my birthday present.

I tucked it safely away and continued on with new found hope. Every few minutes I couldn't resist retrieving the gem from my purse and looking at it. I didn't stay much longer, not wanting to spoil my elation with more hours baking in the barren creek. Nothing else mattered I had my stone, so I set off to show the others.

They too had found tiny pieces, but to them it meant nothing.

They were more interested in getting their bucket finds cut and trying to make money from them. The French boys had been told that cutting in Thailand was far cheaper, so their sapphires were to be stowed away until further notice. My stone meant a great deal to me, although worthless financially I wanted to make the most of it and so headed to the gem shops.

The shops had trays of empty jewellery in which the public could have their stones set. Mine may have been too small to cut, but I was sure it could be clamped into something. After being turned away at several shops, where the owners didn't understand sentimental value, I finally found help.

The two women behind the counter suggested gluing the sapphire to a piece of jewellery, but I was afraid that it would fall off and be lost. After careful selection, I arranged to have it fixed into a sterling silver ring. Happy birthday to me! The silver cost more than the sapphire was worth but I didn't care in the slightest. I left town with a warm fuzzy feeling and a beautiful new ring that to me, was worth more than money itself.

*

My birthday celebrations were far from over and our next destination was a bottle shop to stock up on booze before heading to the free camping in Emerald. This time the ground was near the botanical gardens, a pretty place down by the river. It would have been a tranquil setting, had it not been for the railway overpass and large main road which ran alongside. The drinking began in the parklands, and I was fairly plastered before we even left for the pub.

On our way to the chosen bar I stopped and invited everyone in the camp site to join us, but my rather overenthusiastic, drunken manner must have scared them off. Undeterred, the four off us walked across town in great spirits, led by myself swinging around signposts along the way.

Emerald was dead as a doornail so I wasn't expecting much. All the bars we passed were empty, so I was surprised to find a young and bright crowd inside a hotel. They were chatting loudly, playing pool and upbeat tunes blasted from the juke box.

Aya and I were celebrating victory as we beat the boys at pool, when I noticed a man walking past, proudly displaying what was definitely a girl's handbag. He didn't come across as camp but was clearly enjoying his moment in the limelight as everyone gave him curious stares. Being a nosey little bugger, I made a beeline for him, 'Why are you wearing a girl's handbag?' I enquired, with as much tact as Borat on a bender.

A whole table of people stared silently back at me, before a girl laughed and told me it was hers. We got talking and before long everyone was wishing me a happy birthday, buying me drinks and then the shots came out. The rest of the night was a blur, but I do remember chatting to the topless waitress and making everyone tip her, introducing Aya and the boys to my new friends and then heading to another bar. I believe I then salsa danced with a big fat man in an otherwise empty pub, before being carried home by the French boys. The night finished with me insisting I didn't need a tent, pillow or mattress and that sleeping under the bridge was going to be the best thing ever. The two boys rolled their eyes and lay down nearby. Everyone was almost asleep as I piped up, 'Heeeeeeelllllllloooooooooo, I want a bedtime story.'

And bless them, they actually made one up. I don't think that night could have gone any better if planned. Fate and friendship had seen me happy once more.

*

Hungover and happy we headed for the coast. En route were the Blackwater Tablelands, a national park set high in the mountains, where we spent a couple of days walking, swimming and talking round the fire. The boy's old van hardly made it up the hill and I laughed as they opened up the bonnet to let the engine cool. My Festiva may have been battered and bruised but she still had stamina.

After our days in the national park we arrived in Rockhampton and I let the boys decide where to stay. Maybe not such a good idea, as we ended up camping illegally outside the tourist information office next to a main road and much to my dismay, fifty metres from a graveyard. Although it still had grandeur, as we were sleeping directly over the tropic of Capricorn. After a terrible night's sleep, I said goodbye to Mathieu who was returning home. Adrian, the remaining Frenchman would be staying in 'Rocky' to try and sell the van, while Aya wished to continue with me. I had found my next travel partner.

*

The plan was to head south, stopping at Fraser Island, the world's largest sand Island, before doing a final spate of farming. We agreed to keep in touch with Adrian, and to meet up with him again further down the coast. Just as we set off, rain began to hammer down and I exercised extra caution as we joined the highway. After only a few minutes, once again, I found myself in a life-threatening situation.

Without warning, a huge tractor tyre bounced off a lorry heading in the other direction. Panicking, I slammed on the brakes which screeched loudly as the tyre thudded down in front of our car. It all happened so fast. I only just had time to register that the tyre was going to rebound off the crash barrier and back at us. Barely checking for oncoming traffic, I pulled into the right hand lane swerving around the tyre with only inches to spare as it bounced back across the tarmac. It dwarfed the Festiva and I was shell shocked as we continued on and out of danger.

I had already seen one accident as we were leaving

Rockhampton and now this. We were nervously laughing, discussing our brush with death, when a stone flew up and chipped my windshield. Was this a real life version of *Final Destination*? As we stopped for fuel the girl on the desk told me of yet another crash. It was a dangerous day to be on the roads.

By the time we turned into Agnus Water it was dark. Due to the conditions the drive had taken longer than expected, but I had been recommended a cheap campground right on the beach. It took a good half an hour to find, and we pitched up quickly, trying to keep as dry as possible in the continuing rain.

*

It was still raining in the morning. With not much else to do we walked around town and checked emails in a small but cosy cafe. The owner, Tom, chatted to us and we agreed to meet him for a drink after doing some washing and shopping. The purpose of our visit was to surf. The town was famous for cheap surfing lessons and although I had completed surf camp and failed miserably, I wanted to give it another go. It would be Aya's first time and I thought that she should have the experience.

However, the rain and cold kept us in the cafes and we decided to save the surfing and get to know each other a little better. Aya was fairly outspoken compared to the shy quietness I had experienced with other Japanese girls. She told me a lot about Japan and listened eagerly to my crazy stories. She was fascinated by my 'alternative' way of life. She was particularly interested in sex. Where she came from, traditionally a couple would have to declare themselves an item before they even kissed. She hounded me with sexual questions and we giggled like a pair of teenagers, discussing penises and performance.

One night out drinking she told me she was going to have a one night stand with a guy at the bar. It would be her first.

'Ok,' I answered, a little surprised that she was keen on the older, hairy and rather tubby man. 'You like him do you? That's the type of guy you're attracted to?'

'No!' she replied. 'But it doesn't matter. One night stand is just about sex, yes?'

I put my arm around the poor innocent girl and took her off to explain that even just for sex you have to at least fancy the guy. I had just deprived Mr Hairy of the luckiest night of his life.

That night we joined Tom for a drink at a local pub, and after making some not so subtle hints about our tents being wet and not having showered for days, he offered us his spare room for a night. The house was huge and we happily enjoyed a takeaway pizza and hot shower as the storm raged outside.

Tom and I talked and Aya did her best to keep up. Her English was good, but it was hard for her if we got overexcited and spoke too quickly. Tom was married, but his wife was away. He confessed to having a small stash of marijuana given to him as a present. He never dared smoke it with his wife around, but thought we might like to share some. I've never been much of a smoker, my tolerance is on par with my alcohol handling, one puff and I'm gone (which was why the Nimbin cookies couldn't have been particularly strong), but every now and then I'll have a dabble just to remind myself why I don't.

As none of us normally smoked we didn't have any tobacco or papers, but ingeniously Tom pulled out an empty toilet roll tube and a piece of plumbing gauze. He cut a hole in the cardboard, placed the gauze and weed on top before lighting it and taking a drag through the giant-sized pipe. Somehow it worked and the idea of smoking a toilet roll made me giggle even more than usual.

*

In the morning the rain drove on and all thoughts of surfing were dismissed; Aya wasn't keen on getting wet in the wet. Instead we thanked Tom and continued on our way. The car reeked of dampness, so we cranked up the heat as we hopelessly attempted to dry our wet and sandy tents draped across the back seat.

It was on this drive that we passed through the well-known town of Bundaberg, famous for fruit picking and rum. We stopped briefly at the distillery to take photos and buy souvenirs from the shop, but the tours were too expensive for our budget.

*

The further south we drove, the more the rain eased and we were relieved to come upon the blue skied, coastal town of Tin Can Bay. Another good night's sleep was had at a campground before we rose early and headed to the beach.

The sun was again shining, but we were not there to swim or sunbathe. This was far more exciting. We were going to hand feed dolphins. Two or three came to the bay every morning to be fed by a queue of tourists. The dolphins were light grey in colour and very different to the ones I had seen out at sea. One had scarring on his dorsal fin and I was told they were the marks of a shark attack. I always thought that sharks were scared of dolphins and that if you saw dolphins in the water it was safe to swim. It's a good job I hadn't put this into practice. Apparently, they are not all as brave and reliable as my childhood hero, Flipper.

According to the woman in charge, this breed spent most of their time in bays and inlets, very rarely going out to sea. The pod had been feeding there for over fifty years after locals began to throw fish to an injured male who'd been caught in fishing net. Now it was monitored to make sure that the mammals were not overfed, but locals knew the dolphins well, even their family links and history. There was a big queue to buy the fish and we only got a brief second to drop it into the eagerly awaiting mouth, but it was definitely one for the memory.

CHAPTER 13

ISLAND ADVENTURES

I WAS LOOKING FORWARD to our upcoming trip. We were off to Fraser Island. It was only accessible by four-wheel drive and although the Festiva was capable of achieving incredible things, she definitely wouldn't cut it on a sand dune.

There were three things I knew about the island: firstly, it was the largest sand island in the world and was world heritage listed; secondly, there was a big problem with the dingo population, who after being overfed by tourists were starting to attack humans; and thirdly, it was famous for backpackers getting themselves into car crashes and rollovers. I didn't need another one of those!

Like most of Australia's hotspots, there were a variety of tours on offer, but I had come too far to be paying for backpacker trips again. There was no way I would risk a hire car, they were ridiculously expensive and I had hardly any four-wheel drive experience. All this taken into consideration, I placed an ad online looking for a ride share. If I could find someone who owned a four-wheel drive it would be their responsibility if any damage was incurred and we would simply share fuel costs and good times. This is how we found Cara and Jan, a cute German couple in their late twenties.

Fraser Island was one big natural amusement park, with crystal clear lakes, beaches as roads and even a bubbling creek which you could peacefully float down. One day we hiked up to Indian Head, a hilly mass of land that protruded out into the ocean. We sat there for some time, watching transfixed as large sharks and turtles milled about in the aqua water below.

Then it was onto the champagne pools, the only safe salt-water swimming on the island. We all screamed in excitement as massive waves broke over the rock pools, knocking us back-wards and under. Then later, we gazed in awe as a whale passed by splashing on the ocean's surface.

*

During our time on the island, Cara and Jan slept in the car on a mattress and Aya and I in the roof tent. I'd never seen one before and it amazed me. It simple unfolded on top of the car and a lad-der led up to a spacious tent, with a soft spongy mattress. I loved the first campground which was full of larger than life trees and stumps, surrounded by a tropical rainforest.

The roads were rough and bumpy, adding to the fun, and the Germans let me take a turn driving on the beach. One day, we wandered along the shore watching people fishing. I saw a fam-ily bent over staring into the water. Walking over, I enquired what the fuss was about, and the kindly father responded by show-ing us how to catch sea worms and find 'pipi' shells in the sand. The worm catching was unsuccessful, but we helped Aya gather pipis and watched on in disgust as she ate them for dinner.

One afternoon, I got my first close look at a live snake as it slid over my foot while I was squatting down to pee. Rather than panic, I silently watched enthralled by this gift from nature. As it moved off me I called the others over to see. They all gathered round to look at what was now just a puddle of my urine, the snake having slipped away.

It's interesting observing the different ways in which people travel. Having previously spent time with the French boys, who slept on the ground, ate with no plates and showered in public, it was funny to watch Cara and Jan; they brushed the picnic table clean before every meal, put cardboard down on the car's floor and squealed every time an insect scuttled past. Despite their fussiness they were a lovely couple and Jan continuously made us laugh with his weird voices and impressions.

At Lake Wabby we all messed around, jumping off the high dunes, which were engulfing the lake at a rate of one metre a year. The dunes stood at an impressive sixty-five metres above sea level and young children were sandboarding down them before hitting the water and skimming across the lake.

My personal Fraser highlight had to be the shipwreck that sat on the beach, hauntingly, half buried in the sand. It was the rusty shell of an old cruise liner, which was being towed to Japan for scrap when a cyclone hit and washed it away. Over our three days we passed it several times and on each occasion it looked different with the changing tide. At low tide we wandered around it exploring the holes and crevices, but my favourite viewing was as the tide quickly rose, engulfing it almost completely. Foaming waves exploded as they collided with the barnacled metal, producing amazing displays of froth and water; a clear reminder of nature's power.

*

The campgrounds were enclosed by fences to protect the inhabitants from scavenging dingoes. I imagined the wild dogs staring in at us during the night as if watching a human zoo. The island was covered in signs, warning tourists not to leave scraps or feed the wildlife. There had been reports of dingoes attacking humans for food, but these were uncommon and disputed. One poster in particular caught my attention. It showed a man and his picnic being raided by animals. I told Aya it reminded me of us, as it depicted a crow stealing sausages and a bush turkey raking through the rubbish, both of which we had experienced. As we stood looking and laughing, I mentioned that my favourite drawing was of the possum stealing a Coke can. 'A possum taking cocaine?' replied a confused Aya. Thereafter, drug taking marsupials became the butt of many jokes.

The signs rang true as the island was abundant with wildlife. We peered dubiously into deep tunnels that were dug out and guarded by large, white spiders and we all fell about laughing as a goanna rushed up a tree to avoid us, before the bark fell off and he plummeted back to earth. The poor little mite was unhurt but clearly embarrassed at this humiliation and scurried back into the bush.

*

One evening, we arrived at a camp site which had a towering sand dune rising behind it. On closer inspection we saw that it was possible to climb to the top where there would be a view inland across the island. We started off full of enthusiasm walking up the mounds which concealed small valleys in-between. Down the valley we went and back up the next dune, only to find more dips and hills hidden among them. It was a very long walk and gave us an idea of how dangerous and misleading the desert could be.

It took a long time to reach what turned out to be a very boring view, and by the time we turned back, night was falling. It may have been exhausting going up, but the walk back was pleasurable, heightened by the glowing pinks that filled the sky as the sun set.

At the very end of our trip, on the brief ferry ride to the mainland, we were rewarded with a last farewell from nature as a dolphin pod swam alongside us. It might have been a major tourist destination, but I had certainly found peace and freedom on Fraser.

ALONG FOR THE RIDE

I was now on the final leg of my visa work. I had only sixteen days left to work and had arranged to do them at an organic vegetable farm not far from the Gold Coast. I had been due to start after our Fraser trip, but the host had emailed to ask if I could delay my arrival. With the glitz and glamour of the Gold Coast just down the road, I figured I could find fun ways to pass the time. But there was one problem, I was sure there would be no free camping and illegal camping or sleeping in cars would be met with heavy fines. I couldn't face staying in hostels and the paid camp sites would be miles from town. It was time to try a new way of travel.

The amazing Couch Surfing system was available all over the world and simply involved sleeping on host's couches. There were many benefits. Aside from a warm place to sleep and hot showers, we would also automatically have a great guide in the form of a host. I logged onto the website which allowed me to create a profile and look at those offering couches. Most profiles consisted of photos, details of the host and their couch and most importantly, references from other surfers. No money was to be exchanged and the system ran on a pay it forward basis. This could be interesting. I pitched the idea to Aya, who seemed happy to do anything that didn't involve work on her behalf and so I sent off a few emails.

*

There were two things I wanted to do on the Gold Coast, party and see the theme parks. Currently there was a promotion where we could get an unlimited pass for the three biggest parks. I was sold, and soon we were driving through chaotic traffic that surrounded Surfers Paradise to Movie World.

Aya was fairly relaxed as theme parks were quite common around Tokyo, however for the girl who'd lived on a tiny island for most of her adult life, this was heaven. I ran around like a child on E numbers, poking my head through the crowd as Batman fought off evil enemies and Scooby Doo embarked on a ghost hunt.

There were lots of shows and rides. The queues were long due to the school holidays, but it was well worth the wait. One ride, called Superman, seemed right up my alley. It looked like a basic rollercoaster with a few loops. It started inside a building so we could only see the red carriages as they flew around the track, with a Superman figure at the back 'pushing' them along.

The wait over, we climbed into our seats and buckled up. Aya was anxious, myself, full of nervous excitement. The ride took us through a storyline where an earthquake had trapped us underground and superman was going to push us out. The carriage stopped at the bottom of a steep slope. I waited for the click, click, click, as it steadily rose to the top of the hill. What actually happened came as a huge surprise.

The train shot forwards at a speed so fast, it literally took my breath away. Before I could register what was happening, we were flying over hills and round loops at what felt like the speed of sound. When it eventually stopped we were panting for breath and I was more than a bit shell shocked. I consulted the leaflet which informed me that we had been taken from 0 to 100 kph in two seconds. Now that's what you call a good ride.

There were plenty more amusements, although none lived up to Superman. The park was teaming with various movie characters and one in particular caught my eye. Batman stood by a long queue of children waiting to have their photo taken. I had an idea: maybe he would pick me up in his big strong arms for a picture; that would be hot. Then my mischievous mind took it one step further. While he was holding me I would whisper in his ear, 'Ever had sex in a theme park?' just before Aya took the picture. Imagine his face. Then it dawned on me, batman was masked and any blushing would be concealed. Or maybe, he would take me up on the offer. Luckily for batman the queue was too long to make my fantasies known and we continued on. Anyway, I had a season pass, I could go back and stalk the poor man whenever I wanted.

*

Meanwhile my phone had been going crazy. I had been offered so many couches to stay on I didn't know which one to pick. In the end we settled for a girl called Christy in Coolangatta, 20 kms down the coast. I had no idea what to expect as we gingerly knocked on the door, but we received a warm welcome from Christy and her two male American friends. I was surprised to find that Christy didn't actually live there, but the guys who did were open to couch surfers and we would all be staying for the night. I cracked open a beer and we spent an hour doing the usual chit-chat before heading out to a party.

By this time I had consumed three beers and was therefore drunk. One of the Americans explained that we were going to a company party held in the penthouse suite of the hotel he worked in. None of us had been invited, but the others knew a few people and it seemed pretty laid-back. Very laid-back in fact, as we helped ourselves to unlimited beer and I cautiously began to work the room.

I walked out onto the huge balcony which overlooked a long stretch of beach and the glittering lights of Surfers Paradise. Turning around I saw that Ben, one of the Americans had opened the hot tub. He was looking comfortable in the bubbles, beer in hand, staring out across the sea of lights. I was feeling pretty wasted, so without hesitating I stripped to my underwear, encouraged everyone else to do the same and hopped into the warm water.

It was a blissful evening. I was served beer every few minutes by whoever I could call to and I relaxed in the bubbles soaking up the thumping music which drifted across the party. The twinkling lights and soft-spoken ocean provided a magical backdrop to a great evening. I was a long way from my wet soggy tent.

The plan had been to hit a nightclub, but by the time we left, the five of us could hardly walk let alone dance. Having used my last inch of energy to get home, I was relieved to lay back on our fold-out sofa bed. I grinned stupidly to myself as I drifted off to sleep. One thought repeating in my head, 'Man I love couch surfing.'

*

I wasn't feeling my best the following day, but we had a lot to do. Aya only had a couple of days left in Australia before she had to return to Japan. I turned over to find her sleeping soundly on the other side of the bed and wondered what she had made of last night's party. I last remembered seeing her in the hot tub trying to give away a very warm beer. She had a quality that I lacked; she knew when to stop. I woke her, and after a well needed cup of tea with our hosts, we thanked them a million times before hitting the road.

The next theme park on our list was Sea World, but Water World would have been a more appropriate name due to the pounding rain. Parked near the entrance I suggested we wait for the rain to ease. Twenty minutes later, I realised we could be waiting the whole day and armed with umbrellas we made a break for it.

Inside we squirmed as we touched stingrays, *oohed* and *awwwed* at the polar bears and stood mesmerised as enormous sharks glided past the aquarium window. The rain continued to pour and we were soaked before the log flume had even left its station. Sadly, the bigger rides were closed due to the weather, but we watched a show from a dry refuge and tried to make the most of our day.

*

Again I was inundated with couch surfing offers. We wanted to stay in Surfers Paradise for at least one night, so I chose Laurence who gave me directions to his place in the centre of town. I pulled up at a flashy skyscraper and followed his instructions up to the 25th floor. The apartment was something special: we were faced with another spectacular view and a large lounge with huge sofas, upon which Laurence and his friends were sitting. They were playing a computer game that was projected to enormous proportions onto his lounge wall. It was a beautiful place, the people welcoming and most importantly, it was dry. I made the introductions and was pleased to find we had been upgraded from couch to bedroom, complete with an en-suite.

The only other girl, who was currently winning the game, looked as if she had just stepped out of a beauty salon. I currently resembled the love child of Worzel Gummidge and a drowned rat. The rain, log flumes and high winds hadn't done my hair any favours and so I excused myself to the shower. Aya was exhausted from the previous night's partying and once in our room I told her to lie down and rest; I would be social enough for the two of us.

Hair washed and dried, a change of clothes and a lick of mascara later, I emerged from the room better equipped to meet our host and his friends. Laurence was from Detroit, in his thirties and a little geeky in the looks department. He was friendly enough and was obviously a high-flyer when it came to lifestyle and work. My stomach lurched as alcohol was mentioned, but as a polite gesture I had brought a bottle of vodka. Beer and I were going to be spending some serious time apart.

I attempted to play the computer game and failed miserably, but I think my running commentary, complete with inappropriate swearing, provided entertainment of a higher value. Laurence introduced me to his friends, two guys and a girl, all Australian, before suggesting we play a drinking game, Kings Cup. This was a new one for me and I didn't stop laughing for the duration. We attempted and failed to make up rhymes, dances and followed random rules such as no pointing, not saying names and finally, ignoring Laurence. The loser had to drink the cup, which had been filled with a cocktail of beer, wine and vodka. Laurence lost the first game and drank it like a true champion. I lost the second. Everyone insisted that I just had to take a few sips, but not to be outdone I promptly picked up the cup and necked it.

In the morning, Aya and I were supposed to be visiting the Wet and Wild Water Park. As it happened the heavens were still open and the rain upheld its barrage against the coast. Deciding it would be far too wet to enjoy the wild, we vouched to stay home, watch movies and to stay off the drink for at least a couple of hours. In the basement of the five star complex was an indoor swimming pool, sauna, spa and steam room. It would have been a waste not to take advantage and surely much better than shivering at the water park.

*

I still wanted a night out in Surfers, and for better or worse we had a big one planned. More of Laurence's friends joined us for another round of King's Cup before we hit the town. I dusted off my big green case that had been hiding in the back of a very soggy Festiva (it leaked following the body work damage from the crash) and pulled out my best dress and long forgotten stilettos. I blow-dried my hair to perfection and carefully applied the first full face of make-up I had worn in three months.

The evening passed by in a dazzle of strobe lights, house music and good times. I danced until my legs couldn't take any more, and I threw my head back in ecstasy as the beat pulsated through me. It was good to be back in the clubs.

*

The next morning, my body disagreed. We had sat on the balcony talking crap until the sun came up, but my body, trained to early starts didn't seem to understand the need for a lie in. Although, I had noticed a small miracle, it had stopped raining. Aya was like a kid at Christmas and upon hearing the news, she bounded out of bed preparing for a day at the water park. Unfortunately, the entire population of Queensland had the same idea and the queues were horrendous.

It made no difference to me, I had a year's pass, but Aya was leaving the following day. I would miss her company, but our relationship had endured its ups and downs. Today in particular we were disagreeing about a common topic, money. When Tom had invited us to stay at his house in Agnus Water, I had shared some of my personal beer stash with him as a thank you. Likewise, when we had stayed with Laurence, I suggested we buy him a bottle of wine as a token of our appreciation. Aya told me not to.

Feeling bad as Laurence had housed and fed us for a couple of days, I had bought him a drink in the club. I had also paid the taxi fare and as Aya and I were splitting costs, I was expecting a contribution. The entire night out had cost us $10 each. Aya argued that in Japan if a man takes a girl out then he is expected to pay for everything, we were providing Laurence with company so therefore he should pay. I told her that in the UK we have a couple of names for girls like that. We weren't fighting, just debating. I told her to forget paying me the ten bucks, but in the end she insisted.

That night my liver heaved a sigh of relief as we stayed in and watched a movie. Aya had to be fresh for the flight and I had a farm job to attend, the Golden Coast was to be exchanged for the country, but only for a short time.

CHAPTER 14

A VOLUNTARY EDUCATION

FRESH AND ALERT the next morning, I delivered Aya to the airport. As we hugged and said our goodbyes, I was sad to see her go but looking forward to some alone time. Having a companion twenty-four hours a day, was taking its toll. I was normally a very independent person, so a part of me felt free to breathe again knowing I didn't have to tour guide, translate or entertain anyone but myself.

Sadly my freedom was to be short-lived, as the final leg of my farming stint had arrived. I had arranged to stay at Anne and George's organic vegetable farm which was situated in the mountains behind Brisbane. As with every farm stop, I had arranged to arrive at 5 p.m., late enough to miss work for the day but early enough to catch dinner. I spent the day shopping for anything that took my fancy, and treating myself to lunch in a café before heading for the hills.

My little car grunted and groaned up slopes and past the most gorgeous lush countryside. I had chosen George and Anne as they claimed to provide high class accommodation and ran courses on food and health. As always I was nervous as to what and who I would find. The hills grew steeper, houses grander and finally I turned down the driveway.

The tarmac ran through the middle of the most perfect, immaculate gardens I had ever seen. The grass was neatly trimmed and practically fluorescent in colour. The beds of flowers and vegetables could have been pictures from the seed packets. Among this setting sat a modern, classy house, backdropped by tree covered mountains that stretched as far as the eye could see.

I slowed the Festiva as it approached the first of several homemade speed bumps which punctuated the driveway. It didn't look like a large property, not compared to my previous farms, but it was certainly very, very grand. My nervousness grew and bubbled inside me. Who were these people? They must be perfectionists. How would I handle people, who if the gardens were anything to go by, must be extremely prim and proper? I climbed out of the car bringing my small day pack and walked towards the front porch.

I saw a face at the window but no one came to greet me. The door was open a fraction, so I called out a timid hello and heard a crisp female voice telling me to come in. Removing my shoes to avoid dirtying the pea green carpet, I followed the voice into the kitchen. There stood Anne, in her sixties, with bushy, grey hair and wrinkles which creased her face like one of those little dogs with too much skin. A brunette girl of around my age stood next to her chopping rhubarb. I was introduced to Emily, a fellow worker, before the pair ignored me and continued with their work.

I sat feeling helpless at the table while Anne and Emily made jam. Finally, I excused myself to unpack my car, excited to see my new room but a little put out by Anne's coldness. As usual my concern was premature. Throughout my life I had always been desperate to please people. I am very competitive and always want to do the best, be the best and included in my neediness is a yearning for the approval of others. George and Anne Thornton must have seen hundreds of backpackers parade in and out of their home. I guess warm welcomes had become thin upon the ground.

Arriving in my room I saw that Emily had taken the bunk beds and surprisingly left the double for me. I opened my case and organised my clothes in to little piles on the floor. The room was basic but cosy, and the window overlooked stunning views of the valley which led up into mountains. The bathroom was huge and a large spa bath sat in the corner. The Thorntons had their own room and en-suite, plus an office and upstairs lounge. The lounge was surrounded by patio doors which opened onto a large, curved, balcony. Even from inside the room, the endless forest and mountains were clearly visible, the glass panelled doors seemingly brought the outside world in. It was a spectacular location.

Eventually, I returned downstairs where we ate in the dining room. An awkward silence surrounded us. Emily tried to keep the conversation going and I answered the questions put to me. Mostly the usual, where had I been? What had I done? What were the other voluntary placements like? When dinner was over, everyone headed to bed. My heart felt empty and a 6 a.m. start was due the next morning.

After breakfast we were put to work weeding an overgrown flower bed in the garden. I took the chance to quiz Emily on our hosts. She had been there several months and intended to do her entire 88 days of farm work at the same place. I mentioned the benefits of travelling around for new experiences, but due to her late decision to stay in Australia, Emily was on a race against the clock before her current visa expired. She told me that Anne and George were nice people once you got to know them.

We were to work four hours a day, six days a week. Four hours didn't sound like a long time, well not until I was sitting in a flower bed doing the same thing, minute after minute, hour after hour. Yes, Emily admitted, most of her work was weeding and it was exceedingly dull. What was I letting myself in for? I had nearly three weeks to work. The whole concept of volunteering was to provide labour in return for food, board and experience. I didn't feel I would learn much from pulling weeds. I hoped this would not be a repeat of the farm in Tully. On the upside, after enjoying a fresh organic meal cooked by Anne, we had every afternoon free. At lunch we would discuss past workers and I enquired about the food and health courses. As luck would have it, one was due to start that very week and I was welcome to take part.

Over dinner, Anne and George would remain fairly silent, although if you could find a topic of interest, George would pick up on it and keep going until the food ran out. Although these rants could be dull, they were better than empty silence. The days passed and we continued to weed. In the afternoons, I drove up to the village and filled myself with cake and coffee while using my USB internet (I still couldn't bring myself to get a smart phone, not trusting myself, after my experience with cars, cameras and anything else of substantial value; instead I stood by my so far unbreakable Nokia). The house had a computer but we were only allowed one hour a week online.

With nothing else to do and no car, I wondered how Emily had entertained herself the past few months. 'I read a lot of books,' she told me. Her sister who lived in nearby Brisbane also came to visit occasionally. Surprisingly Emily had little interest in joining me for visits to civilization, but I was happy to explore alone.

I began to run a forest track daily, in an attempt to lose the spare tyre which was again forming after months of beer drinking and cheap, easy food. As mentioned, I have never been good at anything physical, running in particular leaves me breathless at the thought. But here I was, iPod in hand, ready for my race of the day. I always took the same track and timed my run, attempting to beat my previous record. However, instead of a tarmac road or footpath, my trail led down old stone steps, through ancient rainforest, past swamps and waterfalls, even crossing trees with roots so large that I had to climb over them. With my music on full blast and my heart beating hard in my chest I felt transported into a jungle based game. I visualised myself as a Lara Croft pounding through the jungle, but no doubt looked more like a red-faced Mario.

*

Eventually, we gained another backpacker at the farm. I was excited, as Emily and I had practically exhausted all conversation between us. His name was Will and he was French. Dressed in a blazer over a buttoned up shirt, with shorts that hovered around his knees, Will looked like an overgrown private schoolboy. He was actually a teacher but had been volunteering for three years. Yes, you heard me right, THREE YEARS! Not for a visa, not because he was interested in farming or becoming a farmer, but just because he felt like it.

We quizzed him for some time over this but could not come up with any logical explanation, so we made up a few of our own. They varied from him being homeless and penniless, to mentally insane and possibly a mass murderer, depending on how he had been acting that day. I understood that placements could be fun and there was a lot to be learnt, but three years! Come on!

Even with all his experience he was a slow worker, in fact, so slow you practically needed a time lapse camera to see him move. He was also extremely argumentative. I love a good debate but there was no give or take with Will; after an hour of him insulting the British and their 'child slave labour' laws, I nearly lost my cool. I don't know whether it was what he said, or the smugness with which he said it, but had it not been for George calling us in for lunch, I thoroughly believe that Will would have left with a garden fork protruding from his groin.

*

By this time the work had begun to vary. I was enlisted to climb avocado trees and pick the fruit. I loved the challenge, trying to grab branches seemingly far from reach. We also spent a day cutting leaves from huge mountains of rhubarb stems. The rain lashed down; I was glad to be in the sheltered packing shed as Anne drove the small tractor through the downpour, bringing red stems for us to strip and bag. We used small knives and quick slashing movements to send the greenery floating down to the floor. There was something immensely satisfying about that hacking motion.

Anne and George had opened up a little. They were busy people, had both written books and set up several community projects. If the rain was too bad Anne would allow us to stay inside and make jams that were sold alongside the vegetables at market. I used to wake up praying for rain, anything to avoid hours and hours of weeding.

One day I was allowed to mow the lawn. I was thrilled, expecting to ride the tractor which pulled a mower around the grounds. I should have known better. Instead I was given a small hand mower to push around the edges of a flower bed on a steep hill. The mower gave up a few seconds before I did, choking, spluttering and finally giving up any signs of life. I was returned to weeding the vegetable garden.

*

No matter how monotonous the work, nature always seemed to have a surprise for us. Weeding the avocado trees one morning, my hands narrowly missed a snake in the long grass. Another day, Emily and I sat throwing witchetty grubs that we found in the dirt, to a kookaburra. We admired its beauty and the fluffiness of its plump body. Then in a flash of pink, a baby mouse ran out in front of me, within a split second the kookaburra snatched it up and carried it away while the little mite squeaked in fear. Emily and I sat frozen in shock. The poor mouse. We hadn't thought twice about partaking in the murder of the grubs, but the cute mouse being gobbled horrified us. Nature clearly didn't give as much preference to appearances.

Other wildlife came in the form of two guinea fowl, large, plump birds covered in black and white spots. They provided endless entertainment chasing anything on wheels. They would chase Emily with the wheelbarrow, constantly follow Anne and George on the tractor and scare the crap out of any driver who headed towards the house. I had somehow escaped them on my arrival, but every time I drove to the village they would run beside me, dangerously close to my wheels, their little legs going faster and faster to keep up. They always stopped at the driveway, but if someone surprised them by hitting the throttle, they stamped their authority by flying alongside and in front, forcing the driver to slow.

*

The workshops were due to begin and Anne handed me some advance homework. As a sugar junkie, I thought learning about food and health would be beneficial, but unfortunately, it didn't

quite live up to my hype. As I read through the papers, chemi-
cal formulas and exam style questions, I was taken back to my
school days. Any minute someone would tell me to be quiet and
then to begin.

From what I could understand, and I did spend a fair amount
of time trying, Anne and George were teaching us how to get our
soil balance correct. The general concept being, that if the correct
nutrients are not in the soil then the plant cannot absorb them.
Therefore, we would not get the required nutrients from eating them. It was a very good point, but with questions asking,
'Which elements could be missing if your plant is not showing
signs of photosynthesis and what affect will that have on your
crop?' I felt a little disappointed. I had no plants of my own. The
course was stretched over an eight week period. I would only be
around for the first couple of sessions.

During the evening Emily and I had to help set up tea, biscuits and name badges. We had great fun guessing the personality behind the names. Nigel would be the village idiot and
Daphne a very posh older lady who probably owned horses. In
the build-up to the meeting the jokes went on. Almost dropping
a glass I swore and Emily called out, 'Now, now. Don't be doing
that in front of Daphne, she'll be sending the vicar round to save
you.'

By the time the unsuspecting locals arrived we could hardly
contain our laughter as we handed out their badges. Nigel looked
exactly as we had imagined but was far too confident and business like to fit the roll of idiot. He had been successfully growing
vegetables for some time. Daphne looked like a new age traveller,
crossed with a librarian, wearing a long purple dress and square
framed glasses. She definitely didn't own a horse. There was also
a couple who ran a cattle station and a very butch woman who
had possibly just jacked up on heroin. Both Emily and I noticed

her head falling and eyes rolling back, during George's speech. Whether that was due to drug use or boredom, I guess we'll never know.

But they all had one thing in common, they wanted to grow produce. I think the actual detail into which Anne delved baffled them almost as much as it did me, but none the less they all returned a week later armed with soil samples for analysis. That was the highlight of the meetings, finding out who already had what it took and who would be doomed to fail or suffer huge expense in order to succeed. By my final session I was regretting having signed up and glad that I would be leaving before the end.

*

Over dinners and lunches I had gradually learnt more and more about the Thorntons. They were pillars of the community and Anne had met George in the UK where she was originally from. They began to grow on me, well a little anyway. As on Ducks Meadow every meal was freshly picked and the food delicious; I began to dream of a veggie garden of my own. Who would have thought, the out of control party girl wishing she had her own patch of dirt.

One night the Thorntons were off to a meeting. An international organisation was encouraging people and communities to become self-sufficient. Emily and I were invited, and I thought it sounded interesting. It was held at a nearby house and featured a similar group to the course seminar; in fact, Nigel himself was present.

The expected was discussed, buy local products, support each other etc., but the theory rang a bell, 2012 was coming! A scary video was shown about the depression in America, depicting starving families sleeping by disused railway lines and dramatically telling us we were heading for another one now. After the video we were asked to suggest ideas to save our future.

Hands flew up. Push bikes would have to be stored for when fuel ran out. They needed to draw up a skills list. Who could make clothes and shoes? Who knew how to repair a bicycle? How would they protect themselves from flood victims climbing the hills? Of course global warming would cause seawater to destroy the towns below.

It was backed up by speeches given by several men who worked in finance, I have no idea what sector; they could have been a clerk at the local bank for all I knew but they sounded very serious and convincing. It was all dramatised by slide shows, more video and even role-play. After an hour, I was completely enthralled and even put forward some suggestions. Maybe it was extreme, but they were harmless and it wouldn't hurt to keep a spare can of fuel in the car. With the Festiva's great economy, I could surely make it to the nearest hill village when the time came. I went home sleepy and smiling. Who'd have thought, prim and proper Anne and George helping to set up a commune.

*

Eventually, much to my relief, my farming time had come to an end. It had been a great experience and I'd learnt a lot, but was sick of having my schedules and travel routes ruled by farmers and immigration. When George signed off my form, I felt relief and joy that had previously been saved for passing GCSEs and driving tests.

I must admit I was not in the least bit sad to go. I had felt sorry to leave Ducks Meadow and knew I would miss my hippy friends up at Airlie, but although George, Anne and Emily were nice enough, they were just not my kind of people. So it was with a very happy heart that I guided my little car down the green leafy hills and back towards the ocean.

CHAPTER 15

FREEDOM, FEELINGS AND
FAST CARS

I HAD DECIDED TO revisit the Gold Coast to watch the famous V8 car race. Laurence had invited me to again stay at his apartment which overlooked the racetrack. I had naively presumed I would return to the luxury room complete with en-suite. My illusions were shattered when I called him and was told that the room had been taken, but I could sleep in the lounge. With the large cream sofas and plush carpet I agreed it wouldn't be a problem.

As I drew nearer to the high-rise I had to pass through security. The roads were currently being turned into the racetrack, but luckily Laurence's street was available for parking. Once again I sailed up to the 25th floor and walked into what was formally known as Laurence's apartment. It now resembled a hostel; backpacks were strewn everywhere, travellers sat in pairs talking, others cooked in the kitchen while a few were watching the press helicopters dance about in the sky. What on earth!

'I just can't say no,' Laurence told me. 'They are all couch surfers; the hostels are full for the races.'

Now maybe I had misjudged him, but for a successful 34-year-old man to let anyone and everyone stay, free for all, in his luxury apartment seemed a little unusual. Then looking around I noted that nearly all of the guests were female. Later I got talking to the only two males who told me they had tagged along with some girls, and Laurence hadn't been expecting them. *Hmmmm*, there seemed to be something a little sleazy about this.

An hour or so later, the cars were on the track warming up. The helicopters buzzed like bees, darting in and out of the sky-scrapers, and the noise from the cars was almost unbearable. I sat on the balcony soaking up the sun and enjoying the vibe, but I couldn't quite click with anyone. Considering they were all happy to crash at a stranger's house, everyone seemed rather antisocial.

*

Later in the evening Laurence's friends, whom I had met during my previous visit, appeared. I recognised Maria and Brendon a young couple, and we decided to go out and leave Laurence entertaining his 20 female guests. Maria and I bonded and again we hit the clubs. The night was a blur of dancing and drinking, and when it came to a close Maria asked if I would like to stay at their brand new riverside home. As we had left Laurence's, two backpackers had been setting up a bed in his closet. I was more than happy to have somewhere else to stay. So instead of spending a sleepless night on a lounge floor with twenty other travellers, I found myself being cosseted in the spare room of a million dollar home. I awoke to Brendon cooking us breakfast, before my kind hosts dropped me back to my car.

*

I decided to drive on to Sydney alone. Even though I had only spent a few weeks there, the city felt like home away from home and it was nice to be heading somewhere familiar. Exhausted from months on the road, I would drive at my own pace, stopping and resting whenever I wanted with no one else to worry about. It was a shame I had to retrace old ground, but I wanted to visit Emma who was now living in Sydney, before driving across the south coast. Then I would go up the west side, completing a full circuit of Australia's costal roads.

Once again I was headed to Byron Bay. I planned on sunning myself on its pale yellow beaches and to meander in and out the jewellery shops. I smiled to myself as I passed the 'Welcome to New South Wales' sign, before the grin slipped as I noticed a weighty grey cloud looming up ahead.

Arriving in Byron I could have continued with my beach plans, although I would have been extremely cold and wet. To put it nicely, it was pissing down. I found an official campground and pitched up quickly, before getting a takeaway and an early night.

The next morning, I awoke to find that it was raining both inside and outside of my tent. Great! I put my soggy sleeping bag into the car, threw the tent in the bin and headed for town, hoping for a camping store. I was in luck, not only was there a shop but it had a spacious, double skinned tent for a very good price. If only my leaky car was as easy to fix. I spent the day around the shops and once again took full advantage of Byron's cafes. The beach was still off the agenda, so long for a few days of sun and sand.

I decided to stay one more night and pray for the weather to stop holding out on me. I chose a different camp site and paid for a pitch with electricity. Tonight I would camp in style. After a hot shower I settled into my large new tent, feeling very content with my inflatable mattress under me and warm duvet over me. I plugged in my internet stick and made the most of having a signal. I ordered takeaway again and lounged in bed, watching movies, grateful that the rain was making pattering noises on my tent and not dripping through it. It was the camping equivalent of a night in on the couch.

*

In the morning, the sky was dry but still an angry grey. I hit the road with no destination in mind, simply taking my time and watching the kilometres on the Sydney signs, get lower and lower. Emily had recommended the small village of South West Rocks as a good place to stop. It was picturesque with a beautiful campground right on the beach front. Sadly it came with a price tag that was a little out of my budget. Thankfully the owners were kind enough to direct me to the nearest national park. I was very wary of staying in the forest alone, it didn't seem safe, but I thought I may as well take a look.

The site was on the edge of the ocean, with just a small strip of creamy gold sand separating the camp from the water. There were plenty of people about, plus coin operated showers. With families surrounding me, my worries disappeared and I felt relaxed enough to stay. From my tent I could see directly out across the water and the sun was finally making an appearance. I walked along the beach watching crabs scuttle away, before laying down with my book and nodding off in the sunshine.

That evening I made myself dinner on the picnic bench and watched kangaroos graze lazily around the various tents and vans. This was relaxation. Sleep took me into a deep world of peaceful dreams, and reality was just as good as I awoke to a glittering sea of blue.

*

The following day I headed towards a beach called Seal Rocks. The drive there seemed to go on forever, short distances alone felt like days. Although when I say short distances, I really mean a four hour drive. I had by now become almost Australian in my driving. Oh it's only 500 kilometres! Whereas, back home in Europe a two hour drive was a long way to travel.

Arriving, I found a camp site, although it looked a little run-down. However, it was right on the beach and hidden among sand dunes, which made for a beautiful but isolated location. I felt a little uneasy; the place was almost empty and had a creepy atmosphere. Clots of bushes and trees were dotted around, separating the camping pitches and casting eerie shadows.

After pitching up, I kept my eyes and mind alert as I went in search of the showers. I had a map of the grounds clearly marking the shower block and toilets. I walked past an old shed with a tin roof, balanced on stilts. The map stated the shower block should be right there, but I couldn't see it. I continued to look around when it dawned on me. Oh no! Those were the showers.

I dubiously peered in. Spiderwebs clung to the walls and the echo of dripping water bounced around the large and otherwise empty 'building'. A large huntsman spider scuttled across the wall. The showers were coin operated, one dollar for three minutes. My first dollar did nothing, a second gave me about a minute and a half of cold water which dribbled lazily out the rusty fitting. This was the Hotel California of camp sites.

I cheered myself up with a walk down the beach. The sun was setting and the noise from the crashing ocean soothed me as always, the sand was deserted except for myself. Then I noticed a dead bird in the sand. It was grey with a black beak and roughly the size of a gull. I felt sorry for the poor thing as it lay with its neck twisted in a horrifically unnatural position. It was covered in sand, the feathers matted with seawater. Then I glimpsed another bird, and another, and another. The whole beach was littered with bodies. This place was getting creepier by the minute.

I took a brief stroll up and down the long stretch of sand which was bookended by sharp cliffs and headland. Between the beach and campground rose the rolling dunes. Up in the dunes I noticed the figure of a man who seemed to be standing, watching me. I kicked myself, come on Julia don't frighten yourself he's probably just come to see the sunset. A few minutes later I looked again, the man was gone.

The sun was low in the sky and I decided to get back before the light became too weak. On the way to my tent I bumped into an older German couple. I asked if they had any idea what had happened to the birds. The man told me that they migrated every year from Antarctica to Canada, but due to bad weather, general weakness or destruction of landing grounds, many of them exhausted, fell into the sea and drowned. What a sad way to die.

I was retrieving a few things from my car, ready to settle down for the night when I turned around to find a bare chested tattooed man standing behind me. It was the man from the sand dune. He introduced himself as camp site security and told me that if I had any problems in the night to run to his hut. Problems in the night???? What was this place? Ironically, he told me he wanted me to feel safe. I was getting more freaked out by the second. He then invited me, in a strange stuttering voice, over to his place for a drink. I declined and went to bed with my torch and rape alarm within reach.

*

Having survived the night, I spent the next two days at a beautiful, safer camp site on the edge of a lake further down the coast. It was expensive, but the showers were spider free and there was a cosy pub nearby. I wrote, drank wine, had cheesy garlic bread and watched a movie before bed each night. Then it was time to return to civilization, where people didn't live out of cars, camp at the roadside or shower at truck stops. The bright lights of Sydney would be upon me once more.

*

Emma and Bruce from my Great Ocean Road trip had now moved to Bondi Beach. As they were currently away in Thailand, I could stay in their room for the next week. I was now not only in need of a rest but also a cash injection. I hoped to find a room to rent in Sydney and a job for a few months, before exploring the rest of the country.

I passed by the large town of Newcastle, wanting to stop but not having the energy. The roads grew wider, the traffic thicker and before I knew it my Satellite Navigation system—that Nik had laughed at in the desert—negotiated me through Sydney's maze of tunnels and toll roads. I tried to keep calm, follow the directions and not cause an accident, but the packed roads closed in on me and panic rose. The impatient drivers and beeping horns came as somewhat of a culture shock and I wished for the simplicity of the desert. My colourful car—which had now been signed and covered in messages from Aya, the French boys and a host of others whom I had met during my trip—certainly drew some stares in among the slick city traffic.

Relieved to have arrived safely, I finally pulled into the driveway of the large detached home. Painted white with big windows, it was a typical beach house. One street back from the famous Bondi strip, this would be the perfect place to rest and regain some energy. In fact it turned out to be more perfect than I ever could have imagined.

*

Emma had given me the number of her housemate Hec, who would let me in and give me a key. Within minutes of my call he bounded across the road barefooted, in long board shorts, his head topped with a mop of bleached blonde hair. His big, blue eyes combined with an even bigger smile had me relaxed within minutes.

I was exhausted from the long drive so planned to be as polite as possible before excusing myself for a siesta. We hauled my luggage out of the Festiva and crammed it into Emma's already cramped room, before crashing out on the couch. Hec was easy to chat with; he listened intently to my travel stories, asking questions, keen to know more. He made me laugh and soon my siesta was long forgotten. We talked and talked and talked and talked. Before I knew it, evening had come and Hec was inviting me out.

It was Halloween and his friend was hosting a party. If I was going to live in the city, I might as well start making friends. I put together a vampire costume, raiding my bag and the dollar store down the street. Hec's costume proved to be more difficult. He had purchased 40 rolls of toilet tissue and was going to become an Egyptian Mummy. How he had planned to wrap himself, I don't know, I guess he was hoping for my help.

It took the best part of an hour to cover him from head to toe in paper. The tissue kept ripping and I had to use a whole roll of tape to hold it in place. The wonderfully simple idea was fast turning into a nightmare, but we giggled the whole way through. Walking up to his friend's house things became worse, as the wind and movement left trials of loo roll flying around Bondi's streets. We raised a lot of interest as we passed busy pubs and restaurants.

By the time we arrived at the party, most of our hard work was gone. Much to the amusement of the guests, Hec was now naked, bar a tight pair of flesh coloured boxers and random bits of sagging tissue. One of his mates had the great idea of covering him with fake blood, to redeem the Mummy like effect. Later, someone asked him why he was dressed as a tampon.

Fancy dress disasters aside, I had a great night. Most of the guests were from the Surf Life Saving Club, a voluntary organisation which helped the full-time lifeguards patrol Bondi Beach. Hec was also a member. By the end of the night we were both the worse for wear and staggered back to the house.

Throughout the evening, I had felt myself becoming more and more attracted to my gorgeous blonde host, and back home on the sofa I noticed Hec's hand on my leg. After a very brief 'is this a good idea?' moment we were embracing in a passionate kiss.

That night he slept in my bed, and when Emma returned to her room a week later Hec asked me to stay in his. I liked him, but it seemed a little sudden. However, after handing out CVs I found a job in a nightclub. I finished at 7 a.m., just as Hec was leaving for his plumbing job, so we would have the bed on time-share. A risky move, but what did I have to lose.

Hec was amazing. Like me he was free spirited and passionate about life, he made me laugh and drove me wildly insane with his gorgeous looks and body. Weeks turned to months and we celebrated New Year's Eve with a huge party in our back garden. I had planned to set off for the rest of my trip in January. I still had the West Coast and Tasmania to conquer, but I couldn't bring myself to leave.

Instead I stayed in Bondi living and working. I attempted to continue surfing and failed miserably. Hec and I enjoyed walks on the sand hand in hand, laughing, kissing and making everyone around us feel sick. We went to festivals and dinners, rode the big wheel at Luna Park and visited Manly on the ferry.

What was I doing? I was an independent traveller, turning her back on the road and sacrificing her singledom for a

24-year-old beach bum. However, something about Hec made me stay. He giggled like a toddler, he saw the simple answer in everything and he was, as I like to call it, a little bit blonde. One day a group of us (yes I had begun to acquire friends) were talking in the lounge and I mentioned my very first visit to Spain. 'It was the first time I had been abroad,' I explained to my friend.

'Where's that?' asked Hec.

I burst into laughter.

'I'm not stupid, I just don't know where abroad is.' Hec continued, 'Is it in Europe?'

In his defence, the Aussie term is overseas, not abroad. His accent was nearly as strong as those in the outback. He was my authentic Aussie, with the carefree spirit to match, and happy to help anyone at any time.

We had so much fun together. I loved the fact that we were both so young at heart (well him in body too) and like me, simple things made him very happy. He appreciated and loved life, with an affection and delight that people normally save for kittens and babies. Living together worked well, everything was perfect. I lived with my best friend and my boyfriend. What more could I want.

*

Time flew past and Emma and Bruce moved up to the Gold Coast. I remained in Sydney. In fact, over a year after my arrival in the city, I am still here. Hec and I are still together and we still live in the Bondi beach house. My trip came to an abrupt end, but at the same time a new part of my life suddenly began.

I started up a veggie garden in our backyard, using the course information that bored me so much at Anne and George's farm. Inspired by the Airlie Beach community I have a worm compost, and I'm addicted to the bio-dynamic yoghurt which is sold at our local store—I try not to think about the cow horns filled with shit when I eat it. I dream of a self-sustainable house. Unfortunately my fear of spiders has returned and even Hec has to chase them with the vacuum cleaner. Needless to say, I'm still a very cautious driver.

During my Australian journey I discovered a passion for the environment; it is an interest that Hec and I share and treasure. My family will be overjoyed to hear that I am giving up the title of *Traveller and General Dosser*, to study environmental management. Hopefully, I will gain a career helping to protect the country I fell in love with. I remember cringing at the thought of three months farm work back in the Kings Cross hostel. Who could have known that not only would I do it, but that it would change my life forever.

When I was on the road people always asked me, 'Are you travelling or are you looking for something?' To be honest it's always been a bit of both, which would naturally pose the question, 'Have you found it now?' Well, who knows, but the city that always felt like home, finally is, and I'm more than happy to hang up my travels for now. Through our relationship, I have been granted a de facto visa and I have no plans to leave the country or man, both having won my heart in equal measure.

So what about the end of my trip and the rest of Australia? Well let's just say we have already discussed the camper van, we'd both love to see the West Coast and for the rest, you'll just have to wait and see.

TO THE READER ...

For those of you who skipped the first few pages, a little reminder to look *up Kangaroos and Chaos* online if you would like to see pictures from the trip. I look terrible in almost all of them but I'm hoping you'll enjoy the insight. On my website/social media I also share 'deleted scenes' that didn't make the cut; a 'where are they now' section to let you know where my fellow travellers ended up (spoiler alert: there's been a few babies born since this story), alongside all the awesome photos you send me of K&C being read during your own travels. Social media-wise I generally post random, funny and educational stuff about Australia and will attempt to keep you updated on my current adventures. Please click, 'like', 'follow' etc. and continue to share in the chaos.

Most importantly, thank you for picking up (or downloading) this book. Please feel free to get in touch or leave a review (I try my best to read and reply to them all). Comments, stories and random thoughts from across the world put an instant smile into my day.

Finally, never be afraid to bring a little chaos into any walk of life, who knows where the adventure could lead!

JULIA BROOKE

Julia left the UK at the tender age of 17. She then spent many years living in Spain and its various islands, in-between backpacking and exploring the world, as much as her bank account would allow.

In 2009, aged 27, she began her Australian adventure with absolutely no idea it would lead to such a life changing transformation, let alone the publication of her first book. Six years after her arrival down under Julia still resides in Sydney, although her relationship with Hec eventually came to an end.

Julia continues to follow her passion for the land, has obtained an Advanced Diploma of Environmental Management and is now in her final year of a Bachelor of Environment. She is taking baby steps to make that dream of owning a piece of land and an off the grid, self-sustaining house a reality. When it eventually happens she would like you all to come and stay or visit during your travels.

ACKNOWLEDGEMENTS

To everyone who was a part of my trip, thank you! To all the farmers and workers who put up with my dubious skills, to each person who I spent a random drunken moment with and to those special people who shared my Ford for ridiculous amounts of kilometres; there would be no story without you.

Nico, thank you for so many things, time or distance will never take away from experience. Leonie, you are a legend, I am so lucky to have met you, please move to Australia! Yuko, thanks for putting up with my terrible driving and for the cultural exchange. Jan... what can I say, you're crazy, possibly even more so than me, don't let go of that.

Erin, Ben and all the family. Thank you for your ongoing support and all the messy adventures. Erin thanks for being there for all these long years and for spending hours correcting my terrible spelling and grammar.

Hec, your passion for life continues to inspire and ignite my own. For all those nights you went to bed alone while I sat at the computer, for your never-ending patience and continued support, thank you.

Edwina for the hours of reading and corrections, your feedback drove me on in times when I doubted myself.

To my wonderful editor Belinda Pappin thank you for being a part of this book's journey and for encouraging me to take the next step.

Damonza for my interior and cover design. You did a wonderful job of translating my ideas into designs. I am immensely happy with the results.

Andrea (for the feedback and sharing my environmental passion), Shiho (for inspiring me to make dreams come true), Tasha (for human soup and British humour) and the rest of the hula hooper community, life in Australia would not be the same without you. Mathieu for sharing my love affair with Sydney and for the glitter you bring to her. Leonie for our crazy friendship, may the nail salon stories continue. Dale for inspiring me to put energy into creativity, there's never a dull moment around you. Tristan, 'life's too short to leave this book sitting on the shelf', thank you. Scott, for helping me go off the rails when I need a break from being on them. Joe, there are no words to thank you for the support and friendship you have given me—may P&E grow old ungracefully.

Faye 'my hubby', years don't change our friendship, they just change the appropriateness of my behaviour, thank you for being understanding and loving when others would judge. Hollie what happens in Vegas ... actually please remind me my memory seems a little hazy ... for being there when I need you no matter what, long time. Dad, for all the years of phone calls, house moving, car advice and for your unconditional acceptance and support, thank you!

Printed in Poland
by Amazon Fulfillment
Poland Sp. z o.o., Wrocław